Steve Waugh's Ashes Diary

FOREWORD BY SHANE WARNE

IRONBARK

Steve Waugh's Ashes Diary

FOREWORD BY SHANE WARNE

PHOTOGRAPHS:

All the colour photographs in this book, with the exception of the final three photos in section two and the photo of Mark Waugh in Ireland (which were taken by Michael Thomas), are the work of London-based Australian photographer Philip Brown.

Phil also provided the following black-and-white photos:
Pages: 13, 14, 15, 18, 22, 30, 33, 34, 37, 39, 43, 44, 45, 46, 53, 57, 58, 61, 63, 65, 73, 81, 82, 84, 85, 87, 97, 99, 103, 105, 107, 115, 118, 129, 133, 137, 144, 145, 147, 148, 149, 151, 153, 155, 160, 164, 169, 172, 176, 178, 182, 183.

The remaining photos were taken by Steve Waugh, or, in some cases, by other members of the touring party using Steve's camera.

AUTHOR'S THANKS:

Special thanks must go to the members of the Australian team — the players, coach and management — for their support.

Thanks also to:
- Phil Brown, for his superb photographs
- our scorer Mike Walsh, for providing answers to my many questions concerning statistics.
- Errol Alcott, for taking the various dressing room celebration photos.
- Tim May, for his proof reading, and for contributing one day of this diary.
- Rob Craddock, for his support during the tour.
- Alan "Lannie" Jones and Harvey Davis for providing the newspaper cuttings from the tour.
- Ian Russell, for compiling the tour record at the end of the book.
- and the people at Ironbark, for giving me the chance to write this diary.

First published 1993, in Ironbark, by Pan Macmillan Publishers
Australia, a division of Pan Macmillan Australia Pty Limited
63-71 Balfour Street, Chippendale

Copyright © Steve Waugh 1993

All rights reserved. No part of this book may be reproduced or transmitted in any form or by any means, electronic or mechanical, including photocopying, recording or by any information storage and retrieval system, without prior permission in writing from the publisher

National Library of Australia
cataloguing-in-publication data:

Waugh, Steve, 1965-
Steve Waugh's Ashes Diary

ISBN 0 330 27465 1

1. Waugh, Steve, 1965- — Diaries 2. Cricket players — Australia —
Diaries. 3. Test matches (Cricket)
I. Title. II. Title: Ashes Diary.

796.358092

Typeset by Letter Perfect, 541 George St, Sydney
Printed in Australia by McPhersons Printing, Mulgrave, Victoria

CONTENTS

Foreword 7
Itinerary 9
The Cast 10
Prelude 11
Early Days 13
The One-Day Internationals 39
Towards the Tests 46
The First Test 57
'Ears to McDermott 65
The Second Test 77
Ups and Downs 87
The Third Test 97
To Leeds via Dublin 107
The Fourth Test 129
Mark Taylor Can't Bowl! 137
The Fifth Test 145
Playing from Memory 155
The Sixth Test 165
Winding Down 173
Memorable Moments 176
Tour Record 183

DEDICATION

*To my parents, Beverley and Rodger, for their encouragement
and support over the years, and to my wife, Lynette,
for the sacrifices she has had to make in order for my
career to take the shape it has.*

WORD by Shane Warne

...eatures of the Australian cricket team's tour of England in 1993 was ...iary. Every day, Steve would be hard at work, recording the events ...apping a photo of an unsuspecting tourist. For some, the diary was ...y were never exactly sure what Steve was putting down on paper. ...I'm sure everyone will be happy with the final product.

...en Steve asked me to contribute the foreword for the book. He has ...cket right from the first time I played with him, on an Australian XI ...991. We've kept in contact ever since, and I've come to know and ...He's the ultimate team player — always offering encouragement, ...what's best for the entire side.

...dent involving Steve that happened in a Test against the West Indies ...as bowling to Desmond Haynes. The field was a little damp, and I ...with a rag in my pocket which I was using to dry the ball. After ..., I returned it to Steve who ran in and bowled a ball that sailed way ...n's head and straight into Ian Healy's gloves. Heals didn't have to ...ooked funny, and everyone had a laugh — except Steve, competitor ...ked straight at me and said: "Thanks Warney."

...w the ball back to Steve I made sure it was dryer than the Nullarbor. ...c Ashes series in 1993, although there was a period, as he records in ...ggled a bit because of a lack of opportunities. It can be a problem batting at six in a side that can reach 500 with only three wickets down, as we did at Lord's. Even in the county games, where guys like Matthew Hayden and Damien Martyn were scoring heaps of runs, Steve didn't always get a look in. But when we really needed him, on the final day of the third Test when he batted for most of the last two sessions to save the game, he came through. And then he followed up with a brilliant century at Headingley, where he and Allan Border put on an unbroken 322 for the fourth wicket.

To see Steve and Allan in that partnership was one of my highlights of the trip. AB was an unbelievable help to me on tour — in fact I can't say enough about what he has done for my entire career. He understands the way I think. It's uncanny the way he is able to work out when I should come on, what fields should be set, and the way I should bowl. He's fantastic — on and off the field — and a genuine inspiration to me, and all the guys. I hope he keeps playing until he can't walk.

The tour was full of great performances and memorable moments. I can remember Steve telling me, at the airport in Melbourne before we left for England, that we would all experience some personal highlights, and the four months of the tour proved him right time and time again. The whole Ashes tour experience was fantastic, and while my favourite memory will always be being part of such a brilliant team, there were also moments of personal success that I'll always treasure.

One of those occurred at Edgbaston, during the fifth Test, when I bowled Graham Gooch around his legs. I had put the idea of going around the wicket and bowling wide of Gooch's leg stump to a AB the night before, and although my captain wasn't overly keen (he thought Gooch would just kick the ball away) he said it could be worth a go.

When I did go around the wicket, the first ball pitched on a length just outside leg stump and Gooch padded it away. But the second was fuller, and wider — wider, in fact, than I had intended. Gooch barely bothered with it, throwing no more than a token pad at the ball. But I'd put plenty of spin on it, and it pitched, bit back, and took the leg stump. To see his wicket shatter was fantastic, and I just lost control and ran at AB, pointing at him and celebrating over what I had just done.

As great a moment as getting that wicket was, it wasn't quite as exciting as my first wicket of the series — Mike Gatting, bowled by my first ball of the first Test, at Manchester. In his diary, Steve has some very complimentary things to say about that delivery, which I really appreciate. The memory of it is something that will stay with me forever.

At the pre-Test team meeting, we'd gone through the strengths and weaknesses of all the English players, and while we'd decided it would be a good idea to get me on at their number four, Robin Smith, as soon as possible, there was no preconceived strategy for me to bowl at Gatting before he was set. When I came on, I was nervous, all I wanted to do was find my rhythm and confidence, and pitch the ball roughly in the right place. That was the plan for the first couple of overs.

As history now shows, things worked out a lot better than that. The first ball pitched outside leg stump, spun past the batsman's bat and pad, and clipped the off stump. Gatting was stunned ... and so was I. In the space of one delivery so much had changed. My confidence was now sky high, I was pumped up and rock'n'rolling. That one ball set the stage for all the things that ran for me throughout the series.

At the beginning of the tour, all I wanted was to do well in the early county games and then, hopefully, play in a few of the Tests and be a part of it all. To capture more Test wickets than any Australian leg-spinner had previously taken in an Ashes series in England, and be named the Australian player of the series, were achievements beyond my wildest dreams.

As I read Steve's diary, the thing I was constantly reminded of was the fabulous spirit we had among the team. It was a brilliant tour on the field, and off it. We shared many a joke and a party, and had a whole series of good times, without ever losing sight of the fact we were in England for one reason — to retain the Ashes. To achieve that goal, and be part of such a happy and successful side, was (and remains) an unbelievable feeling.

I think it's great that Steve, through this book, has had the opportunity to tell the story of our Ashes experience in 1993. I just hope, like everyone else who was involved in the tour, that I get the chance to go back in '97 and do it all again.

ITINERARY

APRIL
- 25 — Arrival in London
- 26-29 — Practice, at Lord's
- 30 — v England Amateur XI, at Radlett

MAY
- 2 — v Duchess of Norfolk's XI, at Arundel
- 3 — v Middlesex, at Lord's
- 5-7 — v Worcestershire, at Worcester
- 8-10 — v Somerset, at Taunton
- 13-15 — v Sussex, at Hove
- 16 — v Northamptonshire, at Northampton
- 19 — First Texaco Trophy One-day International, at Old Trafford
- 21 — Second Texaco Trophy One-day International, at Edgbaston
- 23 — Third Texaco Trophy One-day International, at Lord's
- 25-27 — v Surrey, at The Oval, or Yorkshire, at Headingley (depending on Benson & Hedges Cup quarter-finals. If both counties involved in Cup quarter-finals, either Northamptonshire or Nottinghamshire to be alternative opponents)
- 29-31 — v Leicestershire, at Leicester

JUNE
- 3-7 — First Cornhill Test Match, at Old Trafford
- 9-11 — v Warwickshire, at Edgbaston, or Nottinghamshire, at Trent Bridge, or Somerset, at Taunton (depending on Benson & Hedges Cup semi-finals)
- 12-14 — v Gloucestershire, at Bristol
- 17-21 — Second Cornhill Test Match, at Lord's
- 23-25 — v Combined Universities, at Oxford
- 26-28 — v Hampshire, at Southampton

JULY
- 1-6 — Third Cornhill Test Match, at Trent Bridge
- 8 — v Minor Counties, at Stone
- 10 — v Ireland, at Clontarf (Dublin)
- 13-15 — v Derbyshire, at Derby
- 17-19 — v Durham, at Durham University
- 22-26 — Fourth Cornhill Test Match, at Headingley
- 28-30 — v Northamptonshire, at Northampton, or Lancashire, at Old Trafford (depending on NatWest Trophy first-round matches)
- 31-August 2 — v Glamorgan, at Neath

AUGUST
- 5-9 — Fifth Cornhill Test Match, at Edgbaston
- 11-13 — v Kent, at Canterbury (or one-day match v Kent on August 13 if Kent involved in NatWest Trophy semi-final)
- 14-16 — v Essex, at Chelmsford
- 19-23 — Sixth Cornhill Test Match, at The Oval

THE CAST

Allan Border
— AB

David Boon
— Boonie/Babs

Matthew Hayden
— Hulkster/Jurassic

Ian Healy
— Heals/Barney Rubble

Wayne Holdsworth
— Cracker

Merv Hughes
— Swervin'/Hilly

Brendon Julian
— BJ

Craig McDermott
— Billy

Damien Martyn
— Marto

Tim May
— Maysie

Paul Reiffel
— Pistol

Michael Slater
— Slats/Sybil

Mark Taylor
— Tubs/Tails

Shane Warne
— Warney/Hollywood

Mark Waugh
— Junior

Steve Waugh
— Tugga

Tim Zoehrer
— Ziggy

Errol Alcott (Physio)
— Hooter

Bob Simpson (Coach)
— Simmo

Mike Walsh (Scorer)

Des Rundle (Manager)

PRELUDE

APRIL 23, the day before our departure for England, was a day of gearing up, getting ready, and looking after final business. All the players and team officials had assembled in Melbourne for final preparations. As has probably always been the way on the day before the departure of an Australian cricket team to the UK, we found ourselves heavily into promoting the upcoming tour and also looking after some early promotional work for next season's domestic program.

My first stop was Illusions Studio, where the opening batsmen had already been interviewed by Channel Nine, filmed in action and photographed — both in yellow one-day uniforms (for 1994 domestic consumption) and Test match whites. By 10am, when the middle order was before the cameras — a line-up consisting of Martyn, Border, M. Waugh and S. Waugh — we were already an hour behind schedule. What looked like a simple procedure of filming a few set-up cricket strokes dragged into hours of takes. Seemingly trivial matters such as adjustments to the lighting, the changing of camera angles, the re-applying of make-up and "sweat", and the changing from one-day gear to Test match gear, all ate away at the time.

Inevitably there was a focus on the theme of the twins together, and Mark and I had to oblige by being filmed side by side — with Mark taking off his pads and me putting them on. Our patience was faltering by the time we finished, one-and-a-half hours late. Next stop for me was a visit to my cricket equipment sponsor — Gunn & Moore — where I picked up a few items of clothing and a cricket bag.

Back at the hotel, each player was given a new "coffin" (hard cricket-case) filled with training shirts, casual wear, tracksuits, cricket creams and a collection of XXXX accessories to use and give away on tour. Like 1989, XXXX, one of Australia's biggest-selling beers, is our major tour sponsor. I had guessed poorly on the amount of clothing we were to receive and now had far too many clothes and bags in my possession.

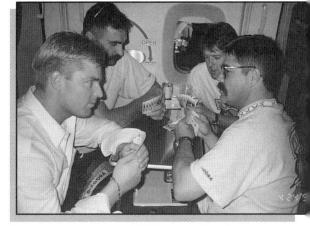

The plane has not long left the ground, and the first of countless tour card schools is underway. The four sharks are (left to right): Shane Warne, Merv Hughes, Tim Zoehrer and David Boon.

It is always hard to judge the right amount of gear to take away on tour and what type of clothes to pack. I have a bad reputation for getting my climates mixed up. On the last Ashes tour I forgot to take a jumper — and when we arrived it was snowing! On the last West Indies tour, I took three jumpers — and walked straight into a heatwave. The bulky jumpers I had in the Caribbean were as useful as a chocolate teapot.

After a careful sifting process I filled one of my soft cricket bags with items that I figured I wouldn't need — and sent it back to Sydney, leaving me with a luggage content of: 1 coffin, 1 large suitcase, 1 soft cricket bag, 1 carry-bag

Quite sufficient for four-and-a-half months on the road, I reckoned.

The day's schedule was a hectic one, and to complete it we attended the Australian Cricket Board's farewell dinner, along with the current Board members and team sponsors. For the occasion we donned our newly-acquired suits, which had been especially selected by Ian Healy and Errol Alcott (the team physiotherapist) to give the side a more updated image. There was general agreement that they give the team a smart and professional look.

The function turned out to be an entertaining one, even though it didn't finish until 12.30am. There were inspirational film clips from past Ashes confrontations, film of the Wallabies' World Cup rugby union victory and a tribute to Allan Border, featuring highlights of his career. The unique feeling of being part of an Ashes campaign was starting to sink in again, especially when one of the guest speakers used the phrases: "It's a chance to create your own piece of history", and, "You can carve your own niche in Ashes folklore". I think all the players realised that ahead lay a chance to change the course of their lives. The '89 series was briefly discussed and the fact that it was four years ago was emphasised. There was quick and unanimous agreement that the entire focus must now be on the '93 tour — not on something that had happened in the past.

The only mishap on the night, predictably, involved the team's "Master of Disaster" — Tim May. One of the waitresses spectacularly off-loaded some alcoholic beverages down the back of his suit, to no-one's real surprise or concern. Tim is regarded as being a bit accident-prone.

Departure day, April 24, 1993, arrived, and, with hours to kill, we headed to the hotel's gymnasium for some fitness work. As usual, we were early at the airport, arriving two-and-a-half hours before take-off. On hand were a sprinkling of fans and media to bid us farewell. The lads, health-conscious as ever, raced off to the airport's McDonald's for a quick fix.

When we finally boarded there was some disappointment — the seat allocation had us dotted all over the place. The flight traditionally is a chance for some of the new players to get to know everybody a bit better, and the seating arrangements undermined that to some extent. Undeterred by this slight hitch, a card school was almost immediately in full swing with Merv and Boonie taking on Warney and Ziggy. It turned out to be a titanic struggle that lasted the whole journey.

A few of the lads slept for most of the trip. I find sleep near-impossible on planes and, with a few of the others, tried to stay amused by reading, writing or swapping cricket stories.

The tradition of the Aussie drinker on the flying kangaroo was not adhered to on our flight; no-one appeared anywhere near as thirsty as Boonie had been four years before. However, another tradition was kept safely alive — that of the "Dumb Quick Bowler". On the Singapore stop, debutant tourist Wayne Holdsworth purchased a Sega computer game. Unfortunately there was a small hitch ... the baseball game cartridge was in Japanese. For the next 13 hours, Cracker happily played a game he couldn't understand. Fast bowlers can do those sort of things.

The setting up of the team's Social and Fines Committees was arranged, in the usual manner — i.e. one experienced tourist as the leader and two others, at least one of whom will be making his first tour, as the back-ups. The line-up is:

Social — Zoehrer (Leader), Hayden and Julian.

Fines — Reiffel (Leader), Hughes and Slater.

Hughes was elected onto the Fines Committee only because he has been a continual pest at previous meetings when not a member of the official line-up. He would hurl abuse at the hierarchy and cause general chaos on most occasions.

The flight finally ended at 5.35am. Our greeting lay in a typical English day — overcast, cool and with light rain falling.

It was great to be back!

EARLY DAYS

DAY 1 (April 25)

THE TEAM was welcomed by representatives from XXXX, the English press, the team liaison officer from '89, Geoff "Gunner" Wilkins, and baggage man, Tony Smith. It was a very subdued affair with the media this time — a much different feeling to that of 1989, when there had been a great deal of keen questioning about the nature of the team and what our chances were. Airport duties over, we headed to the Westbury Hotel, courtesy of our team bus (which includes a TV, toilet, cooking facilities and a lounge at the back, which was immediately claimed as home for the quick bowlers).

My first room-mate is Tim May who happens to be, among other things, a notorious snorer — and especially after a pint or two. Despite this, he's one of the best roomies going around.

A press conference and introduction of the team at our hotel (which, fortunately, only lasted about an hour) was followed by a buffet lunch and player interviews. All the guys were weary but we knew the best thing was to exercise, and wait for nightfall before going to sleep. Most of the team went to the closest gym where we used the treadmill and weights room, followed by a spa and swim. Undoubted highlight was Merv and his Orca the Killer Whale impersonations which saw most of the water end up out of the pool.

Craig McDermott and Wayne Holdsworth later experienced first-hand some of the aftermath of yesterday's massive IRA bomb blast in London, when they were diverted by police while jogging in Hyde Park. There was talk of another bomb in the vicinity. They still made it back for a brief but to-the-point six o'clock team meeting which sorted out our objectives and attitudes for the tour.

Afterwards, we dined at a Mexican restaurant called Break for the Border, where Matt Hayden and Brendon Julian ordered a meal entitled "Border Blast". It was a promising portent.

I was glad to get to bed. However, Maysie's "anti-snoring device" — a plastic ring he inserts up his nostrils — unfortunately dislodged during the night, allowing the chainsaw to cut loose at a particularly high decibel level.

Merv Hughes and David Boon pose for the press, outside the Westbury Hotel in London.

DAY 2 (April 26)

THE DAY dawned to an overcast sky, a temperature around 15 degrees and the prospect of rain. Today we went to Lord's and the feeling of excitement was evident among the players, particularly the younger blokes. But not *just* the young blokes; Bob Simpson declared that he still gets a thrill each time he arrives at Lord's ... even after 30 years.

Our first session was designed to get the aches and pains from the long trip out of the system, and to get a feel of the local conditions. Everyone was nice and relaxed, with the only concerns being Merv Hughes and Tim May, both of whom are recovering from knee operations and have to take it easy for a week or two, and Paul Reiffel, who's down with a stomach virus.

As is expected in an English cricketing summer, the rain came, causing us to change location to the indoor nets for our afternoon practice session. All the guys were pleased that the first day's practice was over, and that it has all begun — although we all know we'll wake up stiff and sore tomorrow morning.

After practice we barely had time to shower before our next appointment was upon us — a get-together with representatives from our tour sponsor, XXXX beer. We were briefed on our responsibilities on tour, which include pub visits, golf days, quiz nights and corporate days — with each player expected to participate in at least 6-8 functions. Once again, we received a mountain of gear — and it was of excellent quality, especially the suede and leather bomber jackets.

I was finally able to contact my wife, Lynette, after calling four or five times. As always it was great to hear her voice and learn that everything is okay at home.

Our allowances for meals are 19 pounds for dinner and nine pounds for lunch on non-playing days; it isn't all that much considering the price of food and alcohol in London.

News of the allowances caused some panic among the lads — and it looks like we'll be eating pub food rather than restaurant food. Out for a stroll, Tim May, Brendon Julian and I stumbled upon The Dog and Trumpet pub, which was hosting an ANZAC Day boat race competition (drink sculling). Our team, admirably captained by Tim May, and boosted by two ring-ins, pulled off the impossible and won the event. We walked away with a collection of prizes ... and potential headaches.

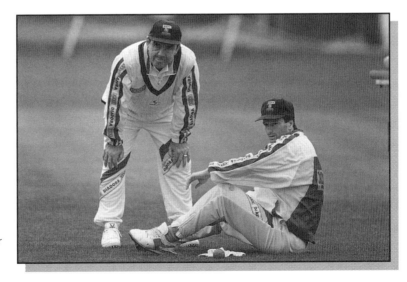

With coach Bob Simpson during our first day's practice, at Lord's.

DAY 3 (April 27)

THE COACH to Lord's left at 9am sharp for an all-day practice session. The index finger on my right hand has almost recovered from the break and ligament damage suffered during the recent New Zealand tour, so I was hardly restricted. But it'll be another two weeks before I can bowl again though. The session was quite impressive, with all players finding some sort of form. The fielding sessions particularly were of a very high quality. Afterwards we lined up for a photo with the team's car sponsor for the tour, Peugeot — who are supplying four cars for the players' use during our stay.

Golf is going to be a popular pastime on the days off, and all the lads play to a reasonable handicap, except Merv and Cracker, who are shockers. Merv's happy with that though — he claims he gets better value for his money as he plays more shots than anyone else. Golf-wise, we're being looked after by a local company, who supplied 20 sets of clubs which can be purchased by the players very cheaply at the end of the tour.

We dined tonight at the Hard Rock Cafe, with hamburgers and thickshakes the order of the day ... just for a change.

No sex please, say Aussies

A SEX ban has been slapped on Australian players bidding to retain the Ashes this summer.

Allan Border's 17-strong England touring squad have been told wives and girlfriends cannot stay overnight at team hotels during the six Tests.

Skipper Border imposed the same restrictions on Australia's last tour here in 1989 and it worked ... they won 4-0.

The ban means players must fork out for alternative accommodation for their partners, some of whom are due to arrive in June and stay for the rest of the summer. But there are no complaints.

"We're here to concentrate on playing cricket and winning the Ashes," I was told. "Having the wives in different hotels is going to cost us money but the cricket comes first."

Meanwhile, as rain played havoc with the tourists' first practice at Lord's yesterday, the TCCB rejected their request for a third umpire to rule on run-outs and stumpings in Tests.

The innovation was used on Australia's winter tour to New Zealand and manager Bobby Simpson insisted: "We've changed our views since that visit because at first we thought it would slow the game down. It doesn't.

"It has added a new, exciting dimension to the game and the spectators get very involved."

But the TCCB said experiments will be limited to televised matches in the three county one-day tournaments. Lord's officials want to try a system where the third umpire's decision is communicated to his on-field colleagues by two-way radio rather than the red and green lights, visible to fans, employed by the Kiwis and South Africans.

Ball-tampering was also raised at a rules meeting between the two camps.

English county regulations now state umpires must inspect the ball at the end of each over and allow the batting side to choose a replacement if bowlers are caught tampering. Umpires are also required to say why they've changed a ball.

But in the Tests, the laws of cricket — which led to cover-up and controversy during last summer's Pakistan tour – again apply.

Inspections will be random, the replacement ball must be similar quality and if the ICC referee intervenes there will be no public statements.

● Aussie pace aces Craig McDermott and Merv Hughes are unlikely starters in early tour games. Both have had surgery since the Kiwi tour – Hughes on a knee and McDermott on a long-term groin problem that last season prevented him joining Yorkshire.

Report by GRAHAM OTWAY

DAY 4 (April 28)

THIS MORNING I established a new UK breakfast-eating record, downing my food in around 60 seconds, which enabled me to be on the bus at 9 o'clock for the trip to Lord's. Training was again of a high standard, but fairly relaxed; we're all settling in to the new conditions. Personally, I'm feeling confident, with my feet moving well. My timing is getting better with each session.

A hasty shower gave us enough time to make it to the British Sportsman's Club luncheon. The boys could hardly wait! Surprisingly, it turned out to be an entertaining affair, with the highlight being a speech by the former British Prime Minister, Sir Edward Heath, who, unexpectedly, took the mickey out of his fellow Poms.

Most of the lads believe one function a week is too many. But today held a special treat, with the MCC welcoming dinner programmed for the evening. We were surrounded by cricket fanatics at the dinner, most in the twilight of their lives, and all of them trying in four hours to extract as much information about our careers and the team's chances in the forthcoming series as was humanly possible. In his address to the gathering, our team manager, Des Rundle, livened up proceedings by breaking out a couple of his favourite jokes. Des did well; he had some of the elderly members choking on their cigar smoke.

Maysie was in top snoring form after the dinner. Unfortunately, a suitable replacement for his plastic "anti-snoring ring" has yet to be located in London. The inevitable noise pollution required some adjustments to the location of our beds — i.e. moving them as far as possible apart — before I could get some sleep.

The front covers of the menus for our lunch at the British Sportsman's Club (right) and dinner with the members of the MCC. The Sportsman's Club cover features a caricature and the autograph of the former British Prime Minister, Sir Edward Heath, who chaired the luncheon.

DAY 5 (April 29)

WE HAD an early start today — 8am for head-and-shoulders photos for our sponsors, XXXX. Within an hour we were on the bus and off to Lord's for another practice session — our first game is tomorrow.

Simmo finally grabbed his chance to introduce a few of the new members of the team to one of his torturous fielding sessions. Brendon Julian was not quite sure what had hit him after taking about 50 outfield catches, followed by some ground fielding. He was left gasping for air and praying for no more.

The highlight of the session was undoubtedly the accidental smashing of three windows in the corporate boxes — a small payback for last evening's punishment at the MCC members' dinner.

The Fines Committee has come up with a tipping competition incorporating the AFL and the rugby league competitions back home. It's 20 quid in — first prize, 180 pounds. And a game of golf, at the Moore Park course, was organised for this afternoon, and attracted about eight starters. Unfortunately, I can't play yet because of my finger. So it was off to the gym with Tim May for a one-and-a-half hour session, followed by some shopping to buy a few new CDs. The 15 I brought with me have already had a fair work-out on Maysie's portable CD player.

Tonight we went to the theatre to see Phantom of the Opera, on first-rate tickets that had us so close we reckoned we could have picked off the Phantom with a well-thrown malteser. It was the third time I'd seen the show, and for me it was every bit as good this time around, although it didn't seem to impress some of the other lads, who wanted more action. After the theatre it was off to a local pub for a few pints and a post-mortem.

Below: AB, enjoying our last practice session before the first game of the tour.

18

DAY 6 (April 30)

THE FIRST game of the tour, against an England Amateur XI at Radlett, was played today, but, as I was not required, I grabbed a rare chance to sleep in 'til 9.15. The other players not on duty were Merv, AB, Pistol and Maysie.

During the first six weeks of the tour, the whole squad is required to attend games as a unit. After this period, the extras can play golf, see their wives and/or girlfriends — or go anywhere they choose. Pistol took the wheel on the way to Radlett, former home ground of the infamous bodyline captain, Douglas Jardine, and not unexpectedly, we took a wrong turn on the motorway and turned a 40-minute drive into one-and-a-quarter hours.

At the game we witnessed first-hand the intense rivalry between beer companies in their quest to outdo each other and grab a bigger market share. With XXXX being our sponsor, Foster's obviously will attempt to pull off some sort of stunt at any game they can. Today was no exception, with a Foster's hot-air balloon hovering just outside the ground and offering people free rides.

The game turned out to be a pleasing first-up effort, with Matt Hayden scoring a superb 151 in his initial game in the baggy green cap. Michael Slater also did well with 41 in his first appearance, and Wayne Holdsworth took 3-28 off eight overs.

As is the case at virtually all English grounds, there were facilities today to place bets on every sport imaginable, including cricket. For the sake of an interest, I took a peek at the odds on the Aussie batsman scoring the most runs in the Test series — and considered myself at 8/1 and Matt Hayden at 20/1 fair value. I had 25 pounds on each of us.

The Social Committee presented Ian Healy with a 29th-birthday cake after the game, and the locals staged an evening of entertainment in our honour. Merv was on fire with his array of Pommy jokes and at one point had two local club members enthralled. Things were going so well he pulled out his favourite whale joke, which involves Merv asking a series of questions to his victims, such as: "What noise does a gorilla make?" — to which they reply with an appropriate sound. Then it's a horse, dog, cat, dolphin ... and finally a whale. At this point they are sprayed with beer from Merv's mouth as he imitates a whale blowing water.

The bus trip home turned into a scene from World Championship Wrestling, with the lounge at the back of the bus transformed into a makeshift ring. There were some monumental clashes, with Matt Hayden bouncing off the window, Mark Taylor falling victim to a Merv Hughes sleeper-hold and Boonie finding himself set upon by McDermott and Hughes, with additional back-up from Holdsworth. Amazingly, there appeared to be no injuries upon pulling up at the Westbury — only words of insult and ridicule which I'm sure will guarantee many more battles on the motorway. It's only a matter of time before blood is spilt — hopefully, not mine.

DAY 7 (May 1)

TRAINING this morning lasted the usual couple of hours, with a few of the lads complaining of soreness. It had nothing to do with the previous day's play, but plenty to do with the keenly contested bouts on the bus.

Today we travelled to the famous Wembley stadium — my fourth visit to the hallowed turf — for the Silk Cut Rugby League Challenge Cup Final between Widnes and Wigan. The unique atmosphere of the place, jammed with 77,000 spectators, made it an experience none of the guys will ever forget ... except for Warney, who fell asleep. Wigan finally won the match, their sixth successive win in the Cup Final.

Dilip Doshi, the former left-arm orthodox spinner from India, now living in London, entertained us at dinner at his favourite Indian restaurant, the Bombay Brasserie, reputedly the best in London. I must admit I'm a little sceptical about Indian cuisine, particularly after the rating by our resident experts, Tim May and Mark Taylor, that a top quality curry is one which makes you sweat profusely, causes your lips to swell and makes you visit the toilet at least five times the following morning. But my fears were dispelled — the food was first-class, and it turned out to be a very enjoyable evening. Even so, it was good to get to bed. I still feel a bit dazed from the flight and hectic schedule so far.

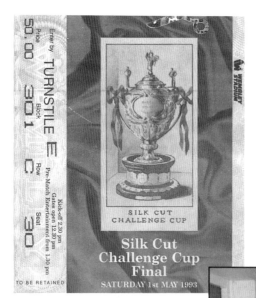

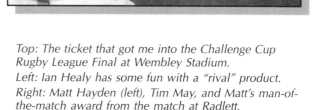

Top: The ticket that got me into the Challenge Cup Rugby League Final at Wembley Stadium.
Left: Ian Healy has some fun with a "rival" product.
Right: Matt Hayden (left), Tim May, and Matt's man-of-the-match award from the match at Radlett.

DAY 8 (May 2)

WE WERE up early, ready for a 7.30am departure for the picturesque ground at Arundel Castle, Sussex, to play a one-day match against the Duchess of Norfolk's XI. Unfortunately, our room service arrived at 7.28 — so we were off to a poor start for the day. The Duchess team was a strong combination, containing the likes of Ian Botham, Joel Garner and a host of ex-internationals, ensuring a good contest for the record 12,000 crowd.

We managed to recover from a poor start to tally a respectable 203, with Ian Healy playing a fine team innings of 47 not out. I got 59 off 72 balls — a pleasing start to the tour. In reply, the opposition fell just seven runs short — with Australia almost managing to snatch defeat from the jaws of victory. Fourteen runs came from the last over. Mark Waugh was the most successful bowler, capturing 5-32 and there was good support from Shane Warne, backed up by some quality fielding.

As usual with a game of this nature, there were a few relaxing drinks with the opposing team at the end. On this occasion, it was a great experience for our younger members, who got the chance to mingle with two of the greats, Botham and Garner.

The trip home turned into a singalong at the back of the bus, with Wayne Holdsworth taking control of the lead vocals and providing some interesting alterations to the lyrics. It proved again that Cracker is a man of many hidden talents. Once again, the Golden Arches (i.e. McDonald's) grabbed the attention of our driver and the lads piled out of the bus for yet another gourmet feast.

DAY 9 (May 3)

TODAY WAS a big day — our first game at Lord's. Even more importantly, the first State of Origin rugby league match was on at midday our time — with 50 pounds of my money riding on the NSW Blues.

The match was a limited-overs affair against a strong Middlesex outfit, and Allan Border won the toss and elected to bat first on a good-looking wicket. It turned out to be the correct decision as we accumulated 243 off our 55 overs. Matt Hayden and Damien Martyn scored 122 and 66 respectively in a highly entertaining and classy partnership. I must admit, my 25 pounds (on Hayden) looks an even better proposition after today. In reply, Middlesex stumbled early and never really recovered, despite an impressive 32 from Mike Gatting, which ended with his run-out. Obviously Gatt was keen to do well and found himself unable to control his emotions after his dismissal. On his return to the dressing room, he proceeded to put an arm through a plate-glass window, cutting himself so badly that he needed 25 stitches and a 2-3 week vacation to fix the damage. He was ruled out of the one-day internationals which start in 16 day's time.

During today's play someone suggested that this touring party could be the prettiest ever to leave our shores. It was subsequently decided to split the team into two sides for a series of events and competitions throughout the tour. Side one is to be called "The Nerds" and will be captained by Tim May, who is over the moon about his selection (although he was considered an absolute certainty by the rest of the lads). Maysie's teammates qualified by being either: — ugly — poor dressers — good drinkers — non-users of gel in their hair; or, as in the case of their captain, all of the above.

The other team is to be named "The Julios" (after Julio Iglesias) or "Pretty Boys", and will be led by Errol Alcott, with qualifications being that they must: — use hair gel — carry a pocket-sized mirror in their pants at all times — have posed as a model for a newspaper article — walk as if they're carrying a watermelon under each arm.

May's team (The Nerds) is: Taylor, Boon, Border, S. Waugh, Zoehrer, Reiffel, Hughes and Healy.

Alcott's team (The Julios) is: Hayden, Slater, M. Waugh, Warne, Holdsworth, Martyn, Julian and McDermott.

The tiring schedule of the first week continued this evening with a reception at Australia House. There was barely time for a shower at the conclusion of the game. This function turned out to be better than expected for four reasons — short speeches, plenty of food, fellow Australians present and an endless supply of XXXX.

Great news! State of Origin I — NSW 14, Queensland 10.

Maysie ignores the attention of one of his fans at Lord's.

Hard at work on the pages of this book.

DAY 10 (May 4)

OUR ROOM this morning was a monumental mess. The floor was covered in clothes, bags and newspapers, making the task of packing a tough one, especially for me as I estimated that it was 90 per cent *my* mess.

We checked out at 9.30am, after paying our bill which consisted of a few phone calls home at the going rate of six pounds per minute. That left me about 100 pounds in the red already.

By now, the positions on the bus are just about set, with the management down the front, accompanied by a few non-smokers. Next comes the card school of Boon, Hughes, Zoehrer and Warne, who occupy four seats opposite each other. At the back is Billy's lounge, which he occasionally rents out if hassled by someone who is looking to share.

The journey to Worcester passed quickly, thanks largely to a showing of *The Commitments* on the bus video-system.

Unbelievably, there were no reservations for the team on our arrival at the hotel, leading to a one-hour delay. We filled in time by signing 100 bats for a sponsor. First glance at our room — or should I say kennel — made it apparent that my roomie (May) and I would have sleeping problems. The beds were about 15 centimetres apart. Maysie immediately scurried down to the local mall in search of an anti-snoring device. I've stayed in some tiny rooms before, but this one definitely ranks as a grand finalist. You'd get bigger in prison. Paul Reiffel reckons they're taking the mickey out of him as his room number is 303.

We trained this afternoon — a fairly relaxed affair with the highlight being a Nerds vs Julios touch footy match, which ended in victory for the good guys (Nerds) to the tune of 5-3. Most of the guys dined out at a local steakhouse, with all of us looking forward to our first serious match which starts tomorrow against a strong Worcester side.

DAY 11 (May 5)

I WOKE up feeling a little dazed, probably because I only had about three hours sleep. Maysie had been in top form — so much so that I thought he was going to suck the curtains from the windows. At least I got the opportunity to listen to my new CD — *Unplugged* by Eric Clapton — on the headphones as I lay there, trying unsuccessfully to get to sleep.

Today was the first day of a three-day match against Worcestershire. The six players to miss out were Hughes, May, Border, Slater, McDermott and Zoehrer, leaving us with a fairly young and inexperienced side, but one with loads of talent. Mark Taylor won the toss and elected to bat on a wicket that looked full of runs. It did four years ago, too — and we were bowled out for 103 on the opening day! Matthew Hayden, coming off successive centuries, got a reminder that cricket is a great leveller when he was out for three. The ball before Matt was dismissed, he and Tails had their usual mid-wicket conference discussing the merits of the upcoming bowler, with Matt telling Tails: "He's a left-hander so he'll probably take the ball away from us towards the slips; we'll just rock forward and belt him through the covers for four, mate."

The first delivery did *exactly* as predicted — except the ball flew off the outside edge of Matt's bat and straight into the gully fieldsman's hands. It re-inforced the old message that you should *never* make bold statements when you're batting as they'll nearly always backfire on you.

Australia finished the day all out 262, with Worcester 1-12 in reply. The highlight was David Boon's 108, on what turned out to be a difficult batting strip. My 49 not out provided just what I needed — time in the middle.

The only mistake I made today was listening to number 11 Cracker Holdsworth when he joined me at the crease, with me needing one run for my 50. His first words were: "Trust me Tugga, I'll be here for a while." The first ball he faced was a nasty inswinger, which he tried to nullify by attempting a six over cover. It missed the stumps by a coat of varnish. He followed that textbook stroke with an edge straight to second slip, earning himself a duck.

Just for a change, we had a function to go to — after-game drinks with the opposition and club officials. Thankfully, it was over in 45 minutes, just enough time for the lads to polish off the food and throw down a quick couple of pints. Tea this evening was of the Italian variety, at a place just around the corner from our pub. The eight of us who went were all pleased with our choices at the end of the night — even Warney, a man who can live on toasted cheese sandwiches, chips, sauce and strawberry milkshakes for weeks on end.

DAY 12 (May 6)

THE DAY began superbly for our bowlers, with Worcester being bundled out for 90 in 33.5 overs. Reiffel, Julian and Holdsworth exploited the favourable conditions to take three wickets each and were backed up by some excellent catching. By the time lunch came around, Worcester were 1-21 after being forced to follow on. The talk in the dressing room was of an early getaway tomorrow. At that point it appeared a formality that we'd wrap the game up today.

Well, someone forgot to give the batsmen the script. In the next session we failed to take a wicket, making us, I would think, the first team in the history of the game to take 10 wickets in a session and then follow up with nil wickets in the next.

The last session was a little more even, Worcester ending up 3-308, with Graeme Hick not out 163 after being dropped three times. He batted with brilliance and awesome timing.

Looking back on the day, we should have finished in a winning position instead of having the game hanging in the balance. Shane Warne encountered his first bad day for a long time, at the hands of Hick, but this wasn't such a bad thing as it will make him even more determined next time they meet.

Hick hammers Aussies

Report by GRAHAM OTWAY

GRAEME HICK gave the Aussies their first taste of his new-found confidence with a brilliant century at New Road yesterday.

On the fifth anniversary of his record 405 not out against Somerset, England's great Ashes hope thrilled a sun-baked crowd for over four-and-a-quarter hours for an unbeaten 161.

Hick's scintillating innings rescued Worcestershire from crisis after they followed on after being bowled out for 90 in 30 overs. The tourists will curse themselves for allowing Hick to take a psychological edge over their bowlers.

And Hick said later: "Obviously it's useful to have had an early sight of their bowlers but the Test matches will be very different in pressure and atmosphere. But it's nice to get a big score under my belt and spend some time at the crease."

Hick gave the Aussies two early chances at 17 and 31 but they were spurned by Ian Healy and David Boon. And by the time he offered a third he had already passed his 100 off only 136 balls.

By the close of the second day, Hick had struck 26 boundaries and two effortless sixes and had buried his three other single figure innings this summer to earn Worcester a lead of 139 with seven wickets in hand.

It was a far cry from the morning session when the Worcester first innings, Hick included, was decimated in under two hours by the Aussie second string pace attack of Wayne Holdsworth, Paul Reiffel and Brendon Julien, who took three wickets each.

But Hick roared back with help from his skipper Tim Curtis and the scoreboard will make happy reading for Ted Dexter and Co.

Ball spells Test havoc

THIS summer's Ashes series between England and Australia could be reduced to three-day contests dominated by fast bowlers, it was forecast yesterday, writes Graham Otway.

That's because one of the types of ball being made available to the two sides – the "Twort", made by British firm Dukes – conforms to recently tightened TCCB legislation but can turn ordinary seam bowlers into unplayable demons.

The Aussies were using a Twort at New Road yesterday as they skittled out Worcestershire for 90 in 30 overs.

One Worcester player told me: "If they use those balls in the Test matches they won't last more than three days."

The problem with the Twort balls is the pronounced seam, which stays hard far longer than the stitching on the other types of balls available for the Tests, made by Readers.

Before the Ashes series starts next month rival skippers Allan Border and Graham Gooch will be asked which ball they wish to use.

● Television replays to judge marginal run-outs and stumpings could be used in the Ashes series.

DAY 13 (May 7)

HICK STARTED proceedings with the same dominance he showed last evening and took his score to 187 before being dismissed. Once again, Warney copped the brunt of Hick's aggression, going for 19 in one over. But Warney could still see the lighter side of the caning he took, especially as he made the statement to me before the start of that particular over that he was feeling confident of taking Hick's wicket.

Worcester finally put us out of our misery by declaring at 4-458, leaving us to score 287 off 55 overs — a fairly tough assignment.

But we made it. Boon scored another hundred, making it a superb double for the game. Taylor rattled off a quickfire 40 and Hayden fell four short of yet another hundred. We found ourselves needing 12 off the last over with Healy and myself at the crease. I edged the first ball for four, followed by a single and then a Healy single. Luckily, the next ball was tossed up and I dispatched it over mid-off for six to wrap up a very good game and place 2000 pounds in the team kitty.

Michael Slater excelled in his first game as 12th man for Australia, wearing his practice hat on the field when called out to the middle. He then decided he needed a hair cut and got one of the other players to cover for him while he had a shampoo and style-cut down the road. The Fines Committee were excited by this news and seem sure to lighten Slats' wallet at the first meeting.

The two-hour bus trip to Taunton, in Somerset, went quickly, thanks to a full 80-minute video of the first State of Origin rugby league match. The battle between the Blues and the Maroons was tame compared with the mauling and physical abuse handed out on the bus during the journey. McDermott, in particular, turned in a man-of-the-match performance, taking out a few of the NSW boys with a series of Chinese burns to the ears, kidney punches and general thuggery — something which he apparently showed some promise at when playing rugby in Ipswich.

We checked in to the Castle Hotel in Taunton, an impressive, older-style building with plenty of character, and immediately headed next door to a pub for a few post-match celebrations. My new roomie is Matt Hayden. It'll be a chance to get to know each other better; we've only met a few times before this tour.

Wayne Holdsworth, first man to receive Plucka Duck

DAY 14 (May 8)

IT WAS five years ago that I was the overseas professional for Somerset, and I still have a special affinity with the county club that helped me launch my career. As we prepared for our three-day match against them, I was looking forward to scoring some runs.

Allan Border won the toss on another fine, sunny day and elected to bat on a good looking strip. Somerset, like most county teams, are made up of about eight or nine English-born players with the rest coming from countries such as The Netherlands, Zimbabwe, South Africa and New Zealand. Most of these players want to make a living out of the game and county cricket gives them that chance — as well as the chance of qualifying to play for England after a seven-year wait.

The Somerset opening attack of Van Troost (Holland) and Caddick (New Zealand) proved to be one of the quicker new-ball partnerships in England and had us in immediate trouble, with Tails being caught for a duck. He arrived back in the change rooms unhappy at his quick dismissal. There, far worse news awaited him — that he was now the new caretaker of a Plucka the Duck doll (from the television show, *Hey! Hey! It's Saturday*), taking over from Wayne Holdsworth, the previous incumbent. Tails must now carry Plucka to and from the ground each day until someone else scores a globe.

Michael Slater scored a brilliant 122 on debut, an innings featuring glorious strokeplay on both sides of the wicket, coupled with superb timing. The whole team performed above expectations, scoring around five per over to reach 431, an hour before the end of the day's play. The arrival of drizzling rain then put a stop to proceedings. M. Waugh (68), Border (54), S. Waugh (38) and Hughes (36) all contributed quickfire knocks to keep the scoreboard attendants busy.

Today Heals offered Merv Hughes 20 pounds if he could hit a six to the longest boundary — with an additional five pounds for each one thereafter. It was more than enough incentive for the big fella, who proceeded to club two enormous sixers, one of which sailed out of the ground ... to the dismay of Heals and a huge grin and salute from Swervin.

Back at the hotel, a longstanding tradition was continued when the Australian captain received a whortleberry pie. The story dates back to the 1930s when Sir Donald Bradman fell ill during a tour match against Somerset. Upon hearing this, a local lady baked a pie made from whortleberries (which are found in the Quantock Hills just outside Taunton) and sent it to the Castle Hotel in the hope of reviving The Don. Bradman was very impressed, not only by the gesture, but by the quality of the pie, and ever since such a pie has been presented to the Australian team captain. On this occasion, with whortleberry out of season, an SOS had to be sent out, and a local gent came to the rescue with five pounds of whortleberries from his deep-freeze. Thus the tradition was kept alive.

Tonight I caught up with a few of the Somerset guys for a beer and later rang home to Mum, as it is Mother's Day in Australia. I think she was surprised that I remembered.

DAY 15 (May 9)

AWOKE TO find the weather has turned sour — with steady rain falling and a grey menacing sky. There was no need to leave the hotel as there was no chance of play until at least after lunch, and that brought a smile to the lads' faces.

With a couple of hours to fill, it was decided to hold our first fines meeting of the tour. These meetings are a good way to get team spirit going, to raise money for an end-of-tour night out, or to buy videos to watch on the bus trips.

Cracker, obviously excited at his first meeting, tried to nail everyone else in the team during the 20-minute session in which the committee throws it open for us to fine each other. Cracker has now put himself in an ugly situation, as his new enemies will be watching his every move, seeking revenge.

The highlight of each meeting is undoubtedly the awarding of the "Daktari" outfit to the person who commits the stupidest act of the week. It was won on this occasion by Tubs. The Daktari was purchased by Tom Moody and myself on a tour of Zimbabwe 18 months ago and has been awarded ever since on overseas tours. It is so bad to wear, it embarrasses the wearer and provides amusement for the rest of the team. The Jungle Jim-type outfit must be worn after the game, to wherever the team decides to go for that particular evening — normally to a restaurant followed by a bar. The plan is to make the wearer squirm for as long as possible.

The team finally headed down to the ground for lunch which, in England, is normally a three-course meal such as soup followed by a roast and vegetables and finally an ice-cream with fruit. It's very easy to pile on the kilos if you aren't careful.

Play eventually got under way at 2.30, in freezing conditions cold enough to prompt most of the players to wear long-johns and a couple of jumpers. Somerset ended up at 4-151 by the close, but not before an occurrence rated as being about as common as catching a glimpse of a Dodo bird — Tim May accepting a caught and bowled opportunity!

Michael Slater, after scoring a century in his first first-class game in Australian colours.

29

DAY 16 (May 10)

DUE TO the loss of three hours' play yesterday, the two captains consulted before the start of play and organised to set the game up by way of declarations so that a result could be reached.

Somerset declared immediately, and we replied with 0-40 before also declaring — setting them 321 to win in 80 overs — a not unreasonable target, but one that proved beyond them. Warne and May each picked up four wickets in impressive displays, extracting turn and bounce from the wicket. However, our quick bowlers struggled to find rhythm, particularly Merv who hasn't fully recovered from his knee operation as yet, and, to a lesser degree, Billy, who, during a frustrating spell, had a run-in with AB which was picked up by the Channel 7 cameras and microphones. AB and Billy thought nothing more of it until they were swamped by the media after the game. The incident was soon in danger of being blown way out of all proportion.

The situation became even more ludicrous when a Channel 9 crew arrived at our hotel from London, a three-hour drive away, looking for interviews. Next morning every single paper ran stories under big headlines, suggesting the Aussie camp was in upheaval. The exaggeration of this minor incident was not surprising as the English press love digging up dirt on the players — particularly if they're Australian ... and winning.

Dinner tonight was at Porters Wine Bar, courtesy of the XXXX rep, Ray Phillips (a former Queensland player and 1985 Ashes tourist), who shouted myself, Junior, AB, Boonie, Heals and Billy to an enjoyable evening talking cricket, and debating the upcoming second State of Origin league game. I challenged Ray to a double or nothing bet on the match. It was now a 100-pounds result if NSW could win by more than one-and-a-half points.

We headed back to the team's watering hole, directly opposite the pub, where Tubs was making a mockery of the Daktari. The thing actually looked *good* on him.

AB tells Craig McDermott to change ends, an order which led to a minor, but highly-publicised argument between the pair.

DAY 17 (May 11)

THE SIX-WEEK period necessary for the healing of the ligament damage to my finger is up, and the splint is no longer required. But there is a downside, as my top joint has stiffened. It will be at least a week before I have full movement back.

This morning we travelled to Hove, in Sussex — a four-hour bus trip. Half the team travelled by car, as they were booked to play a round of golf just outside Brighton. The occupants of the bus were soon asleep but quickly woke after a couple of hours with the news of a foodstop. The service station was taken by storm as the boys pillaged sandwiches, drinks, chips and chocolates. You could have been excused for thinking it was their last supper.

The trip was livened up by a viewing of the movie, *Good Morning Vietnam*. But our driver is in for a huge fine, for speeding past Stonehenge without stopping or pointing it out to the lads. It didn't seem to worry Merv too much, who enquired: "What's Stonehenge?" He was assured it was only the pile of rocks that Chevy Chase knocked down in *National Lampoon's European Vacation*.

We checked into the Imperial, with the roomies the same as last stop, and the prospect of a day off. I went with Matt Hayden for a gym workout, followed by a walk along the promenade and a stroll out onto the fun pier at this resort town in the south of England.

Once again, we had an official engagement — drinks with the management of the hotel for an hour. It looks like Des Rundle, our manager, will have to delve deep into his wallet at the next fines meeting for agreeing to this one. After that, we had tea at a Mexican restaurant, followed by the worst movie of all time — *National Lampoon's Loaded Weapon I*. Billy, Pistol, Maysie and BJ were unanimous in their disapproval.

Mark Taylor with the prized double — the "Daktari" outfit and Plucka Duck.

DAY 18 (May 12)

BREAKFAST AT the hotel was reported to be pretty ordinary. However, I was unable to confirm this as I left my run a bit late and only had time to grab an orange juice and some Coco Pops.

The news today of the composition of the English team for the one-dayers came as something of a surprise — with the selectors following our lead and going for youth rather than the older, more experienced players they've tended to rely on in the past.

Training was affected by the miserable weather, ruling out our hopes for a centre-wicket session. Instead, we settled for practice on an artificial wicket, along with a fairly intense fielding routine, which was inspired by our poor efforts in the recent two first-class matches. During the fielding session, Simmo put me into an advertising board while I was attempting to take one of his catches. It was not the first time. In fact, Simmo has got quite a few players over the years, with Tim Zoehrer being his prized possession. Zoehrer was once left hanging on a barbed-wire fence in Gwalior, India, as he took a spectacular catch above his head.

My roomie has picked up a touch of the flu which he generously passed onto me. I feel sapped of energy, and had a sleep this afternoon. I perked up by dinner time and headed into Brighton for dinner with Junior, Heals and Tubs. We ate Italian, then spent a happy hour-and-a-half watching *Mr Bean* videos at the pub just down the road from our hotel.

Two of the younger members of the side, Cracker and Marto, who were wearing their Australian bomber-jackets, were set on tonight by a couple of local thugs who proceeded to use our lads' melons for soccer practice via their Doc Martens. The attack resulted in a collection of lumps, cuts and bruises and a firm endorsement as to the sturdiness of Dr. Martens boots.

Brendon Julian gets the very first wicket of the tour, against an England Amateur XI, at Radlett.

Matthew Hayden receives a standing ovation from the Lord's members, after scoring 122 in a one-day match against Middlesex.

Mark Waugh, bowling in the nets at Lord's.

Craig McDermott, with Umpire Harold "Dickie" Bird, during the third limited-overs international, at Lord's.

A single to fine leg, during my first century of the tour, against Sussex at Hove.

David Boon, during his first-innings century against Worcestershire.

Captain Allan Border, at Edgbaston during the second one-day international, when he, with Mark Waugh, guided Australia to a brilliant victory.

There's no end to the tricks Shane Warne can do.

DAY 19 (May 13)

THE COUNTY Ground at Hove, the venue for today's match against Sussex (a three-dayer), is another ground with a huge slope running across the full length of the oval — not ideal for cricket, but very common in England. Sussex won the toss and elected to bat on a wicket that had been used the previous day. The thought is that it will be good to bat on for two days, but then should turn and keep low on day three. Our team for this match is very strong in the bowling department, with four quicks plus Tim May, and myself to help out if needed.

Today was one of those days when the ball seemed to follow me around in the field. I covered more kilometres than the Leyland Brothers. By the end of the day, Sussex had managed to total 353. The final wicket didn't fall until 6.45pm, after six hours and 45 minutes of cricket. It felt like a week in the field in the cold conditions. BJ was the pick of the bowlers with 5-63, showing signs that he could be the find of the tour. He can swing the ball both ways and possesses awesome power with the bat, all backed up by good hands in the field.

Our reserves had a tough day with Mark W. heading off to the races, where he lost his cash. Boonie and Tubs went golfing, leaving Warnie and Cracker to hold fort at the ground. But it was probably fortunate the whole team wasn't here — the away dressing room at Hove would be comfortable for a six-man team. For a touring squad it's a nightmare. Half the gear from my coffin is missing already, scattered among the bags and bodies which clutter the mini-sized room.

Tails heads for the nets.

DAY 20 (May 14)

THE MEDIA are nothing if not persistent. Today, they were still hounding Allan Border over his brush with Craig McDermott at Somerset — to the point where everywhere AB turned, a camera clicked. Fortunately, the TCCB (Test and County Cricket Board) have demanded Channel 7 make an immediate apology, otherwise they'll be banned from entering any of the Test-match venues during the upcoming series.

Our opening pair of Slater and Hayden began the run chase in warm sunshine and proceeded to tear the opposition attack to shreds, reaching their 100 partnership in only 20 overs. The ferocity of the strokeplay was such that Merv put forward the thoughtful suggestion that Matt Hayden's bat should be tested for steroids.

We ended the day at 3-303, after the last session was washed out with Marto on 79 and me on 41. The off-field highlight of the day was the 80 pounds a few of the players had on a horse which won in the last stride, a result which brought forth a huge cheer as we kicked it home on TV. The fleet-footed nag also caused a hold-up in play. Allan Border, who was about to take strike, pulled away and looked for confirmation that his 10 pounds had turned into 65.

Most of the team met at the Sussex Cricketers' Club after dinner tonight for a couple of thirst-quenchers. The spirit in the side is excellent, and all the young guys have slotted in very well.

Michael Slater, exercising at Hove.

DAY 21 (May 15)

THE BREAKFAST staff still haven't located any Vegemite or peanut butter but have come up with an adequate replacement in Marmite to keep the lads happy. Four of the reserves, Tubs, Junior, Warney and Boonie, made the trip to Wembley today for the FA Cup Final between Arsenal and Sheffield Wednesday — much to the envy of the rest of the team.

The final day's play didn't lead to a victory, but plenty of positives came out anyway, with Marto and myself scoring hundreds in a 200-run partnership, and Maysie taking three wickets in another impressive display. And there was further success on the racetrack — the 80 pounds five of us had on a hot tip given to Boonie romped home in the last at Thirsk.

The last session of play was played out in arctic conditions, with the temperature low enough for anyone with any commonsense to stay indoors, let alone stand out in the open waiting for a cover-drive to snap a finger off. The team couldn't get off the ground quickly enough when a result couldn't be achieved, and headed straight for the dressing room's communal bath to thaw out. However, before long Merv decided to make it his own little play-area, scattering all the occupants.

By seven o'clock everyone was on board the bus for the three-hour trip to Northampton, armed with a replay of the FA Cup Final, plenty of XXXX and 15 pounds worth of peanuts and crisps. However the food quickly disappeared and a pit stop was required halfway up the motorway where Burger King was raided. We struck a restaurant full of Sheffield Wednesday fans on their way home from the Cup final.

At Northampton it was straight to bed. We have another game tomorrow — which will make 10 days of cricket out of the last 12.

DAY 22 (May 16)

A GOOD crowd had arrived even before play this morning for our one-day match against Northamptonshire. The home side won the toss and elected to bat, on a pretty ordinary-looking wicket devoid of grass; a low, slow bounce of the ball was the anticipation. Yesterday might have been cold, but it was paradise compared with today's almost unplayable conditions. The 55 overs in the field seemed like an eternity, and when they had been bowled Northants' tally was an impressive 2-273. More disturbing was the fact that Merv's knee had locked up in the cold conditions. He's off for a scan to see if there are any more problems that need attending to.

We gratefully retreated to the changeroom, to be greeted by the now-customary sight of hundreds of bats that require signing by the end of the day's play. Most of these autographed bats are used in raffles or given to sponsors. The proceeds generally go towards a local player's benefit year. Hidden among the bats today were a couple of soccer balls, also to be autographed. Before that happened, the change-room was turned into a replay of the FA Cup Final, with scorching shots and crunching tackles being executed. Finally a stray shot sent a light fitting crashing to the floor, and the game was over.

Everyone in England seems to be an avid autograph collector. People wait in hotels, next to the team bus, or anywhere they think a player might be found in order to get that vital piece of memorabilia.

When we batted, Mark Taylor and Mark Waugh continued their good form together at the top of the one-day order, scoring 89 not out and 74 respectively, joining the rest of the batsmen, who all have at least one good score on the board. It's a great sign for the upcoming internationals.

We moved to 2-183, needing 91 off 16 overs to win, when heavy rain put an end to proceedings for the day. Unfortunately we were a couple of runs behind the required run-rate, and so it went down as our first loss, even though we would have cruised to victory if we had received our full quota of overs.

A quick getaway was required, as we faced a two-and-a-half hour trip up the motorway to Manchester — plus half an hour for tea — meaning an 11 o'clock arrival at our next destination.

Alan Fordham in century form against the Australians at Northampton
Picture: PHILIP BROWN

DAY 23 (May 17)

TRAINING WAS scheduled for 9 o'clock this morning at Old Trafford, the venue for this Wednesday's first one-day international, but it was apparent very early that we were no chance. The rain was steady and there wasn't a patch of blue sky to be seen. In the hotel, though, there were plenty of sunny faces as the players realised it was a day off!

I hadn't bowled for six weeks before yesterday, and the four overs I sent down against Northants took their toll. I was stiff and sore in the lower back and needed some treatment from our physiotherapist, Errol Alcott. Errol has now been with the side for the past eight years and continues to put players on the park who wouldn't be able to play except for his expertise. This afternoon I went to the gym for a tough one-and-a-half hour session of weights and stretching.

While I was there, Ian Healy rang home to get the State of Origin II rugby league score. To the disbelief of the Queenslanders it was another Cockroach (NSW) win, which almost certainly guarantees reprisals from the Banana Boys on our next bus trip, to London.

We did some promotional shots in the hotel foyer for XXXX and for an Aussie food promotion. Crocodile steaks, yabbies and kangaroo meat will be on the menu over the next three days in the hotel's restaurant. Afterwards we had drinks and dinner with the hotel management. It was much appreciated as the allowances are running short for most of the guys.

Merv teaches Warney the finer points of photography.

DAY 24 (May 18)

WE TRAINED for three hours at Old Trafford in our most impressive practice session of the tour so far. All the bowlers were flat out, searching for the rhythm so vital to their performance; the batsmen worked just as hard, striving not to be dismissed. In the fielding drills Simmo, as usual, pushed us to the limits.

I went to the shops this afternoon, and then saw a movie, *Indecent Proposal*, with Ian Healy. At 6.30pm the entire touring party gathered at the hotel to run through our game plan for the first one-day international tomorrow. We talked about the basics, such as the fact that the team which scores the most singles in limited-overs cricket wins 90 per cent of matches, and we focused on trying to rectify our weaknesses of the past 12 months — which have been our middle 20 overs in the batting and our last 15 overs when we bowl.

The 12 players for the match were announced with Zoehrer, Holdsworth, Slater, Warne and Julian missing out. It must have been an extremely tough selection process, but it means that, in all likelihood, Matthew Hayden will play his first international tomorrow.

As is traditional on the night before a Test match or the start of a one-day competition, the team dined out together, on this occasion at Pier 6 — next door to the hotel — where the dockyards had once been. The atmosphere was relaxed, with all the players very keen to get on with the serious part of the tour. We are confident of victory in this first match.

Quite a few of the guys chose to have a beer at the Pump House pub before settling down for the night — and this gave Marto the chance to lighten his pockets via the fruit machines.

The team bus, and "Huey", who, with his son Simon, drove us around Britain.

38

THE ONE-DAY INTERNATIONALS

DAY 25 (May 19)

UNLIKE IN Australia, the one-day games here are played in whites, with the traditional red ball. It gives the game a different feel, almost as if it is part of a Test match. The more traditional feel creates an atmosphere vastly different from a one-dayer at the SCG or MCG under lights. Today's international, at Old Trafford, was the first of a best-of-three series for the Texaco trophy. The second match will be played on Friday at Edgbaston in Birmingham, and the third on Sunday at Lord's.

The 12th man for today's international was announced during our pre-game warm-up, and Damien Martyn was something of a surprise choice, especially after his last innings of 136 against Sussex. The fact that we could afford to leave a player of his calibre on the sidelines certainly meant that the side was a strong one

We batted first, after Gooch had won the toss. Our innings was punctuated by some excellent periods of play followed by poorer passages, but overall we were pleased with our final score of 258 off 55 overs, highlighted by the efforts of Taylor (79) and Mark Waugh (56) plus a string of 20s from the lower order.

England reached 3-160 in reply and looked to have the game under control. The crowd became very vocal around this point, particularly targeting Billy. After a simple misfield by him, the crowd began some donkey imitations and chants of "Ee-aw, Ee-aw" rang out — which Billy misinterpreted as them having a go at the size of his ears. And quick bowlers wonder why they're labelled thick!!

The last 15 overs produced a huge turnaround — as is so often the case in the one-day game — with England eventually falling five runs short of victory, thanks to some superb catching and intelligent bowling. Billy took 3-38, and I finished with 3-53 after bowling the last ten overs straight from one end. Personally it was a pleasing performance.

The dressing room erupted into immediate and loud celebrations, with the team's music machine blaring out the boys' favourite tunes such as *Khe Sanh* and *Bound For Glory* while our sponsors' product, XXXX, flowed freely. Everyone in the team was relieved at winning such a close game — something we haven't been able to do recently. Most importantly, the sense of camaraderie and team spirit evident in the room after the game indicated that when things get tough in the future, the team will pull together — a quality that can turn a good side into a great one.

We were joined in our celebrations by John Monie, the Aussie coach of the Wigan rugby league team and Andy Gregory (the Leeds and ex-Great Britain halfback), a player we've cursed when Australia have played the British in a football Test. Off the field he seems like a good guy. We were also joined by the Sheffield Shield players, Chris Matthews (Tasmania) and Stuart Law (Queensland). Both are over here playing league cricket.

Three hours later the team boarded the bus for home. Then came the celebrations, at Henry's (a pub), and later a few drinks with the players of the Premier League soccer champions, Manchester United, at a private party.

DAY 26 (May 20)

THIS MORNING, on the bus for Birmingham, more than a few eyes that looked like road maps. There were some nasty hangovers around. It was clear some of the boys had over-dosed badly on the "old tonsil varnish". However, the Queensland contingent finally got some joy from the video screen, watching the Brisbane Broncos come back from the dead to beat Illawarra 24-22 in an exciting rugby league premiership game.

Grey skies greeted our arrival. We're getting used to this, and when the rain came spilling down our planned training session was washed out. After my 10 overs yesterday my back hasn't pulled up all that flash and required some treatment from Errol, followed by a series of strengthening exercises.

Not surprisingly, a quiet night was had by all, with most guys ordering room service, and watching the replay of the FA Cup Final. It, like the drawn first game from last Saturday, turned out to be an average game.

My roomie this week is Ian Healy (alias Heals or Barney Rubble), one of the characters in the side. Heals is always good for a laugh and a great team man. He's also very fastidious about his appearance on the field. In fact I suspect he cleans his boots more times than the guards at Buckingham Palace clean theirs.

McDermott's hostility provides sense of foreboding for England

Hick's 85 brings Gooch praise

DAY 27 (May 21)

WE WERE greeted by a freezing cold Edgbaston day as we prepared to (hopefully) clinch the Texaco Trophy. On such days, warm-ups are vital — especially groin and hamstring stretches; they are the muscles most prone to tears on the sort of slippery surface we faced today.

Before a capacity crowd, we won the toss and sent England into bat on a wicket which we reckoned would provide some early movement off the seam. There was some assistance, and we got away to a great start to have them 4-120 off 33 overs at lunch — mainly due to the bowling of May and McDermott. It was a big morning for Merv too. He found some form, and *also* worked out the chant which has become a regular event whenever he bowled. Originally Merv thought it was simply a song to spur on the England batsmen, but today he realised that when the fans were chanting "Sumo! Sumo! Sumo!", it was because they had perceived a likeness between the fast bowler and those large Japanese wrestlers. Actually, the tune is quite catchy!

At lunch, if anyone had tried to tell me that England were about to take 112 off the last nine overs, I would have bet my house against it ... and thus ended up homeless. It happened, with Robin Smith, who played one of the all-time great one-day knocks, finishing with an unbeaten 167, off 163 balls, out of a total of 5-277. Paul Reiffel and I copped most of Smith's wrath, with the ball being returned from the paying customers more than once. It felt like we were bowling in the highlights package. On the completion of the England innings, the team was in shock from the ferocity of Smith's innings, and from the final total — which was 60 more than had looked possible at the break.

The team's attention was drawn back to our last tour here, when we chased 279 at Lord's and won. We knew that with a mix of discipline and aggression, the target was still a very reachable one for our powerful batting line-up. The key was for someone to make a hundred and the rest of the players to build on that stability.

However, the tea-time score was not looking too promising; we were 3-95 off 25 overs, with Junior and AB at the crease. The atmosphere in the viewing room was tense, but as is so often the case, Merv broke the ice with a joke ... to be followed by Cracker and Maysie, each trying to out-do the other, until they finally could think of no more. We had two hours of continuous laughs, in which time the two batsmen moved to within 15 runs of victory before Junior was dismissed for a magnificent 113. From there AB (who finished 86 not out) and I cruised to victory with two overs to spare. It was one of the greatest one-day victories I've been associated with.

The dressing room was once again the best place on earth to be, as we celebrated our series win in the traditional way — with Boonie up on top of the bench leading us into our team song. It's a moment that always sends shivers down my spine and makes me proud to be an Aussie.

This was the fourth time England have been beaten in the Texaco series, which is now in its eighth year. And we're super-keen to make it a clean sweep at Lord's in two days' time. A great day ended with a meal and some celebratory drinks.

DAY 28 (May 22)

THE DOWNSIDE of life as a touring cricketer is the time spent away from your family, especially for those guys with young children. Only this morning, David Boon's daughter asked her mother: "Where's Daddy? He's been away so long ... Is he in heaven?" It's times like this when players wish they could have their families with them, but we accept that being apart from family is a price that has to be paid under the rules and lifestyle demands of a professional sport such as cricket. On this tour, wives and families are not allowed to stay in the team's hotel until the last two weeks of the campaign. They can, of course, live in England if they choose, although that isn't much of an option, as they only end up trekking around after the team without spending much time with their companions — at a great financial cost.

Training today was optional — and I took the chance to give the body a much-needed rest after the pretty hectic schedule so far. Most of the players who haven't played much cricket recently went to the nets along with the keenest member of the squad — Simmo, a genuine lover of the game. He can't get enough of it.

The *Sunday Mirror* newspaper made enquiries today about an interview and I agreed to it after a few stipulations. I'm pretty wary. The tabloid press over here go out of their way to create scandal, and seem to misquote you at every opportunity in order to sell their papers. Already Shane Warne has learnt that the hard way — one of the papers over here stitched him up with false statements and complete fabrications of comments he made during an interview.

The heroes of Edgbaston — Allan Border (left) and Mark Waugh.

DAY 29 (May 23)

LORD'S TODAY was packed to capacity one-and-a-half hours prior to the start of play in the final one-day international, despite the outrageously expensive ticket prices. The average seat costs 37 pounds ($82 Australian) — about three times as much as the best seats in the house in Australia.

At this famous ground many traditions are kept alive, including one which insists that no women are allowed in the Members' enclosures. And they insist that all teams must wear whites during practice — the only cricket ground in the world to have such a rule.

Also unique is the route the players have to take from the dressing room to reach the playing field. You go via a couple of sets of stairs, through the famous Long Room, invariably packed with members smoking cigars and wearing "egg-and-bacon" (orange-and-yellow striped) ties, then down another set of steps and finally out onto the ground. It's a procedure that proved to be too tough the first time I played here for Somerset, and resulted in me entering the playing arena via the wrong gate, much to my embarrassment.

AB has a dose of the flu and Marto replaced him, with Mark Taylor taking over as captain. And Pistol was dropped from the side, giving Brendon Julian his chance.

England won the toss and bowled on an unusually soft-textured wicket — in the hope that it would seam around in the morning session. Runs were hard to come by early, with Caddick, Cork and Jarvis bowling more accurately than in the previous two encounters. At lunch we were 2-105 off 35 overs, probably about 20 less than we had expected.

The Lord's lunch lived up to its billing as the best on the county circuit, featuring lamb chops and mint sauce, vegetables and chips, followed by apple pie and custard.

Back on the field we managed a competitive total of 5-230, with Tubs scoring 57 and Boonie 73 in a fine partnership. But the highlight was a dazzling innings of 51 not out from Marto, off only 43 balls, just when the tempo needed to be raised.

In reply, England got off to a "flyer", taking nearly five per over from the first 20 overs, before Gooch was out for 42 when the score was 96. Even when Smith was stumped off Tim May soon after tea, to make it 2-115, the home side looked to be in a comfortable position to wrap up the match. The early batsmen had been especially severe on BJ, who, in his first international, had copped a bit of a hammering, conceding 27 runs off his first

Celebrating with keeper Ian Healy and Brendon Julian, after Heals had caught Graham Thorpe off my bowling late in England's innings.

On the pavilion balcony after winning the one-day series 3-0. In the centre is Matthew Hayden, whose catch of England tail-ender Paul Jarvis was the talk of Lord's. With England eight-down, but still in with an outside chance, Jarvis had skied a ball from McDermott to deep cover. Matt misjudged the flight of the ball, but, as the ball flew over his head, he leapt backwards to grab the chance with an outstretched hand. The other Aussies are (left to right): Damien Martyn, Shane Warne, Steve Waugh, Bob Simpson, Mark Taylor and Allan Border.

three overs. But he was comforted by all the boys telling him not to worry — we reassured him that we were positive he could pull it back to six or seven an over after tea.

Somehow England managed to pull off the impossible and self-destruct, losing their final eight wickets for 82 runs. Once Hick was bowled by Julian, attempting a carefree cover-drive, you could feel the tension rise. As each successive wicket fell, the pressure increased, resulting in an easy target of four runs per over turning into six per over, against an opposition which suddenly sensed a kill in the offing.

As the wickets continued to fall, the crowd became quieter and quieter. It was as if they were ready to concede defeat, as if they didn't really expect their team to fight back and win. After his early mauling, BJ staged a remarkable recovery to take 3-50 off 11 overs, while I bowled the last 11 straight from one end, to take 1-43 and do my bit in another tremendous Aussie victory. The day showed once again that fighting spirit and a never-say-die attitude count for plenty when it comes to influencing the crucial moments in a match.

Celebrations tonight were much more subdued, mainly because our attention has already turned to the Test matches. But we're happy; it's a fine achievement to win a one-day international series 3-0 in England.

The team happily accepted an invitation to join the Australian TV personality, Ian "Molly" Meldrum, for drinks at the Regent. Molly is a long-time cricket supporter and as usual, he looked after the guys — shouting drinks and food all night, which was much appreciated by all.

TOWARDS THE TESTS

DAY 30 (May 24)

TODAY WE had the luxury of a sleep-in until lunch-time — it was one of our few days off. Most of the guys opted for the golf course but, unfortunately, my back pulled up too sore for me to have a round, so for me it was a routine of exercises, followed by a hot bath, to try and help the problem. I lunched with my manager over here in England, Jonathon Barnett, at Henry's, a trendy eatery overlooking London's Green Park, not far from our hotel.

Back at the hotel there was trouble. My roomie complained my junk has encroached onto his turf, and demanded an immediate assessment of the situation, resulting in the desk being cleaned so he could at least keep up with his personal diary. There was also agitation for a path to be made so he could reach the mini-bar and suggestions we should try and find the lounge, thought to be somewhere in the room. Our situation can be likened to that of Oscar and Felix in *The Odd Couple* — Heals is very orderly and neat while I prefer the laidback approach to living in a hotel room.

Dinner tonight was at one of the newly-opened chain of restaurants called Planet Hollywood, owned by Sylvester Stallone, Bruce Willis and Arnold Schwarzenegger. It's a place featuring movie memorabilia such as the knife from *Psycho* and the mask Hannibal Lecter wore in *Silence of the Lambs.* The owners looked after the boys with free hats and shirts, and best of all we didn't have to line up outside, which saved us two hours of queuing in fairly chilly conditions. Afterwards, a few of the non-playing personnel took a peek at Stringfellows, one of the top nightclubs in London and a place where they charge like wounded bulls for drinks.

DAY 31 (May 25)

TODAY'S MATCH against Surrey turned into something of a farce. All their frontline bowlers cried off with injuries, as well as a couple of their batsmen — resulting in them putting out a virtual second-string combination. And this despite the fact that any county team beating Australia can earn 4000 pounds. It wasn't that unexpected, as the average county player has very few days off and any opportunity to have a rest is accepted. However, you would expect players to be keen to make an impression against high-quality opposition such as a visiting Australian team.

Once again, our dressing room was a joke, being one-sixteenth the size of the home team's, even though we have 17 players and a mountain of gear. The lack of space resulted in the reserves — of whom I am one — seeking alternative accommodation out in the hallway.

At lunch, Australia were 3-130 (Mark Waugh not out on 55, Martyn on 30), after the top order failed for the first time on tour.

Being one of the reserves usually means adding a couple of kilos to the waistline, due to the double-barrelled reason that you aren't exercising as much and there is always food available in the change rooms to nibble on. To compensate, we usually use the gym facilities at the grounds, planning a one-hour session after lunch. During our workout today, Australia added 130 runs (in an hour!), with Junior scoring 105. It was a display that had the members ducking for cover as they were peppered with high-quality strikes over the boundary.

Mark eventually cruised to 178, with Marto playing a disciplined knock of 84. However, most interest surrounded the handing over of Plucka to Paul Reiffel after he was caught at slip before he was able to trouble the scorers.

Thankfully, Merv found a way to occupy his day without continually pestering all the other reserves. He played Monopoly, at which he is a very fine exponent — mainly because no-one else can get a word in, and also because any argument is settled with a headlock or a Chinese burn to the ears.

In a visit to the Ladbrokes betting office I backed Warney to take 10 wickets in the match at odds of 20/1 — a very fair quote I reckoned, considering the nature of the pitch. Late in the day, in a quest for quick runs, we lost our last six wickets in swift succession to be out for 378, and Surrey reached 20 without loss before bad light stopped play. Shane will get the chance to chase my money in the morning.

Tonight was my first XXXX function, with Cracker, Marto and Warney, in London, so it was straight from the ground to the pub. The evening turned out to be a good promotion, although the format of the trivia quiz meant the night took far too long to reach a conclusion. After a series of knock-out rounds, one player teamed up with two people from the crowd until a winner was found. Eventually Marto's team won the night.

DAY 32 (May 26)

IT WAS another very cold day, and my hamstrings felt as tight as guitar strings during the warm-up. When play began, Surrey struggled on a wicket already deteriorating and slumped to 7-135, before rallying to total 231. The follow-on was avoided courtesy of a wild swipe by their number 11 off Warney, which cleared the boundary with ease — and sent the Surrey lads into a state of ecstasy, not because of the importance of the runs, but because this particular batsman definitely wasn't renowned for his artistry with the blade. We were assured he could comfortably wear any of the following designations: bunny, rabbit, ferret or Jack.

Today's lunch scaled new heights, and was achieved by overcooking the chicken by about three hours. The bird came with no gravy or sauce, requiring each player to reach for the chainsaw to make the first incision. Then came the tough part — chewing it without losing all fillings and/or teeth. The choice of green vegies was extraordinary, being peas, peas or peas. They were slightly overdone, darkish in appearance and bearing an uncanny resemblance to rabbit droppings. Capping the feast were the potatoes from last week's fixture.

The afternoon was spent at the gym used by the team when in London. It's just down the road from our hotel and has excellent weight-training facilities, bikes, swimming pool, spa and sauna — all the requirements for a good workout.

In the last session of play Australia scored quickly. Tubs was in good touch, finishing on 56, but Slats was contemplating suicide after being dismissed by the last ball of the day. At the close we were 2-150.

The evening was spent at Caspers Restaurant, which has an unusual theme. Revolving around each of its 100 tables is a telephone so that you can call any table you might care to have a chat with. Dean Jones, who is in England coaching the Durham Second XI, caught up with us over dinner. I guess it was tough for Jonesy, as I know he'd love to be touring with us instead of being a spectator.

DAY 33 (May 27)

IT WAS cold again; it seems weeks since we've had a warm sunny day on which to play cricket. The pitch at The Oval was breaking up by the start of the day's play, with the ball bursting through the topsoil due to the groundsmen not rolling the wicket enough. Tubs went on to make 80 before we declared at 4-171. By lunch we had Surrey in trouble at 3-45 — with all the players positively sprinting off the ground in eager anticipation of another top-class feed!

Merv, Heals, and myself being reserves, and, coincidentally, members of the Nerds, decided to take the afternoon off, and settled on a game of golf at Moore Park. We were told to get onto the A4 to Oxford, but to go via Marble Arch in Central London. They were simple instructions, but almost as soon as we left the ground Merv spotted the A4 Oxford sign and was convinced this was the direction we needed to take. But Heals was adamant we had to find Marble Arch, as advised by Simmo and AB. So we pressed on in bumper-to-bumper traffic. Thirty minutes of increasing abuse among the Nerds found us circling Marble Arch and, hopefully, on the right path, although there more than a hint of pessimism in the car. There was joy at last as we stumbled across the elusive signpost, one hour and three minutes into our travels.

But there was misfortune for our wicketkeeper. Upon closer inspection, Merv concluded that it was the very same sign we had passed an hour ago! Luckily for Heals the big fella was behind the wheel so there was no way there could be any immediate reprisals. But this proved a fairly serious error in judgment, as Merv began to re-enact a few scenes from *Wayne's World* as well as refining some skills generally needed only in go-kart racing. After another wrong turn which cost us a further ten minutes, we eventually found the golf course. By now we only had time for nine holes, and what's more, just as we parked, the car the heavens opened up.

Waugh and Hughes ended up the losers in a particularly poor display of golf, with Healy the only player to show any hint of form. There was nothing left but for the losers to drive home *and* buy McDonald's on the way as payment for the defeat.

Back at the hotel we caught up with the team and the news that we had had a convincing win by bowling Surrey out for 144. Tim Zoehrer created a new Australian record by bringing off eight dismissals in an innings, six catches and two stumpings. Everyone was very pleased; Ziggy has had only limited opportunities on this tour.

Team sponsors XXXX shouted us to dinner at Planet Hollywood but made a fatal mistake by encouraging the guys to sample the cocktail list, which they proceeded to do with great enthusiasm, starting off with a few Terminators and ending with a round of Beetlejuices, with a few others in between. Upon the arrival of the bill there was a feeling among the players that perhaps we've had our last free dinner from the sponsors.

DAY 34 (May 28)

I WOKE to find I'd scheduled my time pretty poorly. I had just 30 minutes to pay the bill, pack my bags, eat breakfast and sign 150 bats. I went amazingly close to bringing it off, brought down only by a mistake in the bill which left me five minutes on the wrong side of departure time.

On the motorway, the second State of Origin league video was put on — and it soon had the Queenslanders pulling their hair out as they watched three certain tries bombed and disallowed in the first half. Amid much cheering the Blues come to life in the second half and set up a handy 10-point lead. Queensland stormed home, but fell short, and there was much abuse hurled across the aisles, with claims of dodgy refereeing. The happy NSW supporters gave no support to such a theory ... or sympathy.

We checked into yet another hotel that didn't quite have our rooms ready for us — so instead we decided to grab a quick meal at the hotel restaurant which, within 30 minutes, had made Fawlty Towers' service look first-class.

The afternoon was cricket-free, allowing the team to head to the golf course. My partner was Warney, a burglar off an 18 handicap (I'm off 12). We were opposed by AB, off 9, and Ziggy, off 14, a combination who have declared themselves the team to beat. The match turned out to be a cliffhanger, settled by a successful 1.5-metre putt on the last by yours truly which earned the winners 15 pounds each — plus the guarantee of a couple of hours' torment at the bar for the opposition.

Earlier in the day, we received a hot tip at an evening race meeting. We all crowded into a bookie's shop, but watched in dismay as it went down by half-a-length to a roughie, after looking the winner.

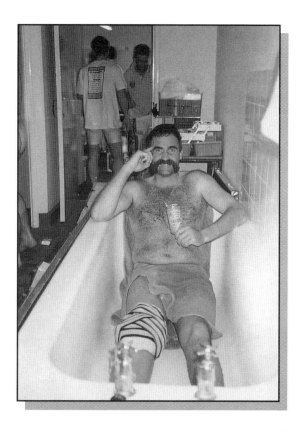

Merv applies some ice and anaesthetic to his injured knee.

DAY 35 (May 29)

IT WAS a familiar story as the curtains were opened in room 393 at 8.15 am: heavy rain clouds, with no sign of blue sky. The hotel staff kept up to yesterday's standard of service — none — with a cup of tea taking 20 minutes to arrive, and the toast barely making it on the half hour. We trekked off to the ground, for the match against Leicestershire, feeling in need of a bite to eat.

AB won the toss and decided we'd bat first on a wicket that obviously hadn't been attended to by the groundsman. It is soft and lacking in any preparation. The Leicester side decided not to play their overseas professional, Winston Benjamin (West Indies), a trend which is becoming increasingly annoying as there seems to be no point in playing against all these counties when they are putting up second-string opposition who usually tend to cave in when the going gets tough. These days it seems the only reason the counties want to play Australia is to draw the crowds through the gate to fill their coffers — and for some testimonial-year player to get 10 to 15 autographed bats signed by our team to enable him to make a few pounds.

Despite the pitch, Slater and Boon continued their excellent form, scoring 91 and 123 respectively in a 200-plus run partnership. It was a wicket that required patience and good technique. During the partnership, some of the lads became a little bored, and decided to have some fun and games on the telephones. Not surprisingly, Merv was at the centre of the sting, along with Paul Reiffel.

From the umpires' room they rang our dressing room, asking for Shane Warne. Warney picked up the receiver to be welcomed by a *News of the World* reporter claiming to have a scandalous story which was about to be released on the front page. Warney began to get hot under the collar, and let fly with a torrent of abuse; his tormentors retaliated with even more outrageous fabrications, and Shane got even angrier — much to the delight of the rest of the team witnessing the set-up. Merv and Pistol finally put Warney out of his misery and confronted him, sporting huge grins. He vows revenge.

AB and I managed to be unbeaten on 42 and 44 respectively at the end of the day, although we both struggled to score early against probably the best spell of bowling we've struck so far on tour — by Alan Mullaly, an ex-Aussie now playing county cricket full-time. The score at the end of the day was very healthy considering the conditions, 3-323, with a declaration on the cards in the morning to give us the time to bowl Leicester out twice.

Slater now favourite to open in first Test

by Pat Gibson

MICHAEL SLATER yesterday inched ahead of Matthew Hayden in their final eliminator for the right to open Australia's batting in the first Cornhill Test. Vice-captain Mark Taylor, who is sure of his place at Old Trafford on Thursday after averaging 83.90 in the last Ashes series here, stood down at Leicester to let the two youngsters get on with it.

And it was Slater, the nimble-footed 23-year-old from Wagga-Wagga, who seized the opportunity, sharing a second-wicket stand of 214 with David Boon and missing his second century of the tour by only nine runs.

Hayden, two years younger but more experienced than Slater, had begun the trip with two one-day centuries and won the vote for the Texaco Trophy internationals.

But he went for two, caught behind off Alan Mullally, the spidery left-arm seamer born in Southend but raised in Western Australia, where he made his first-class debut in a Sheffield Shield final. Mullally bowled an impressive opening spell and Slater had to work hard to survive, so much so that he made only six of Australia's 20 in the first hour.

But then he cut loose, taking 14 in one over from Mullally, including three fours, two cracking cover drives and a superb cut.

Mortified

It still took him 155 minutes to reach his 50 but he celebrated in style, skipping down the pitch to drive Adrian Pearson for an effortless six over long-on.

Boon, meanwhile, took a minute longer over his half-century before taking full advantage of Leicester bowling that was growing more nondescript by the over.

His second 50 came in only 51 minutes as he had struck 19 fours in his 123 to confirm his status as the strong man of Australia's batting before he threw his wicket away. It is conceivable he could revert to his old opening position to make room for the gifted Damien Martyn in the middle-order.

So Slater must have been mortified to drive a return catch to Vince Wells when he had been there just over four hours for 91, including that six and ten fours.

It probably left the selectors undecided but as Allan Border and Steve Waugh took the Australians to 323-3 their problems, compared to England's, were minimal after an almost trouble-free build-up.

They have won three of their four county games, to put them on course for a £50,000 Tetley Jackpot, as well as the three one-day internationals.

"We are pretty pleased with the whole thing," admitted coach Bobby Simpson. "But that doesn't mean we're underestimating England and we'll be doing our homework to make sure we've got the best side and the best tactics to beat them. We've got long memories going back to the last time England won the Ashes in 1986-87.

"Right up to the first Test they were not very impressive to say the least — which shows what a fine line there is between success and failure."

SCOREBOARD

Leicester *Australia won toss*

Australia First Innings
M Hayden c Nixon b Mullally		2
M Slater c & b Wells		91
D Boon c Parsons b Wells		123
A Border not out		42
S Waugh not out		44
Extras (b4 lb3 w8 nb4)		21
Total 3 wkts		323

Fall: 2, 216, 227.
To bat: I A Healy, B P Julian, M G Hughes, S K Warne, T B A May, C J McDermott.
Umpires: O Sharp & B Leadbeater.

52

DAY 36 (May 30)

ANOTHER FREEZING cold day dawned, and AB declared at the overnight score, with the plan being to bowl Leicester out before the follow-on target (173) and then, hopefully, to bowl them out cheaply again, with the spinners being the trump cards.

However, the first session saw only about half an hour's play. The teams were on and off the field a couple of times, forced off by rain which was falling almost horizontally due to the gale-force winds. The end of the day was reached, surprisingly, without anyone suffering from frostbite or hypothermia — Leicester limping to a score of 7-168. The Earl of Twirl (Maysie) and the Sheikh of Tweak (Warney) snared three wickets apiece. But, because of the weather, it was a miserable day — on an enjoyment scale, it was roughly equivalent to a visit to the dentist knowing you have to have a root canal filling on your wisdom tooth.

Most of the excitement was confined to the Coral's bookmaking tent where Junior, the team's lunatic punter, backed horses all over the country, along with side bets on the cricket — with disastrous results.

The evening meal came courtesy of the colonel at Kentucky Fried Chicken, where I was joined by Swervin and Pistol, which we followed with a quiet pint and game of pinball at the local pub.

The brothers Waugh.

DAY 37 (May 31)

AS IS the case in a lot of county matches — which used to be over three days until this year — the only way to achieve a result in a three-day touring match is for the two skippers to get together before the start of play and discuss a course of action. Leicester today decided to declare at their overnight score, and we scored a quick 80 runs, with Slats unbeaten on 50 — capping off another fine match for him, and perhaps clinching a spot in the first Test team.

The final equation left Leicester needing 243 off 72 overs to win — a target which proved too tough for a side that didn't appear to have a great desire to fight when the chips were down. Their final total was 97 runs short, with the last five batsmen being dismissed in the softest possible ways. It was almost as if they were even keener than we were to end the match.

We were barely on the motorway to Manchester — our next stop — when the bus, as if possessed, pulled into McDonald's. With the sounds of Bon Jovi blaring, we sped on in a great frame of mind. All the guys have now become great mates and we were looking forward to success in the fast-approaching Test series.

The bus pulled into our hotel, the Copthorne, at 8.15, and almost immediately, BJ, Heals, Junior and I headed off to the movies, directly across from the pub. We watched *Groundhog Day*, armed with the usual boxes of popcorn, sweets and litres of Coke, but were slightly disappointed with the entertainment.

The Nerds. Standing (left to right): Simpson, May, Hughes, S. Waugh. At front: Zoehrer, Healy.

DAY 38 (June 1)

NINE O'CLOCK training was interrupted by continuous rain which allowed only a brief net session, although we managed to squeeze in a fairly intensive fielding workout. Later in the day, Heals, Matt Hayden and I visited an indoor centre in town to use the gym facilities and indoor nets as the rain continued to tumble down outside.

Another promotion awaited at the hotel — this time a photo session for Drizabone products, now selling in England. Matt Hayden, being from the Queensland outback near Kingaroy, looked the part in his coat and bush hat, but the same couldn't be said of myself or Heals, who at least provided good entertainment for the passers-by.

The long-awaited clash of the Nerds vs Julios was programmed for tonight at the Manchester Tenpin Bowling Alley, with Nerds skipper May confident of success. We were chasing a 2-0 lead after our touch football victory at Worcester. The afternoon was spent looking for suitable outfits for the contest. This proved to be much harder than first thought, with Heals, Maysie and myself searching for hours before we could locate a shirt that looked bad enough, and was reasonably priced. We probably could have saved all that time by just sending Maysie out shopping for something that he would normally buy anyway. Along the way we stumbled across a novelty store which had the finishing touch required — Nerd glasses — and exactly the right number, six pairs.

The teams congregated in the hotel foyer, with the Julios absolutely gorgeous in their team blazers and RayBan sunglasses, and the Nerds looking so ridiculous that even other guests couldn't control their laughter. We were transported to the bowling alley aboard the team bus, with much sledging and threats of physical abuse coming from both sides.

The challenge finally got underway with a fair crowd in attendance. It was a titanic struggle up until the seventh frame, at which point the Nerds cracked under pressure and ended up going down 706 pins to 691. The big disappointment was Merv, who we had thought would be our trump card. Instead, the big fella was more interested in seeing whether he could smash the pins apart with brute strength rather than mucking around with finesse. He gave the floorboards quite a pounding but didn't score too heavily. Maysie, being the team captain, took the loss heavily and immediately made his way back to the hotel to examine the stats and look for answers.

Both teams headed to the Samuel Platz pub for a XXXX promotion and ended up having a few drinks with the staff to celebrate Mark and my 28th birthday, with Heals making a speech. Even though we couldn't understand him, the gesture was much appreciated.

The Nerds and the Julios, preparing for the summer's most important sporting event.

DAY 39 (June 2)

IT RAINED again — restricting us to half an hour's light fielding, undertaken when a rare break in the weather allowed us to take the field. The Old Trafford ground staff's equipment here is unique in that they have inflatable covers which allow hot air to be blown in from two portable generators, creating a hothouse over the wicket which keeps the wicket square dry. In a climate like Manchester's they are a great improvement on the the traditional covers which sit directly on top of the grass, and hold in the moisture.

Browsing in the novelty shop yesterday, I spotted a plastic set of ears not dissimilar to Billy's real ones, although perhaps slightly larger. After consultation with Maysie, it was decided that we must go back today and purchase 10 sets of the ears with a view to putting them to good use in an upcoming county game. The plan is that when Craig is about to begin his opening spell, the remainder of the team will produce the false ears, and pop them on. Hopefully everyone will have a good laugh at Billy's expense. Unfortunately, there will be certain repercussions, and Maysie and I will have to keep a keen eye out.

A 6.30pm meeting brought the whole squad together for the pre-Test naming of the 12 players, together with a run-through of the opposition's strengths and weaknesses. The vacant opening spot was a toss-up, with Slats getting the nod over Matt Hayden, probably on his performances against Leicestershire. The selectors named both May and Warne in the 12; they have been the form bowlers so far. My roomie of the moment, Brendon Julian, won selection and will make his debut tomorrow along with Slats.

As has seemed normal, the Poms had a last-minute withdrawal. The Kent fast bowler, Alan Igglesden, strained his groin at training today and was replaced by the experienced Phillip De Freitas. After our team meeting, in which everyone seemed positive about the next five days' cricket, we dined at Pier 6. But everyone's attention has turned to the day that is crucial for us — the first day of the Test series.

It was an early evening for all, with a minor hiccup occurring outside room 442, where my room-mate became increasingly frustrated when our door card refused to work, leaving us locked outside our room. This event caused BJ to act like a good sort until one of the hotel staff was summoned. He immediately recognised the problem — the card was from the Hinkley Island Hotel in Leicester. BJ was left looking just a little red about the cheeks.

The "blow-up" covers at Old Trafford.

THE FIRST TEST

DAY 40 (June 3)

I WOKE up this morning feeling like I'd gone five rounds with Mike Tyson. My head was throbbing and the rest of my body was aching. Hopefully, I'll pick up, but the rush to get to the bus this morning didn't help. I thought I was bad at waking up in the morning, but BJ has me well covered in that area and, as per usual, we had about ten minutes to devour breakfast — about 20 minutes short of what we needed.

The atmosphere in the dressing room before the game was tense. That's always the case on the morning of a Test, but even more so today as the run-ups for the bowlers were saturated, causing a one-hour delay to the start of the match. England are fielding a side which includes both spinners, whereas we made Maysie 12th man. Leaving Tim out was a choice that was agonisingly tough, as the Old Trafford wicket has something of a reputation for aiding the spinners. But with all the rain we've had here, the wicket should also help the speedsters — and this was obviously the stronger opinion.

Graham Gooch won the toss and sent us in. By lunch, we were in great shape at 0-60, with Slater, in his debut Test, looking as comfortable as he would playing for Lake Albert in the Wagga Wagga competition. Mark Taylor too was looking very confident.

Slater departed after lunch for 58, an impressive debut. With Taylor growing in authority and Boon grinding the English bowlers down, we reached the commanding position of 1-183 with about 90 minutes remaining. At this point, the wicket began to turn sharply and the whole mood of the day started to change dramatically. Boon departed for 21 followed shortly after by Junior for 6 and then Tubs for a magnificent and potentially match-winning 124.

With 40 minutes' play left, I entered the unique atmosphere that engulfs Test matches between the two countries. I was soon retracing my steps to the pavilion after being bowled by a sharply-turning delivery that I should have covered with bat and pad close together.

On being dismissed in such a manner at such a vital time (there were 15 minutes to go in the day), a rush of emotions go through your head ... anger, disappointment, self-pity. More than anything else you wish time could be turned back 10 minutes, so you could have another chance.

The end of the day saw Australia at 5-242. Neither team has gained the ascendancy. But the wicket is turning sharply, and I would say we probably have our noses just in front.

My health deteriorated further during the day and I was advised to take a course of antibiotics to try and clear up the virus I've picked up. I headed straight back to the hotel and ordered room service, but it ended up untouched as my appetite has gone.

I rang Lynette, who is due over in two-weeks' time, to try and finalise her arrival and accommodation details that need to be tied up. I'm looking forward to her coming over. Late into the night, I ended up watching *Cape Fear* on the in-house video system when I couldn't get to sleep.

Mark Taylor, on the way to his crucial first-day century at Old Trafford.

DAY 41 (June 4)

I HAD another very poor night's sleep, with most of the evening spent looking at the ceiling or tossing from side to side. I probably only had about two hours' decent shut-eye. Things were no better at the ground. There I was experiencing hot-and-cold flushes and was excused from doing the warm-ups.

The morning session was a poor one for us. Our remaining five wickets fell for only 47 runs, with BJ becoming the new owner of Plucka. The English team would have been very happy with their comeback considering we were 1-183 at one stage last evening, and looking like scoring at least 350-400 in total. The big success story for England was their new off-spinner, Peter Such from Essex, who bowled with great accuracy and flight to take 6-67 off 33.3 overs. It will be interesting to watch his performance in the second innings, as his fingers will no doubt be sore after such a long spell. He'll also have to cope with the high expectations he now carries.

The Fleet Street press were up to their usual tricks this morning, giving Gooch a serve for sending us in after winning the toss. They didn't mention that we would have done exactly the same if we had called correctly. It seems the press over here love to see England losing. When it happens they can create a ridiculous headline, or put their players under the microscope and slowly dissect them until the team members are either sapped of all their confidence or dropped altogether, to make way for new scapegoats.

At tea the honours might have appeared fairly even, with England at 3-99. But in fact we had grabbed a huge psychological advantage. With his first ball in a Test in England, Warney had completely bamboozled Mike Gatting, by producing a delivery that turned from about a foot outside leg stump, beat a textbook-looking forward defence, and clipped the top of off stump. Gatt couldn't believe it! It really was an amazing ball. Long after we've all retired, that one delivery will be etched in the memory of everyone who witnessed it. It was such a ball that it will become part of the folklore that surrounds these great sporting contests.

Another vital breakthrough occurred shortly after tea. Gooch was furious with himself after hitting a waist-high full toss from Warney straight to BJ at mid-on — the fieldsman's first taste of success in a Test match. From there, Warne and Hughes dominated the rest of the session, both putting in long stints of high-quality bowling. England, at 8-202, were in a precarious position at the close of play.

The English team were welcomed into our rooms at the end of the day for a drink, something which has unfortunately almost disappeared from the game at this level. It was a pleasant experience to have both teams enjoying each other's company off the field. The rest of the evening was spent having dinner with Mark W. and Pete and Iris Greenalgh, the couple who billeted us eight years ago when we made our first journey to the UK to play league cricket. Now, as then, they looked after us as if we were their own. But, because of the flu, I was unable to eat much at dinner. I decided to have an early night to try and shake the illness off.

DAY 42 (June 5)

TODAY WAS laundry day, but there were no bags from Room 442. BJ is about as easy to wake up as a hibernating bear and I was wasn't well enough to rush downstairs by 8.30 to make the deadline. At the time I felt like I'd had a big night out with Maysie, except it was the flu causing my headache and nausea this time.

The team bus pulled into the carpark at Old Trafford at 9.05am and, despite the time, there was a crowd of about 30 who had obviously sacrificed their breakfast to try and snare those all-important signatures to add to their collections. I realise supporters have an important place in the scheme of things, but having autograph books shoved in your face morning, noon and night can test your patience, especially when the demands come in addition to the hundreds of bats that are always in the change rooms waiting to be signed.

To rub salt into the wounds for BJ, there was a fax waiting at the ground for him from Plucka Duck saying: "I hear you're now looking after my brother — take good care of him. Good luck for the rest of the tour."

The dream debut of Peter Such continued in the morning session, when he took the wickets of Tubs and Slats to have us 2-55 at lunch. But the afternoon session was a good one for Oz. We added 104 in the session for the loss of one wicket, Mark W. for an aggressive 64. Mark's effort was backed up by a typically valuable knock from Boonie, who looked to be in a mood that suggested it would take a lot of hard work to dismiss him.

My tea break was spent on the throne. I only hope the runs keep flowing from the bat as freely as they're coming now! I feel as if I'm back on the sub-continent wrestling with Delhi Belly.

Boonie and AB continued to grind the opposition with relentless determination and concentration, until play was halted for the day, with us in the driving seat at 3-231. The batsmen were 85 not out and 29 not out respectively.

The tension of the afternoon's play was eased when Channel Nine's Tony Greig tried to interview Mark W. directly below the players' balcony. Their discussion was disrupted because they were continually pelted from above with an assortment of fruit. Eventually a grape lodged in Tony's top pocket, which led to the abandonment of the interview due to laughter.

Dinner was once again courtesy of room service, but most of my food was again untouched. I spent the rest of the evening at the movies with Matt Hayden watching *Falling Down*.

Michael Slater, during his impressive Test-debut innings

DAY 43 (June 6)

WE LOST AB in the second over of the morning — to Andrew Caddick, his first Test wicket. That brought me to the crease two deliveries before the second new ball was taken. Boonie then departed in the following over, only seven short of his first Test hundred on English soil. He was desperately disappointed — it's a target he would love to achieve.

Heals began his innings in the usual manner, trying to cut anything ranging from a long hop to a yorker ... with mixed success. But after a cautious start, the partnership gained momentum and by lunch we had added 90 runs. Heals was on 44 and I was 53. The day was shaping well, as we now had a 424-run lead, and intended scoring quick runs after lunch to give ourselves plenty of time to bowl the Englishmen out.

Everything fell into place after the interval. Heals really enjoyed himself, and played shots all around the wicket. He raced to 93 before realising he was on the verge of not only his first Test century, but his initial first-class century as well.

At this point we had a mid-wicket conference, which went something like this ...

"What do you do when you're in the 90s?" asked Heals.

"Stuffed if I know," I replied. "I've only buggered up half a dozen hundreds myself."

Heals, obviously inspired by my motivational chat, proceeded to smash the first ball of the next over, from De Freitas, over mid-wicket and then followed it with an equally arrogant shot over the top of mid-on, to bring up a superb century. It was a special moment for Heals and I'm glad I was batting with him. He had been at the crease for my first hundred, at Headingley four years before.

By the time AB declared in the mid-afternoon, we had put on 180 in 41 overs to create a new sixth-wicket record for matches between the two countries at Old Trafford. The resemblance between this partnership and the one between Dean Jones and me at Headingley in '89 was uncanny, with the running between the wickets being a feature. Hopefully, it's a good omen. It was the same feeling with Tails' batting on the first day — it was so much like his effort on the first day in '89, when he blunted their attack and gave us the upper hand.

The smell of victory was in the dressing room, as we prepared ourselves to go 1-0 up in the series. But Gooch had other ideas and, in a defiant act of controlled aggression, ended the day unbeaten on 82, out of a total of 2-133. But England's chances of survival took a major blow on the very last ball of the day when Mike Gatting was bowled by Merv. It appeared Gatt was expecting a bouncer. Instead, Merv beat him with a good-length inswinger — a dismissal that may prove to be the straw that breaks the England side's back.

My health hasn't improved much in the past couple of days, so it was another early night watching TV and ordering room service which, thanks to a chef who cooks anything we ask of him, was pumpkin soup and toasted sandwiches.

DAY 44 (June 7)

GOOD NEWS as the curtains were parted in Room 442 this morning — bright sunshine, the promise of a full-day's cricket and, hopefully, victory.

Gooch was more cautious in the morning session, adding only 30 to his overnight total. But he looked impenetrable. Our only success was the dismissal of Smith, who had looked uncomfortable in both innings against the turning ball ... which is something he'll be facing at every opportunity in the remaining Tests.

The first session was a very frustrating one with balls continually just out of reach of players and edges falling short of slips fieldsmen. But we knew that if we continued with the same discipline the luck would turn around to favour us.

Eventually the gods did smile upon us, in bizarre circumstances. Soon after lunch, Gooch became only the fifth person in the history of Test cricket to be given out handled the ball. He had patted the ball into the ground off Merv, and turned to see it bounce towards his wicket. Instinctively, Gooch swatted the ball away with his hands. Unfortunately, the hand is the only part of the body which it is illegal to use.

That particular dismissal proved to be a major turning point in the game. We picked up a further four wickets in the session, Gooch's 133 dominating the tea-time total of 7-273. At this stage the team was extremely confident of victory, and the XXXX and champagne were already on ice in the Esky. I was searching for the victory songs in my bag. Bad news — I left them at the hotel. Luckily our baggage man, Tony Smith, volunteered to go back and retrieve the celebratory lyrics.

David Boon has made a habit of taking amazing catches in close. In England's first innings, Chris Lewis turned a ball from Hughes firmly passed the little Tasmanian at short leg. It should have been a couple of runs, but Boonie threw out a hand, deflected the ball up and over his head, and turned around to make a brilliant diving catch.

Boonie (far left) leads the team victory song. The other Australians in picture are (left to right): Errol Alcott, Tim May, Allan Border, Mark Taylor, Paul Reiffel (with back to camera), Craig McDermott (obscured), Michael Slater (taking photo), Wayne Holdsworth (at back), Ian Healy, Bob Simpson, Shane Warne, Steve Waugh.

But for a while it seemed that trip may have been an unnecessary one. What seemed a hopeless situation for England began to look salvageable, as Caddick and Lewis dug in on what suddenly seemed a pretty good batting strip. Finally the breakthrough came, when Warney had Lewis prodding forward to a good-length ball that turned, found the edge of the bat and went straight into the safe hands of Mark Taylor at slip. Then came Such, with the same comical technique he had employed in the first innings. Once again it proved hard to combat and, with Caddick, he fought on into the final hour, in search of a creditable draw. Unfortunately for them, Merv still had enough juice in the tank for a last all-out assault, which included a barrage of short balls and helpful hints to the batsmen on how their techniques were holding up under pressure.

Our determination and patience seemed rewarded when Caddick clipped a ball off his hip to backward-square where Warney dived full-length to his right ... only to see the ball pop out of his hand. But, in an instinctive reaction, he grabbed it at the second opportunity to complete a brilliant catch.

Moments later, the game had ended. Such was finally removed, in the next Hughes over, caught by a diving AB close to the wicket, to complete an outstanding Test match win. Our success will make us very hard to beat in the series, as a victory in the first Test is always a vital psychological break to have on your opponent.

The stumps were souvenired amid a mixture of joyous celebrations and relief. In the end we only had 30 minutes to spare. In my opinion, the highlight of our performance today was the character we showed when things were going against us. It reflected our commitment to the task at hand. All the bowlers looked extremely tired after putting in huge efforts, with the best figures going to Merv (4-92 off 27.2 overs) and Warney, who took 4-86 off 49 overs (including 26 maidens).

The great feeling of winning a Test match is something that makes all the hard training and time away from home worthwhile. The spirit of the side was exemplified when one of the reserves, Wayne Holdsworth, led the team singing for most of the night — although some of the words were changed quite a bit from the original lyrics.

Shane Warne, the man of the match at Old Trafford, celebrates the key dismissal of Chris Lewis, caught at slip by Mark Taylor, on the final day.

Above: A crucial dismissal in the first Test — Mike Gatting, bowled by Merv Hughes off the final ball of the fourth day. Below: Allan Border celebrates his catch that dismissed Peter Such and put us one-up in the series.

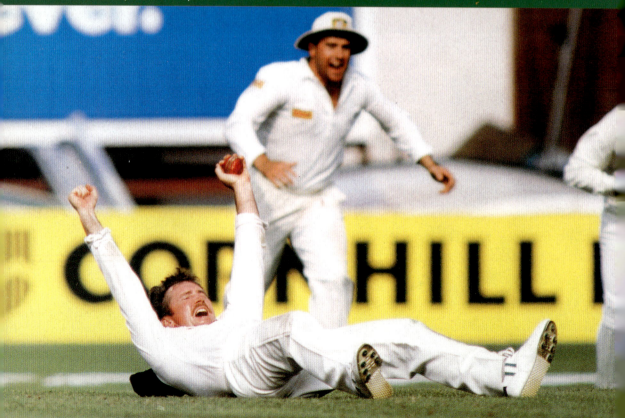

Merv Hughes celebrates the first Test win in typical Merv style.

Allan Border, batting during the second Test at Lord's, watches as Mike Atherton grabs at a defensive shot. The keeper is Alec Stewart.

Above: Robin Smith (centre) waits with partner Mike Atherton and bowler Tim May, while the third umpire studies the video replay to decide whether Smith has been stumped in England's first innings at Lord's. The umpire's decision, the first of its kind in Ashes Tests, went against the batsman. Below: In the second innings, Smith fell to this acrobatic catch at short leg by substitute fieldsman Matt Hayden, again off the bowling of May.

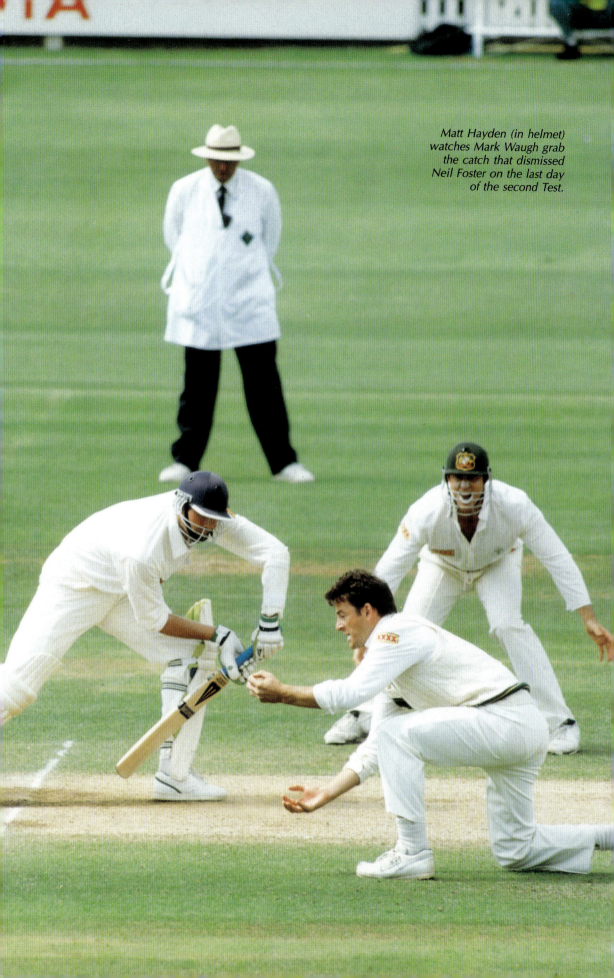

Matt Hayden (in helmet) watches Mark Waugh grab the catch that dismissed Neil Foster on the last day of the second Test.

Above: The final wicket at Lord's — Tufnell, bowled Warne, 0. The Australian fieldsmen are (left to right) Ian Healy, Mark Waugh and Matt Hayden. The umpire is Mervyn Kitchen.
Below: Man of the match from the second Test, Michael Slater (centre), acknowledges the Lord's crowd. The other Australians are (left to right) Tim May, Matt Hayden, Mark Waugh, Brendon Julian, Bob Simpson (behind Slater), Damien Martyn, Mark Taylor and Wayne Holdsworth.

'EARS TO McDERMOTT

DAY 45 (June 8)

THE BUS was scheduled to leave for Birmingham at 10 o'clock, but thankfully I was in the car that would follow — with Heals, Maysie and BJ. We four had no fixed leaving time, although 12.00 was rumoured. More by accident than plan, I woke from my slumber at 11.55am, and found BJ in a semi-comatose state. He's clearly a man who enjoys his shut-eye when he can get it.

Behind the wheel for the first leg of our journey was Heals, who quickly managed to stumble upon a country pub just outside Warrington. It proved more than adequate for our lunchtime needs. The 30-minute journey had obviously sapped Heals of his strength and a new driver was required for the rest of the trip. Yours truly won the position.

By the time we'd been on the motorway all of five minutes, all three of my fellow travellers were pushing out the zeds! Worse followed when a traffic jam, 25 kilometres outside Birmingham, turned our one-and-a-half hour trip into a two-and-three-quarter hour nightmare, which included 20 infuriating minutes spent searching for the Hyatt Hotel once we reached the city.

I have another new roomie for this part of the trip, who happens to be a fellow Bankstown boy — Wayne Holdsworth, on his first tour and performing well. The team for this match, against Warwickshire, is down to 14 players. The remaining three players have been given time off to spend with their wives or girlfriends who have just arrived over here. These ladies will soon be joined by the rest of the girls.

The evening was spent at a barbecue at the pub next door. Cracker and Matt Hayden were happy to give the head chef a few tips on the art of how to cook a decent barbie, but the cook wouldn't believe that a dash of beer on the hotplate gives the meat extra flavour. Later I rang home to make sure everything was OK with Lynette's travel arrangements. I still haven't been able to pin down any accommodation for Lynette and her travelling companion, Helen Healy, when they are in London.

Tim May (left) and Errol Alcott.

DAY 46 (June 9)

I HAD another poor night's sleep, but not because of the bed or pillows this time. Just for variation, our air conditioning unit was pumping out warm instead of cool air and, as a consequence, I felt like I'd lost half-a-dozen kilos in sweat through the night.

Boonie and I have the 12th and 13th man duties for the three-day match that began today, against a reasonably strong Warwickshire side that includes the county's overseas professional, Allan Donald from South Africa. Once again the weather was inclement and the prospect of a full day's play looked to be very doubtful when our two openers, Slater and Hayden, strode to the wicket. Play was interrupted a couple of times in the first session, but even so Slater continued his impressive form, reaching 50 for the seventh time out of 10 innings he's played so far on tour.

None of the lads in the team could believe how quiet it was in the dressing and viewing rooms today ... until someone realised that the world's biggest pest, Merv, was back in the hotel resting his body after his tremendous performance in the first Test. To make the day more entertaining for the guys watching the game, a variety of things were introduced, such as playing cards, reading papers, listening to music and trivia quizzes. I decided to quiz Brendon Julian about the history of Australian cricket. It proved a topic he would be foolish to choose if he was ever a contestant on Mastermind.

My first question was pretty simple. When I asked him who Stan McCabe was, he replied: "Isn't he the guy out of Jake and the Fatman?"

End of quiz!!

The middle session was a positive one for Australia, with both Martyn and Border racing to half-centuries before the tea break arrived. Just before tea, some of the Australian women tennis players and coaches who are in Birmingham preparing for Wimbledon (which is on in a couple of weeks) popped in. Hopefully we'll be able to catch a day's play at the home of tennis after the Lord's Test.

AB was dismissed shortly after tea, and Martyn was joined by Zoehrer under skies that suggested the end of the world was near. We could see massive lightning strikes in the distance, and with an hour of play to go, the heavens opened up, deluging the ground. Within 15 minutes the playing field was a lake, leaving absolutely no chance of further play, which meant Marto will have to wait 'til tomorrow to score the 14 runs he needs for his century.

Back at the hotel we ran into "The Gladiators", a group of super-athletes who take on contestants in a set of events designed to test strength and endurance — in front of the television camera. Apparently, the show had enormous success on TV last year and, even if it didn't, I doubt anyone would have the guts to tell them it was a failure.

Later I had dinner with the under-25-year-old members of the party at TGI Fridays, a popular eaterie in town.

DAY 47 (June 10)

THERE WAS no sign of sunshine as Heals took the warm-ups this morning. Errol was treating AB's back which pulled up stiff after batting yesterday. To make things interesting, we decided to divert from the usual course of jogging around the ground, and disappeared out the first exit available and onto an adjoining paddock — leaving behind a stunned Bob Simpson. There were a few ideas put forward as to where this mystery course should have taken us — back to the hotel, to the movies, to the nearest cab — all of which were quickly, if reluctantly, rejected. Eventually the pack headed back to the ground and into the serious business of preparing to win a cricket match. The net facilities are quite good here and, as such, the boys made the most of it. This was especially so of the boy from Kingaroy, Matt Hayden, who sleeps with his Gray-Nicolls bat at night and spends more time in the nets batting than even Geoff Marsh used to (Geoff would practice shots in front of the mirror in his hotel room at 6am ... just for fun).

Marto continued, more cautiously than yesterday, towards his century, which he finally achieved, continuing his excellent form in the county matches. We declared immediately after his dismissal, to give the bowlers, May, Reiffel, Holdsworth and Julian their chances to push for selection in the second Test side.

The worst possible situation a 12th man can get into (other than not having the beer cold at the end of the day) is for one of the batsmen to get injured seriously enough for that batsman to be unable to field. That happened to AB yesterday and, as a result, I was required for a while in the morning session. But there was a bonus — I escaped Merv, who had come to the ground today, for a couple of hours. AB finally took his place at first slip after lunch, and inspired the side to a fine performance, before another heavy thunderstorm hit the ground. Before the rain came, Maysie had once again turned in a good performance, taking three wickets and enhancing his claims for a Test guernsey.

Most of the players went their separate ways for dinner. May, Holdsworth and I chose an Italian restaurant, where we ran into Neville Oliver, the ABC cricket commentator, who had some interesting information on the English side. Apparently, their selectors are so worried about Robin Smith's inability to play leg-spin that they have sent him away for a week's practice against the only decent leg-spinner in English cricket, Ian Salisbury. It seems a pretty desperate measure, and suggests that, if we can win the next Test, the English selectors will make wholesale changes to their line-up.

DAY 48 (June 11)

THE ALARM went off, with neither of the occupants in Room 1519 showing any signs of life, until Cracker realised that if he didn't make a move we would miss not only breakfast, but the whole day's play as well. I peeked over the top of the sheets soon after, to see the silhouette of Cracker punching the air, followed by a set of cartwheels, and immediately realised there must have been some inclement weather brewing up outside. I joined Cracker at the window, and quickly realised it would be a good idea if we started building the ark immediately, such was the darkness of the sky. Simmo confirmed the obvious when he told us the bus would now be leaving at 10 o'clock, with the likelihood that there would be no play today.

At the ground, which was waterlogged, we were told that the umpires couldn't call the game off until after all the corporate sponsors had finished their lunch. Only at that point would they not be able to claim a refund for the day.

Fish and chips, the traditional Friday lunch, was served at 12.30 and the bus was on the motorway to Bristol at 1.00pm. The two-hour trip gave the Queenslanders a chance for some revenge on the NSW boys, as the third State of Origin game was shown. The Maroons' win was some consolation for them after the previous two titanic struggles ... and Blues victories.

The afternoon was spent lazing around the Swallow Hotel, checking out the gym and, for four of us, receiving a haircut. It will be at least two weeks before these trims can be considered wearable. After recovering from the initial shock of confronting the mirror, another one soon followed. Fifteen pounds ($35 Australian) was the asking price for the damage.

Most of the team ended up dining at Mulligans Seafood Restaurant. Everyone enjoyed the meal except for Marto, who ordered scampi without realising that he actually had to remove the shells himself. He refused to eat them, as he wanted his hands free from their odour. After finishing the meal, we found Marto a burger, and, with steady rain falling outside, decided to go into town and have a few drinks. The Ritzy Nightclub gained our patronage.

A summer's day at Edgbaston.

DAY 49 (June 12)

JUST AS I was about to attack the bowl of sugar puffs on offer at the buffet-style breakfast at the Swallow Hotel, Warney casually strolled up to me, dipped his bowl in the coco pops, and quietly mentioned the fact that he and Simone are now engaged. They had just spent the last three days in the Lake District north of Manchester. Word is he gave the poor girl no option, as he popped the question after rowing their boat out into the middle of a lake, knowing that she can't swim.

Their engagement will mean two things in the short term. One: it has automatically halved his fan club; and two: it guarantees him yet another shot at either the front page or back page of every paper his face has frequented since we arrived. The extent to which Warney's status has grown was emphasised when an Australian paper suggested he was "the biggest thing to come out of Australia since Jason and Kylie". One can only hope the media leaves him alone to get on with his cricket. If they do that I'm sure he'll develop into a champion.

In what is becoming a familiar story, we arrived at the ground in Bristol to find the covers sprawled across the wicket and light rain falling. The game, against Gloucestershire, finally commenced an hour late, after a fairly laid-back warm-up routine. No-one at the time was quite sure what time we would be starting.

The locals fell victim to Mark Taylor's hidden two-up ability, found themselves batting on a wicket we classed as dead (no bounce or speed in it), and proceeded to crawl along at about two runs per over. The former Test opener, Chris Broad, played a long and impressive innings. You would expect that from a man who has played 25 Tests and could easily be part of this series and more than likely perform very well.

To make the game a little more exciting, it was decided to produce the ten sets of autographed Craig McDermott ears straight after the tea break. In order for the plan to come together, the physio was told to take Billy to the treatment room for a few stretches — to give the lads time to have a practice run at fitting their plastic wing nuts on. Getting the ears on could have posed a problem, as they're a cheap and nasty product which could cut you up if not carefully attached to your melon.

After a couple of minutes' practice, the boys were confident they could pull the stunt off. The manager chased down Channel Nine, who were told to prepare for a prank straight after tea and to make sure they got it on film.

Billy returned to the dressing room unaware of the devious plot about to befall him, although some of the boys nearly gave it away with comments like: "Let's 'ear a bit of talk out there after tea." Twelfth man, Cracker, chimed in with "I'm 'ere if anyone needs something", followed by Merv, who told the captain that he was "all ears as to how you want me to bowl", and all of us that "it'll be 'ears and 'ears before we come back 'ere — so let's put on a good show."

The big fella from Ipswich still hadn't twigged, although he couldn't work out why all the other guys were rolling around on the floor laughing. He just joined in the frivolities. The team was led onto the field with ears securely hidden in trouser pockets. It was very apparent that all the players were now much keener and livelier. The first ball after tea, inevitably from Billy, travelled safely through to the keeper. Happy with this first-up effort, he turned his back and began to make his way back to his mark, at which point the plastic ears were simultaneously withdrawn from each player's pockets and attached, amid uncontrolled laughter, from the players and the crowd. Billy, still unaware of the plot, and keen to take his first wicket for the day, turned at the top of his mark and took three strides before spotting that every player possessed a set of ears capable of picking up Sky Channel. He all but tripped over, and a huge grin appeared on his face. Seemingly unperturbed, he carried on calmly until about three metres from the wicket, when he broke up, and ended up delivering a half-paced ball that landed just on the edge of the wicket.

The Australian team that played Gloucestershire at Bristol ... complete with ears. Back row (left to right): Taylor, S. Waugh, Hayden, Hughes. Front row: Warne, May, Healy, Boon, Martyn, M. Waugh. Absent: Craig McDermott.

The 12th man then ran onto the field with a huge plastic bag, and collected all 10 sets of ears, while the good-humoured applause from the crowd clearly showed they had enjoyed the joke.

To his credit, Billy had a good laugh about the prank, though he was a bit concerned his kids might cop a bit of stick at school about their dad's ears. One of the great things about a team sport is that an incident like this can enhance morale — I'm sure it will become a great talking point in years to come whenever the guys get together.

Merv and Warney continued their good work by taking two and four wickets respectively — a particularly impressive effort from Warne, because the ball became soaked, making it hard to grip. The scoreline at the end of play read Gloucester 7-183, after an afternoon on which the less-sober element in the crowd, through their songs, created more excitement than the over-cautious efforts of the home team.

When we returned to the dressing room, several of the members of the side raced to souvenir the plastic "McDermott Ears" ... and claim a rather large and valuable part of Ashes '93 history.

After play BJ, Heals, Billy and I attended another XXXX function, at a local social club. It turned out to be a bit of a fizzer. The venue was a long hall and, because the English are generally conservative by nature, everyone there crammed into the far corners. From our position on the stage, we needed binoculars to spot them.

The highlight of the night was the selection by mistake of a 16-year-old local lad to join one of the teams on stage for the trivia quiz. Obviously keen to make the most of this opportunity, he proceeded to knock the top off about four cans. Soon after, he had to be escorted back to his seat after his team, captained by Billy, crashed to an early defeat at the hands of the eventual winner, the side led by Ian Healy.

There was some joy at the end of the evening when the local XXXX representative produced a large bottle of Southern Comfort for the lads. He had heard we were quite partial to a nip or two during victory celebrations.

DAY 50 (June 13)*

I WOKE up suffering the effects of some Bristol hospitality — courtesy of the good folk of Harveys Wines, where the latter part of the previous evening had been spent. Apparently it is some kind of tradition that touring sides are taken through the cellars and then wined and dined until you can take no more. From my observations, several of last night's guests may have pushed themselves beyond the limits of medical soundness.

Given the circumstances, the day started fairly sedately. All I tried to do was look enthusiastic and presentable when, in fact, all I wanted was to lie down and let some birdlife peck my eyes out. But, with the liver pumping double-time, I managed to throw off the effects of the tonsil varnish in record time, and at the 11 o'clock starting time, I presented a fine picture of an Australian cricketer.

Within half an hour (which seemed like five hours) we wrapped up the Gloucester tail. Hughes had five wickets, and Warne four, while I finished with only one. While bowling tightly, I was about as penetrating as a plastic knife.

Back in the dressing room, I severely over-estimated Billy's sense of humour and ability to have a good laugh. I asked him to autograph my set of jug handles (ie: plastic ears). The request was met with a flurry of abuse, uppercuts, rabbit and kidney punches, and general bruising to most of my body, external and internal. Having managed to keep myself injury-free for almost two months (a career record!), it seemed, at the time, to be a rather disappointing way to end my tour.

Not satisfied with the injuries inflicted upon me, the "Winged One" then set out to destroy my personal belongings. Not distracted by my desperate cries that both physical assault and damaging third-party property are criminal offences punishable by a court of law, Billy, armed with a stick of Pink Zink, proceeded to colour in my sunglasses and other items in the near vicinity.

Fortunately, a good samaritan arrived and told Billy that perhaps the idea of signed "McDermott Ears" at ACB shops across the country could produce a rather generous stream of income. This completely tamed the winged-nut beast and enabled me to escape ... with a pulse, no severed limbs and sunglasses. Upon scurrying to the physio room (where I was later pronounced fit to continue the tour), I tried my sunglasses on. The visual effect of Billy's attack brought back unhappy memories of the early morning.

Meanwhile, Australia were piling on 400 runs in better than even time, with Hayden, Boon, M. Waugh and Martyn all compiling scores in excess of 50. However, some sobering news arrived when we learned that Ian Healy's right thumb, which he had injured in a keeping mishap in the Gloucestershire first innings, has been diagnosed as fractured. With the second Test only four days away, it must be doubtful that Heals will be able to play. But those who know his determination, and pride in the "baggy green", will be extremely surprised if he's not there on Thursday.

The evening was spent with a few quiet drinks at the bar with Molly Meldrum and Plucka Duck who have arrived in England for some footage to be used on the TV show, *Hey! Hey! It's Saturday*.

* This entry was guest-written by Tim May

Shane Warne, who was quickly nicknamed by the British tabloid press as "Hollywood", appears to be auditioning for a part in Young Guns III.

DAY 51 (June 14)

THE NOW familiar menacing sky, with not hint of blue anywhere, was once again hovering above the county ground at Bristol this morning, and eventually led to the day's play being abandoned. The draw puts our Tetley 50,000 pounds bonus in jeopardy, as we need to win 10 out of the 14 county games that we play on this tour. To date, we have won four games and had three (including this one) inconvenienced by rain. Any more wash-outs will leave us with virtually no chance of collecting that bonus, which the team has treated as a huge incentive.

The heavy rain tumbled down just as we were about to commence our warm-ups. We were sentenced to a morning in the confines of the dressing-room, locked up with the likes of Holdsworth, Hughes and a variety of characters who get bored very easily and can create mayhem in a matter of minutes if nothing is happening around them.

Luckily for the team, a saviour appeared in the form of Plucka Duck, who arrived with Molly to get some footage of the boys training. Ever since he was introduced to us by Tim Zoehrer at the start of the tour, Plucka has become something of a team mascot. But unfortunately his "fitness" is lacking, and the initial warm-up lap was almost too much for him. He was suffering after a big night on the town, and was finding the warm environment of his woollen suit very conducive to a technicolour yawn. Some fresh air was needed immediately. Next up was the 10-minute routine of stretches we normally go through, and Plucka added some interesting dance routines to liven up proceedings. This was followed by a fielding exercise that found the duck struggling for footing on the wet surface, resulting in some nasty tumbles that left a trail of feathers on the deck ... and a badly-hungover duck gasping for air, to the amusement of everyone watching at the ground.

The poor weather continued, but the situation that applied at the Warwickshire game applied here too, and the game could not be called off until the corporate sponsors had eaten lunch. To fill in time, Plucka was told to pad up for the cameras — and take the lads on. He looked more than a little apprehensive, as his sight is down to only about 10% due to the fact he can only peep through a couple of slits in his costume.

Batting on an artificial wicket, he successfully let the first ball go through to the keeper. Slowly growing in confidence, the duck began to use his webbed feet to the leg-spin of Warne and collected a couple of boundaries. At this point, the bowlers decided to bring Plucka back to earth. McDermott, in search of his first wicket for two weeks, strove for that extra yard of pace, but was handled with ease — to the delight of the now enthralled crowd. Despite the bowlers' best efforts, Plucka kept his wicket intact and began to look so impressive that one English journalist was heard to say: "Is he qualified for England?"

Both the game and Plucka's exhibition were eventually called off, and we were able to make our way to London via the M4 motorway. *The Blues Brothers* found its way onto the TV screen, which did much to shorten the trip.

My new roomie for this leg of the trip is Damien Martyn, who is having a very good tour with two centuries already under his belt. I settled for a room-service dinner — chicken and soup — a privilege which set me back 21 pounds (about A$46).

DAY 52 (June 15)

WE WERE back at the home of cricket for training this morning, but the conditions didn't allow the bowlers to operate off their long runs. And the wickets were a little damp, due to the persistent rain that has fallen in London over the last three days. Most interest in the session surrounded how Ian Healy's broken thumb would pull up after the practice session. The truth is we won't know very much today as he is only catching a tennis ball to give his hand more time to heal.

Practice was cut short as we had a luncheon hosted by the National Sporting Club to attend. I recalled that this wasn't a bad function back in '89. Sitting directly opposite me at my table was "PC Tony Stamp", (who stars in the TV programme *The Bill*), a man who loves to watch cricket when away from the set. Fortunately, the speeches weren't very lengthy, although the editor of The *Evening Standard* gave a speech that tried to gain a few cheap laughs at the expense of Merv. It didn't go down too well with many of the 740 people.

Des Rundle, the team manager, didn't let us down with his speech, managing to slip in a dirty joke on the unsuspecting cigar-smoking crowd. They seemed to appreciate his effort more so than the elderly MCC gathering at the Lord's dinner earlier in the tour.

The afternoon was spent between the sheets. But, as usual, it was disrupted by a steady stream of callers — all asking for Shane Warne. They were all put through to my room by an operator who didn't listen closely enough to the pronunciation of the name. I also had to put up with the usual couple of faxes that end up under my door, rather than the door of their correct recipient, Mark Waugh.

Lynette is due to depart Sydney for England tomorrow with Helen Healy, on a journey which involves a two-day stopover in Bangkok. My phone call found her struggling to fit all her clothes in the one suitcase she is supposedly bringing with her, but besides this minor problem, everything was going to plan. It will be great to see her.

The real Plucka Duck, all ready to go out and face the best the Australians can bowl at him.

DAY 53 (June 16)

AFTER DEVOURING my room-service breakfast in record time and with 30 seconds still left on the clock to make the bus, I was intercepted this morning by Simmo in the hotel foyer. He explained that training had been postponed until 2 o'clock in the hope the weather would clear up and we would be able to use the turf wicket facilities at Lord's. It soon became apparent the weather wasn't going to clear. I didn't want to lounge around and do nothing all day, so I headed to the gym for a pretty solid workout on the exercise bike and the weights.

With most of the guys going their own separate ways after the tour finishes, it had been left to each of us to finalise post-tour flights and hotel accommodation. Today seemed as good a day as any, so, after the gym, Maysie, BJ and I headed off to the Qantas building to confirm our bookings.

After this was accomplished, we set off for Harrods. We had to wait for 30 minutes to catch the No. 9 double-decker red bus to Knightsbridge, and eventually alighted at this popular tourist attraction in pouring rain. We were only yards from the front door of Harrods, but the lads were feeling the need for some nourishment, so before we entered we stopped for a pitstop at a nearby KFC.

We've now been to KFC so many times we can't be far away from being able to reveal the 11 secret herbs and spices that for so long have remained a mystery to everyone!

With lunch out of the way we strolled into Harrods and headed for the food hall, where Maysie immediately started to behave strangely as he scrutinised the Indian cuisine. With only a glass panel separating him from his idea of heaven, he began to salivate like a dog about to get a bone. Next stop was the confectionery department, a definite weakness of both BJ and myself. Harrods has every imaginable type of chocolate, all of which we were eager to sample ... and most of which we did!

A trip to Harrods wouldn't be the same without checking out the toy department. That task ended up requiring the best part of two hours, and we were enticed into buying a few crucial items — a couple of paper aeroplanes that always come back to the thrower; two Spiderman Action toys that climb down walls by themselves; and a nurf soccerball that nearly cost us a fortune later on in the dinnerware section. A throw at Maysie caught him unawares, and an unfortunate rebound off his head crashed into the Wedgewood display but, thankfully, didn't break anything.

We decided it would be a good idea to leave the store before we were escorted out, and headed back home for a team meeting scheduled for 6.30pm.

The meeting proved much the same as the one before the first Test. It was stressed that controlled aggression and patience were the two key factors required for continued success in this series. The only possible change to our line-up will be the introduction of May for Julian. The Lord's wicket generally favours the spinners, and Maysie has bowled superbly on tour so far.

The traditional pre-match dinner was held at The Big Easy in Chelsea, which is another American-style eatery with plenty of memorabilia all over the walls. The food was in the form of ribs and chicken ... and heaps of it. When it came out on the table, we resembled a group of cavemen about to tuck into our catch of the day.

The record number of rib racks eaten in the restaurant currently stood at seven and a few of the lads were keen to get their name on the honour board. But, unfortunately, our team physio and dietitian, Errol Alcott, was on hand to put an end to any such notion. But Wayne Holdsworth may have set a new vanilla-malt milkshake record during the evening. Six was his tally, before he could take no more.

THE SECOND TEST

DAY 54 (June 17)

THE TEAM bus is always a quiet one on the first morning of a Test match and was even more so today. It is every Australian cricketer's dream to be selected to play in a Test at Lord's. Once inside this fabled arena, you always get a sense that you are in a place that is steeped in tradition. It is rightfully called the home of cricket.

Our starting XI was announced at warm-ups, roughly one-and-a-quarter hours before the start of play, with only the expected change — May for Julian. AB then called correctly, a vital toss for us. We were banking on batting first for two reasons — so that the wicket will have time to dry out, rough up and thereby allow our spinners greater opportunities; and to give Heals a few more days for his broken thumb to improve before he is required to keep wicket.

Michael Slater began the match with a sparkling boundary off the first delivery he received and batted brilliantly all the way to lunch, while Mark Taylor looked as safe as a bank at the other end.

Lunch as usual at Lord's was superb, and I decided to cash in. I didn't think there was much chance of me being needed today, so the double serve of apple pie and ice cream went down nicely. The middle section of play went along the same lines as the first, with the two boys from the southern NSW city of Wagga Wagga doing it easily, thrilling the huge contingent of Aussie supporters in attendance.

With the cricket going so well, a couple of the lads started to feel very relaxed. The Nurf soccer ball flew about in the change rooms until, to the shock of our coach and thousands of spectators, it was accidentally thrown out the door and bounced onto the playing surface. The perpetrator ducked for cover behind his coffin in the hope of escaping a tongue-lashing from the hierarchy. Only one problem — the moustache gave him up straight away!

Slater reached his maiden Test hundred with a flick to fine leg and immediately put on a show Greg Matthews would have been proud of, punching the air, kissing his helmet and waving his bat in the air like an Olympic fencing champion. And rightly so, as it was a superb hundred featuring shots all around the ground played with power and grace. The two undefeated batsmen arrived back in the dressing room at tea to the thunderous applause of all their team-mates. Everyone was congratulating Slats on his century, although I wouldn't be surprised if he doesn't recall it. He appeared to be in a trance-like state, probably from not believing he had actually gone from being a second XI cricketer for NSW 12 months ago to where he is now — a fantastic achievement!

In the dressing room, there is always plenty happening and today was no different. Our physio took a call from a bloke who claimed he was Sir Donald Bradman, and couldn't work out if it was fair dinkum or not. One of the play-

A triumphant Michael Slater returns to the Australian dressing room at tea on the opening day, having already reached his maiden Test century.

Gooch made to wait five hours for breakthrough as luck deserts his side at Lord's
Australian openers punish England

By ALAN LEE
CRICKET CORRESPONDENT

LORD'S (first day of five; Australia won toss): Australia have scored 292 for two wickets against England

ALL the threats and exhortations came to nothing. Roused by fighting talk from captain, manager and chairman, England still needed five hours to take their first wicket on the opening day of the second Test match at Lord's yesterday. There was no lack of effort, no lack of the required passion. Luck deserts habitual losers.

Graham Gooch, who has left nobody in any doubt what this game means to him, lost the toss and the chance to impose control. England bowled well, better than at any stage of the first Test, and might easily have taken wickets while the new ball was moving off the seam. But, when the tide is running against a team, the edges never go to hand.

Mark Taylor and Michael Slater took their early good fortune and took over the day. In their contrasting ways, the neat, acquisitive left-hander and his ebullient young partner led hungrily from a good, slow pitch. Their stand of 260 was the highest for any wicket in an Ashes Test at Lord's, decidedly not the tonic which English cricket craved.

Slater, playing only his second Test, made 152 with a range of stroke and clarity of purpose suggesting it will be only the first of many. For Taylor, centuries in England are becoming more routine. This was his second in successive Tests, his fourth in eight games in this country.

There has only been one bigger first-wicket stand by Australia against England and that was the 329 Taylor and Geoff Marsh put on at Trent Bridge in 1989, when their side completed the last of four wins in that series.

The bookmakers had formed a low opinion of England's prospects even before a ball was bowled, quoting them at 7-1 to win the game. By lunch, they had drifted to 12-1, by tea, it was 33-1 and, if Ladbrokes' betting tent at the Nursery End had not been shut due to a licensing mix-up, they would have accommodated anyone still wishing to back England by close of play at 100-1. Even at such fancy odds, few sound men would have been tempted.

Mick Hunt, the groundsman, had been up all night with his staff, mopping up the effects of Wednesday's deluge. Through their efforts, play could begin on time; in the morning sunshine and England, having, like Australia, opted to play two spin bowlers, knew that early inroads were crucial. It might easily have happened, for Neil Foster and Andy Caddick were a handful for an hour, Slater being taken on the glove by Foster and all but flipping on to one from Caddick that darted back off the pitch.

This was quality bowling, almost every ball compelling a shot. But it brought England nothing and, at 50 for none, Gooch summoned Such. His first ball turned enough to prompt spin at both ends and, when that produced no instant dividends, Gooch brought on Lewis and then even had a rare bowl himself.

By lunch, he had used six bowlers, operating to field-settings that were thoughtful and imaginative. Here was a captain answering charges of shallow tactics and a team responding. Yet here too, was an opening pair enjoying themselves hugely, running aggressively between the wickets and dispatching anything loose unerringly.

Australia should have had one, shortly before tea, when Taylor was drawn down the pitch by Tufnell and hopelessly beaten by one which turned past the inside edge. He was a yard out of his ground when the ball hit Stewart on the arm. It was the second stumping opportunity wasted in successive Tests and with Stewart's batting suffering along with the confidence of the bowlers, the evidence for a proper wicketkeeper is now overwhelming.

Taylor was on 85 then, but Slater was long past his century, a milestone he recorded by punching the air repeatedly, kissing his green helmet and throwing his arms around Taylor.

Slater's strength is speed of footwork, so nimble he looks to be on wheels. It gets him in position uncommonly early, so his favourite on-drive is played from perfect position, no matter the length of the ball. At 150, however, it all suddenly seemed too easy to him and he was caught by the substitute, Ben Smith, at mid-wicket, mistiming a full-length ball as Lewis attacked him round the wicket.

Six overs later, Taylor followed and there was at least a certain justice in his end. Tufnell once more had him in flight, but this time, as the advancing Taylor played for turn, the ball drifted past the outside edge, a simpler stumping which Stewart gracefully completed.

The rest was anti-climactic, with England in no hurry to bowl extra overs and Boon and Mark Waugh intent on nothing other than being in residence when play resumes this morning. They survived the second new ball, now five overs old, and unless the fates decide to favour England this morning, an awesome series is in prospect.

☐ England will play five Tests and five one-day internationals during their winter tour of the Caribbean. After months of negotiations, England won concessions on the start of the tour, which will begin in January rather than February, and on there being four warm-up matches before the internationals.

One that got away: Taylor steers a ball past the outstretched hand of Smith on his way to another century against England in the second Test yesterday

LORD'S SCOREBOARD

Australia won toss

AUSTRALIA: First Innings

	4s	Min	Ball
M A Taylor st Stewart b Tufnell 111	10	323	265
M J Slater c sub (B F Smith) b Lewis 152	18	263	263
low drive to mid-wicket			
D C Boon not out 11	1	85	45
M E Waugh not out 6	—	35	26
Extras (b 1, w 1, nb 10) 12			
Total (2 wkts, 360min, 94 overs) ... **292**			

TEST MATCHES: Feb 19-24: Kingston, Jamaica first day Feb 22; Mar 17-22: Georgetown, Guyana first day Mar 21; Mar 25-30: Port-of-Spain, Trinidad first day Mar 29; Apr 8-13: Bridgetown, Barbados first day Apr 11; Apr 18-21: St John's, Antigua first day Apr 19.
ONE-DAY INTERNATIONALS: Feb 16: Bridgetown, Barbados; Feb 26: Kingston, Jamaica; Mar 2: St Vincent; Mar 5: Port-of-Spain, Trinidad; Mar 6: Port-of-Spain, Trinidad.

BOWLING: Caddick 21-4-61-0 (nb 4) (8-1-23-0, 5-1-15-0, 5-0-22-0, 3-2-1-0); Foster 19-4-59-0 (7-0-27-0, 4-2-12-0, 6-2-18-0, 2-0-2-0); Such 14-1-31-0 (4-1-5-0, 6-0-17-0, 4-0-9-0); Tufnell 15-2-65-1 (nb 5) (4-0-21-0, 7-1-35-0, 4-1-9-1); Lewis 15-1-57-1 (nb 6) (8-1-23-0, 7-0-34-1); Gooch 6-1-15-0 (w 1).

INTERMEDIATE SCORES: 50: 55min, 14.4 overs; 100 111min, 28.5 overs. Lunch: 101-0 (Taylor 36, Slater 60) 35 overs. 150: 179min, 45 overs; 200: 222min, 60 overs. Tea: 212-0 (Taylor 86, Slater 120), 67 overs 250: 262min, 75.5 overs. New ball taken after 89.3 overs at 289-2.

Taylor: 50 in 156min, 126 balls, 5 fours, 1 six; 100: 289min 212 balls, 9 fours, 1 six. Slater: 50: 91min, 80 balls, 6 fours 100: 190min, 175 balls, 10 fours; 150: 289min, 260 balls, 11 fours.

ENGLAND: *G A Gooch, M A Atherton, M W Getting, R A Smith, G A Hick, †A J Stewart, C C Lewis, N J Foster, A R Caddick, P M Such, P C R Tufnell.

FALL OF WICKETS: 1-260 (Taylor 100), 2-277 (Boon 2).

PREVIOUS RESULT: First Test (Old Trafford): Australia won by 179 runs.

MATCHES TO COME: Third Test: Trent Bridge, July 1-6. Fourth Test: Headingley, July 22-26. Fifth Test: Edgbaston, August 5-9. Sixth Test: The Oval, August 19-23.

Umpires: M J Kitchen and D J Shepherd.
Referee umpire: J C Balderstone.

---

ers took over — only to find it was actually an Aussie tourist holidaying in Israel, desperate to find out the Test match score. He thought it was his best chance to speak directly to the players if he said he was the Great One!

After the interval Tubs reached three figures — another extremely important knock for the side. His dig, like Slats', was filled with quality shot-making. Their superb partnership must have had the whole of Wagga Wagga preparing for a ticker-tape parade when the boys arrive home. In many ways it was just like turning the clock back to Trent Bridge in '89 when Geoff Marsh and Taylor put on 329 for the first wicket. That record will stay intact, as this partnership was severed on 260, when Slats was caught, probably as a result of relaxing too much. He seemed to be finding it almost too easy out there. Tubs then departed with around 30 minutes left to play, giving the Pommie bowlers a faint hope that better things might be around the corner.

Late in the day, Merv came out with a thought-provoking comment regarding an article which suggested he has a love-hate relationship with the English crowds. "Yer," he commented, "I love them and they all hate me."

The remaining time was safely negotiated by Boon and Mark Waugh, which left us with a tremendous scoreline and, more importantly, the psychological advantage after the first day once again, an edge which is so vital in Test matches. In the "away" dressing room at Lord's there is an honour board on the wall which features the names of players who have scored hundreds against England at the ground and another for players who have taken five wickets in an innings. We've already added the names of Slater and Taylor to that "batting" board, on sticking plaster with their scores alongside.

Tonight was a quiet one. I was feeling especially tired — I'm sure watching a full day is mentally more draining than actually playing.

DAY 55 (June 18)

THE CUSTOMARY warm-up and stretching routine were forgone this morning, and we headed straight for the nets after a quick team fielding drill. The coach and captain saw today as a vital batting day so and had decided the more batting practice we had the better our chances of reaching a big total. We also had one further "task" to perform before the start of play. As has been the case in most of the previous 31 Australian cricket tours of England, a team photo was taken in front of the Lord's pavilion. As is the usual custom, the most experienced players sat in the front row and the newer members of the party stood at the back.

The morning session was once again dominated by us although it was sprinkled with unsuccessful appeals in the first 30 minutes, which was not surprising as they had the use of the second new ball. At lunch, David Boon and Mark Waugh were still undefeated, and they entered the Members' pavilion and strode through the Long Room and up the two flights of stairs to the away dressing room to a great ovation from all the touring party. After lunch the partnership continued to frustrate the Englishmen, with Boon digging in and looking immovable and Mark W, with shots all around the ground, racing towards his first Test century on English soil.

When Mark reached 99, all the players congregated on the balcony in preparation for a celebration. But, on this occasion, that preparation was tragically cut short. A Tufnell delivery cannoned off Junior's pads and clipped his off stump, robbing him of every cricketer's dream — a century at Lord's.

They say that twins have some form of ESP or that they are affected by events that happen to each other — well, on this occasion, it felt as if *I* had been dismissed one short of 100, such was my disappointment. I'm sure Mark's disappointment would be magnified many more times over. That one delivery will surely be replayed in his mind a thousand times tonight, and all the while he'll be hoping for time to turn back and give him another shot at history.

The Lord's centurions (left to right): Taylor, Boon and Slater.

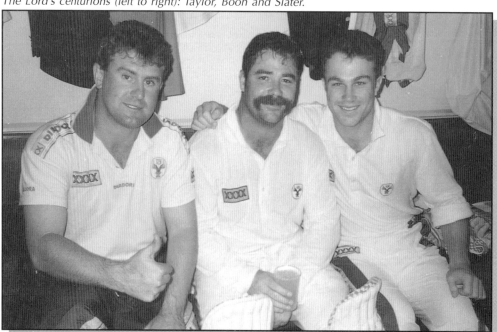

The Australians send a message to Craig McDermott. The men on the balcony are (left to right): Paul Reiffel, Dean Jones, Wayne Holdsworth (at back), Bob Simpson, Matthew Hayden, Errol Alcott, Ron Steiner (from the ACB).

The fact that the score had been mounting so steadily with so few wickets falling caught me short. My gear was all over the room just when I needed it. Fortunately, AB made it through his first over without trouble, just as I was managing to locate my creams from under my coffin.

I might have been panicking, but Boonie was remorseless. His single-minded approach continued to grind the opposition, and, much to his elation and relief, he was finally rewarded with the century that had eluded him on his past two Ashes campaigns and in the first Test of this series. When the total passed 500, AB decided it was time to quicken the tempo, with boundaries flowing from his bat. Before anyone realised it, he had scored 50. Then, with just seven minutes of play to go, AB threw himself into a cover drive and was bowled off an inside edge.

The score may have been 4-591 but that dismissal still sent my heart rate soaring, as I was the one to go in. To make matters worse, the light was very poor and the third new ball has just been taken. As I shaped up to my first delivery, all I could think of was the fact that Plucka was about to get a new owner! But, fortunately, I survived the remaining time, while Boonie ended up unbeaten on 138.

Some people might say we have batted on too long but one of the reasons we continued to pile on the runs was that during the tea interval Craig McDermott had doubled over in agony with stomach trouble. After consultations with doctors, he was immediately rushed to hospital. There were fears of a burst appendix, or possibly complications arising from two previous hernia operations. I don't think I've ever seen someone in as much pain as when I found Craig in the players' toilets, gasping for air and unable to move. He was all hunched over, with tears pouring down his face. All we can hope is that it turns out to be nothing too serious.

After play, the Rolling Stones drummer, Charlie Watts, as well as Molly Meldrum and John Cornell (a movie and TV show producer and one of the leading figures in World Series Cricket, but probably best known as Paul Hogan's sidekick, Strop, in Hogan's 1970s TV shows) came in for a drink with the boys. The three of them are mad cricket supporters. The rest of the evening was a quiet affair, spent at the movies with BJ, watching *The Vanishing*, starring Kiefer Sutherland.

Allan Border bowled by Lewis late on the second day, after a quickfire 77.

DAY 56 (June 19)

WHILE ENGLAND were having another ordinary day in the field yesterday, a few of the lads tried to predict some of the headlines that would appear in this morning's papers. Maysie was almost spot-on with his call of "Waugh Fails". In fact the headline in the *Daily Mail* read "Waugh's 'Failure' Staves Off Ultimate Insult", referring to the fact that if Mark had scored 100, we would have been the first Test team to have the first four batsmen score hundreds in the same innings. This possibility must have crept into one MCC member's thoughts as he backed our first four players to make hundreds at the massive odds of 1000/1 with a 100-pound wager. By falling one run short, Mark cost the poor bloke 100,000 pounds.

Our innings was terminated 40 minutes into the third morning with Boon still there on 164 and S. Waugh 151 less than that.

The England openers started promisingly enough, but then an event thought to be impossible shook the foundations of this hallowed arena. Maysie, thought previously to be only skilled enough to catch a cold, took a spectacular running catch, complete with a tumbling roll, to dismiss Gooch. And he did not appear to have suffered any injury in making the dismissal.

The team erupted into immediate celebration, and everyone waited for a typically dry piece of humour from Maysie to explain his superb piece of fielding. We weren't disappointed. "Which fellow did I get out?" he asked. But after further questioning as to his coolness under pressure, Maysie revealed the truth — that he had stopped breathing a couple of times as the ball was in flight after being top-edged to him at deep fine-leg. I suppose that made the catch all the more meritorious. With his confidence sky-high, Maysie proceeded to capture the next two wickets. In tandem with Merv, he bowled a superb spell that caused a middle-order collapse.

A couple of the English batsmen seem fazed by our bowlers, particularly Robin Smith when facing our spinners and Graeme Hick when confronted by short-pitched bowling from Hughes. This is something that will be hard to reverse given the present frame of mind all parties concerned are in.

The team spirit and strength of our side was highlighted by the continued superb fielding of our substitutes. Brendon Julian was outstanding today. At stumps, England were in a mess, at 9 for 193, after Warney again took over the show in the final session and prevented any type of fightback. The three frontline bowlers have really done a superb job. Their attitude was typified by Merv Hughes' reply after he was asked: "How will you go without Craig McDermott?"

"Well, I'll just have to do enough work for two bowlers instead of one," he replied.

The evening meal was at The Bombay Brassiere, where Dilip Doshi entertained Michael Slater's fiancee (Michael wasn't there, he had a bat contract to sort out), BJ, Tubs, and myself. The only worrying aspect of the evening was the realisation that I'm starting to enjoy Indian food. That itself is not a problem. The trouble is I can't admit it in front of Tubs and Maysie because I'm always giving them a gobful about what it's doing to their insides and their waistline.

DAY 57 (June 20)

LYNETTE WAUGH and Helen Healy, along with 2-year-old Emma Healy, touched down at Heathrow at 5.20am and were settled in their new accommodation with a friend of mine by 7 o'clock. I was woken from my slumber by Lynette at 7.30, happy at the thought that she'll be here for the rest of the tour but unhappy that she cost me an hour's sleep. Seriously though, it is always comforting for a player to have his family with him on long tours. This is especially so for the guys who have young kids.

The capture of the last English wicket took a frustrating 30 minutes of play, after which their two openers, Gooch and Atherton, made their way to the crease needing to bat for two full days to save the Test and some pride. But the stand was soon broken. The vital early breakthrough was achieved by Warne, who had Gooch very well caught by Healy low down. We hoped this would lead to another collapse, but in fact it had the reverse effect. England dug in, and Atherton and Gatting looked determined — something which is, of course, expected at this level.

A crucial moment in the match occurred during in the middle session, just when England looked like clawing their way back into the game. When Atherton was 97, he worked a ball off his hip to the on-side. It looked like being the boundary that would bring up his hundred. But Hughes, fielding at deep backward-square waiting for the sweep, raced around the boundary and picked up the ball only inches from the rope. At precisely the same time as Merv intervened, Atherton turned and headed off for his third and 100th run. Gatting spotted the danger and sent him back, only to see his partner slip and be left tragically sprawled on the wicket, out of his ground. Merv's return was brilliantly picked up on the bounce by Heals, and the stumps were broken — which I'm sure is how Atherton felt. Cricket can be a cruel game sometimes and probably no more so than when Atherton was on his hands and knees trying to scramble back to his crease.

Atherton's demise was quickly followed by the dismissal of Smith, who seems unsure as to whether he should play his natural attacking game or tough it out until he is more sure of his footwork and technique against the spin. This indecision is clearly playing on his mind and his scores are suffering.

Smith's departure was the final wicket of the day, and at the close, England, at 3-220, have a sniff of survival. Long innings by the not out batsmen, Gatting and Hick, appear their main chance of avoiding defeat tomorrow.

Heals and myself caught up with the girls tonight. They're staying only five minutes walk away from Lord's, and we had an enjoyable evening away from the confines of the team hotel's four walls.

The second-innings dismissal of Mike Atherton, run out after slipping over in mid-pitch, for 99. Atherton had turned a ball behind square, run two, but then been sent back by Mike Gatting as he set off for his hundredth run.

Graham Gooch, who, after England's second straight loss, found himself under increasing pressure from the local media.

DAY 58 (June 21)

WE FELT this morning that today would probably be the most important day of the whole Ashes series. We knew that if we capitalised on the previous four days' good work, we'd be 2-0 up in the series and very hard to catch. And we hated to think England might escape with a draw here and gain a confidence boost for the remaining four Tests. The importance of the situation was emphasised before we began our pre-game stretching routine.

Right from the start, the morning session went our way. Gatting appeared a touch unlucky to be given out LBW to Warne, and then an unconvincing 64 by Hick ended when he was caught at slip by Taylor off May's bowling.

The fall of Hick brought Chris Lewis to the crease. In trying to get off the mark, Lewis charged down the wicket, but missed the ball and was stumped. His failure would almost certainly cost him his spot in the England side and claimed the goggles of Mr Magoo at the same time (he'd been out for a duck in the first innings).

The mood in the lunch-time dining area summed up the state of the game, with the Aussie players very jovial and the English side of the room stone silent. The chat surrounded the possibility that we would finish the game well before tea, which was when the Queen was due to be introduced to the teams. This meeting is a highlight of the Ashes tour for the players. Luckily, another strategy had been planned, and we would have met the Queen at Buckingham Palace if it had not been possible at the ground.

England's lower order, along with Alec Stewart, put up a good fight, but the innings ended just before the scheduled tea interval when Warney took the last two wickets with identical deliveries, Such and Tufnell being bowled behind their legs off successive balls. Our victory preserved a remarkable record — only once this century, in 1934, has Australia lost a Test match at Lord's.

There was an immediate scramble for the stumps, with the century-makers grabbing one each and one of the bowlers the other one amid scenes of great excitement and relief among the players.

Before the off-field celebrations began, the players donned their blazers and went back onto the field to meet the Queen and Prince Philip. I stood next to my fellow East Hills Boys High old boy and Bankstown District Cricket Club team-mate, Wayne Holdsworth. Everything went smoothly, with Cracker and myself both greeting the Queen with the customary "Ma'am". However, Wayne had forgotten he was also to meet Prince Philip. With his attention fixed on the other players meeting the Queen, it needed a solid S. Waugh elbow to make him realise that Prince Philip had been waiting for a response for about ten seconds. Cracker, not one to panic under pressure, came out with the following words of wisdom:

"How are you going, mate?"

With the formalities over, and Cracker and I still laughing at his rather casual greeting to the royal family, the serious business of enjoying a Test match win went into full swing. Boonie was up on the table, leading all the boys as they sang their hearts out. The feeling of a Test match win is more intoxicating than any amount of alcohol you can get your hands on — something that you have to be a part of to fully appreciate. Maysie is especially pleased, not just by his own performance but because it is the first Test match team he has been in that has won. And he seemed quite keen to celebrate that fact.

On the way back to the hotel, I dropped into the hospital to visit Craig McDermott. He is hooked up to a drip as he is not allowed any food for a week, which has already affected his weight greatly. He appears in good spirits despite the fact that his tour has come to such a premature end.

UPS AND DOWNS

DAY 59 (June 22)

WE WOKE to find the papers full of headlines calling for half the English side to be axed. But of all the alibis, excuses and reasons given for England's performance in the Lord's Test, the most interesting, without doubt, came from the English chairman of selectors, Ted Dexter. He put forward this theory for their bad showing: "Maybe Venus is in the wrong juxtaposition with somewhere else." Dexter's throwaway line gave the tabloids a headline they dream of.

The British papers really are amazing. Last night, the team had continued its celebrations at our local pub, The Windmill, and then onto Stringfellows, where three of our players were refused entry because the two guys they were with were deemed too drunk. This made page two in one English paper this morning under the headline: "Aussies Too Drunk To Get Into Nightclub". The article did admit it wasn't the team members but their friends who caused the problem — but who cares anyway?! They had the headline they wanted and used it to sell their papers — a style of journalism that is very hard to accept.

Today was one of the few days on tour that is free of any cricket, so the players and wives went to Wimbledon to catch the second day of the championships. The first match on Centre Court was between the defending women's champion, Steffi Graf, and a little-known Australian, Kirilly Sharp. Unfortunately Sharp was completely outclassed and managed only 17 points in the match, losing 6-0 6-0 in next to no time. Graf's display illustrated exactly how we need to approach the rest of the Ashes series — keep the opponent pinned down when you're on top.

Among the other players I had a chance to see were the former champions, Boris Becker and Martina Navratilova, and the Australian, Wally Masur, who won in straight sets. And in the process I was able to devour half-a-dozen ice creams, numerous hot dogs and a couple of punnets of strawberries. The tour party at the championships was made up of about half the guys and their wives and girlfriends. Most of us watched a lot of tennis, while a few of the boys strengthened their forearms in the bar enclosure, taking in as little tennis as possible on their day off.

With Ian Healy, a great friend and tourist.

The whole day was an enjoyable experience, with Heals probably having the best day of all, as he is a huge fan of Steffi Graf. He's even got a picture of her on his coffin. The biggest surprise turned out to be that my wife didn't fall asleep watching the tennis like she had last time she was there. Lynette must be the only person ever to have had a snooze at the FA Cup Final, Wimbledon and the British Open Golf Championship and think nothing of it.

After getting home from the tennis around 8.00 pm, we enjoyed a quiet evening with our wives and a few of our English friends at their home.

The British press was brutal in its treatment of England's chairman of selectors, Ted Dexter, after we went two-up in the series. Only days earlier, the papers had been demanding, in bold and irreverent headlines, the sacking of the English soccer manager, Graham Taylor. Now newspapers like The Daily Mirror (above), and The Sun (below) turned their attentions to Dexter.

DAY 60 (June 23)

I MADE the most of not being involved in the current three-day match against Combined Universities at Oxford by sleeping in 'til nine o'clock. Lynette was under a threat of death if the curtains were opened up before this time.

The three days of the Universities game represent a rare opportunity for Ian and I to spend some time with our wives, who are allowed to stay with us when we haven't got a game. Normally the girls can't stay in the same hotel as the players until the final two weeks of the tour. We spent the morning shopping at Harrods and having a look around London. The wallet was unexpectedly still intact at this stage. In the afternoon, Lynette and I made full use of the gym facilities available to the team, and by the time I flicked the TV to the teletext back in the hotel, Slater had managed to race to another hundred and Hayden had missed his ton by two runs. I just hope the pavilion at The Parks at Oxford is still standing and not in ruins, as I know Matty is desperate for his first hundred for Oz in a first-class game.

The management at Planet Hollywood have looked after the lads while in London and again let Mr & Mrs Healy and Mr & Mrs Waugh straight in without having to endure the hour-long queue outside. This made the evening that little bit more enjoyable, with the food and atmosphere once again excellent.

DAY 61 (June 24)

HEALS AND I gave the shopping a miss this morning. We were, of course, bitterly disappointed, but considered it more important to keep an eye on the teletext screen and support the boys even though we couldn't be with them in Oxford. As an added bonus, Wimbledon was also on TV, and we managed to catch a few sets before the girls arrived back to ask us whether we would like to check out the largest toy store in England, Hamleys, before lunch. Now, this is the type of shopping I don't mind — spending a couple of hours checking out all the new gimmicks, toys and board games — much preferable to trying to buy clothes.

When speaking with Molly Meldrum in the dressing room after the Lord's Test win, he mentioned that Jimmy Barnes was in town for a couple of shows and offered us tickets to one of his concerts at the Forum. I jumped at the chance — I reckon Jimmy's a legend, and after seeing him perform again my opinion of the man has only been enhanced. It was one of the best live performances I've witnessed. His renditions of *Flame Trees, Khe Sanh* and *Good Times* sent the masses into a frenzy.

After the show finished, the record company which looks after Jimmy Barnes invited us back to his change-room for a chat and a photo to cap off a great night.

With another day off tomorrow, we decided to head out after the concert to a disco with an English friend of ours. He managed to get us into the top nightclub in England — Tramps — where we got the chance to meet Kylie Minogue. This made Lynette's night a memorable one — not to mention mine!

DAY 62 (June 25)

THE SHOPPING extravaganza rolled on into day three with the participants taking in Sloane Square and its fine array of clothes and shoe shops. But not even the "50 Per Cent Off" and "Clearance Sale" signs could entice the girls to part with a few pounds.

Lunchtime was spent with Craig McDermott, his wife and two kids who have been staying in the same hotel since Craig's release from hospital last night. Billy's stay in hospital has seen him lose half-a-dozen kilos, as he has not been able to eat anything solid. The operation was quite a major piece of surgery and as a result, Craig would not have been able to play until the final three or four weeks of the tour. So the best scenario was for him is to go home and get himself ready for the next Australian season.

Even though he is extremely disappointed at his tour coming to an abrupt halt, Craig seems in good spirits. I'm sure his absence will be missed greatly by the side. But, every cloud has a silver lining and in this case, Craig's unavailability will give one of the reserves a chance to make a name for himself in the remaining four Tests.

Heals and I had to leave the girls in London with friends and head off to our next venue — Southampton, on the south coast — a reputed 75-minute trip. Somehow our journey ended up taking 195 minutes as a result of heavy traffic and the now customary wrong turn off the motorway.

We checked into the hotel and, thanks to the teletext in the room, discovered we'd won at Oxford, with our part-time leg-spinner, Tim Zoehrer, capturing three wickets. Tim is my new roomie for this leg of the trip, and he has with him an unexpected guest in Plucka. Ziggy failed to trouble the scorers at Oxford.

A quiet pub meal with the boys was followed by the Sky-TV movies and an early night. The upcoming game, against Hampshire, is important for everyone as the third Test is only a week away.

Left: A duck against Hampshire gave Plucka a new owner. Right: Damien Martyn.

DAY 63 (June 26)

OUR WAKE-UP call arrived 15-minutes late this morning, and solved the problem of what to have for breakfast. There was no time left for food. Soon after the team bus pulled into the ground with a large crowd already in attendance and an unusually clear sky overhead. During the day the temperatures reached the mid-twenties — something that would usually be classed as heat-wave conditions in Britain ... with water restrictions only a matter of time if the weather stays the same for a couple of days.

By the time our openers, Taylor and Hayden, made their way to the middle, the ground was at full capacity. The crowd loved their cricket, and the quest for souvenirs. It seemed that every one of the spectators was carrying an autograph book that had to be signed at all costs before the day was over.

Our top-order continued their excellent form, with Matt Hayden hurtling towards a century before he mistimed a pull shot and was out, for 85. After his dismissal, Boonie strolled past three figures for the fifth time on tour in another dominating display.

My chance at spending a bit of time occupying the crease was terminated by a poor decision. I was deemed to have gloved a ball onto my pads and then onto their bat-pad fieldsman. But in terms of the team's performance, my misfortune hardly mattered, as our batsmen scored so quickly throughout the first two sessions that AB was able to declare with one hour remaining, having scored 393 for the loss of seven wickets. Hampshire then lost their first wicket in Merv's initial over, which brought to the crease the crowd's favourite, David Gower, in need of a big score to push his claims for a recall to the English side. Unfortunately for the crowd, Gower fell almost immediately to his favourite cut shot. The hush that covered the ground after this dismissal emphasised the general feeling that it may have cut short this great player's last chance to represent his country, and signalled the end of a magnificent international career.

With Gower's departure, Robin Smith came to the crease. The English media have been calling for his head and he responded in the only way he knows, belting us for 31 not out in the final 20 minutes. By stumps, 465 runs had been scored in the day.

On tours such as this, management receives plenty of invitations for the team to go to cocktail parties and functions, most of which are knocked back due to time constraints. But tonight was an exception, as we had been invited to the Isle of Wight for a dinner party hosted by a very wealthy elderly lady.

The Isle is home to a number of well-off people who live there because of the isolation and privacy. It's about 20 minutes from the coast by ferry. Tonight they put on a good show with great food. They also hired a local to sing us a few tunes, but were very disappointed when our nominated piano player, Ian Healy, failed to tickle the ivories. His rather lame excuse was that he had to get back to the hotel to call his brother before the time difference made it too late to get in contact with him.

A snapshot from the dinner party held on the Isle of Wight.

DAY 64 (June 27)

THE 1,000,000-1 odds of Ian Healy finding the gold nugget that fell off his necklace yesterday while training appeared to be rather slim this morning, especially as the crowd have trampled across the ground during the lunch and tea breaks as well as after the first day's play. However, the gods smiled upon Heals, as he spotted the nugget on the ground while doing the warm-up before today's play. He was a very relieved man, as it was a present from his in-laws.

Robin Smith continued in the same vein as he had finished last evening, and used his awesome strength and quick wrists to hit a succession of boundaries. His only blemish was being caught behind off a no-ball from Paul Reiffel, which proved very costly for us. After reaching his hundred, Smith began to tee off, reviving nasty memories of his carnage in the third one-day international at Edgbaston. Balls started to disappear out of the ground. One particular over from AB had the first ball rearranging the advertising boards, followed by a six that landed in the adjoining backyard of a house. This blow meant a change of ball, to which AB commented: "That wasn't such a bad move losing the last ball, as this one is the best we've had all tour."

Unfortunately, upon its first excursion into the air, it found itself disturbing the guttering of a property behind the stand at mid-off. We required another change of ball.

Smith finally went for 191, an innings that probably saved his Test spot and put Hampshire within 20 runs of our total. We felt they should have declared earlier if they wanted a result from the game, as there probably isn't enough time left for us to set them a decent total to chase tomorrow.

The Australian team created an unwanted record today by allowing 53 extras, the most by any side playing against Hampshire. But the figure is slightly inflated as no-balls count for two runs nowadays, instead of one run as was the case before 1992.

With all our top-order batsmen in good form, the second-innings line-up was reshuffled. Healy opened with Hayden, followed by myself at 3 and Julian at 4. Unfortunately the change didn't come off. First Heals played across the line early on and was LBW and then I joined him back in the shed, after having a mental blank and letting a ball go that pitched marginally outside the line of off-stump but came back enough to send the off-stump cartwheeling out of the ground. Plucka has a new owner.

The Hampshire captain, Mark Nicholas, invited AB to set up a possible run chase tomorrow, in the hope of one side achieving a victory rather than the match dying a slow death. Both captains agreed on roughly the same plan, which is for Hampshire to be chasing around 300 runs off 60 overs.

After the day's play, Heals, Slats, BJ and I watched Sylvester Stallone come out trumps again in *Cliffhanger*. No doubt still pumped up from the flick, we neglected to take the right route home. We became hopelessly lost, owing to a succession of poor instructions as to the right direction home, coupled with Heals' well-kept secret of night-blindness which was exposed when he failed to pick up any clues in the form of road signs. We finally managed to stumble upon the Hilton 40 minutes after we should have.

DAY 65 (June 28)

THE ENGLISH side, or perhaps the more aptly named World XI, was announced today and included a host of new faces: Nasser Hussain, Alan Igglesden, Graham Thorpe, Mark Lathwell, Mark Ilott, Martin Bicknell and Martin McCague. Their selectors are hoping to change the England side's run of seven successive losses (one against Pakistan, three in India, one in Sri Lanka and two against Australia). We consider the most surprising omission to be Graeme Hick, who was starting to look dangerous in the last Test and has averaged over 50 in the last five Tests he's played, 10 runs better than the next best Englishman.

A large crowd was again in attendance this morning, as we performed our daily stretches with a group of women Dutch cricketers keen to take a few photos for keepsakes. During the routine, there was suddenly a lot of commotion and laughter among the girls, and Tim Zoehrer, who spent two years playing cricket in Amsterdam and can speak Dutch, was laughing along with them. We asked the reason for the laughter, and he explained that one of the girls had asked her friend for a favour: "Could you please take a photo of that fat man?" That fat man being Merv Hughes.

An incident occurred in the morning session that could have reduced our tour party to 15 players. Matt Hayden narrowly missed being run out when his total was 99 — a fate that would have seen him hanging from the rafters as he's been twice dismissed in the late 90s already on tour. He eventually departed for 115 in another impressive performance, which reminded the selectors of his ability. But, without doubt, the highlight of the morning for the crowd was Merv's 61 not out, which included seven sixes. It was a display of sheer brute strength and included shots you won't find in any coaching manual.

The expected declaration came at lunch-time, leaving Hampshire to score 288 off 64 overs — a very getable total considering the lightning-fast outfield and easy-paced batting wicket. This fact was emphasised when their openers raced to 167, with 22 overs still available to score the remaining 124 runs. With 10 wickets in hand, a Hampshire win seemed almost a certainty, until a run out saw one of the openers depart. Soon after he was joined by Robin Smith, who was caught behind from the first ball he received.

The whole complexion of the game changed. Tim May struck twice within the space of three overs, at which time the Hampshire captain sent out instructions to abort the run chase. They only required six runs per over, and Nicholas' decision appeared a rather feeble attempt at trying to win the game, especially after the two captains' discussion the previous evening which led to the belief that both sides would try and reach a result through positive cricket. I would hardly say scoring 22 runs off the last 16 overs could be classed as attempting to win a game. Sadly a draw seemed more important to Hampshire than risking a loss in the quest for a victory.

The most excitement or entertainment in the last session happened when our 12th man, Tim Zoehrer, ended up wearing half the drinks he brought out onto the field during the drinks interval. This is one of the pitfalls of being a 12th man, especially when the game gets a bit boring. Some of the lads tend to want to see who can drench the 12th man with the most water, leaving him to walk off soaked and embarrassed.

The bus left almost as soon as we left the field. It's a three-hour trip to Nottingham, but on the way we found enough time to pull into a Golden Arches (McDonald's) to grab a quick fix before re-boarding the bus and resuming the Australia-New Zealand first Rugby League Test which ended in a 14-all draw.

DAY 66 (June 29)

WITH THE third Test at Trent Bridge only two days away, today's training session was fairly arduous, but at the same time relaxed. Most of the squad is in good form and we're confident of victory.

There has been a lot of talk about the possible nature of the wicket. Most people are speculating that it will be a seamers' wicket, with plenty of grass to aid the pacemen, rather than the first two Test pitches, which have helped our spinners.

The Trent Bridge groundsman seems keen to help the quicks. He was quoted in the paper as saying, "We are two down in the series and, for an Englishman, that's not very pleasant. I would sure like to change that. Of course, I've been influenced by what team has been selected and I'm doing my bit to help England. It's okay provided it's done in a sensible manner."

Little wonder England left out their left-arm spinner, Phil Tufnell, and added an extra paceman to their squad.

But I'm not convinced they're on the right track. After looking at the wicket to be used in the Test, I can't believe how everyone keeps saying it will suit the quick bowlers. It appears similar to the wickets we've come across so far, except for the fact it has a tinge of green about it.

Just as the wicket might fool a few people, so too does the rest of the ground. The outfield at Trent Bridge appears on TV to be carpet-like but, in fact, it is one of the most uneven surfaces I've played first-class cricket on. There's every chance of someone turning a knee or ankle on the undulating turf.

I spent the afternoon at the headquarters of my sponsor, Gunn & Moore, getting a couple of bats made up to my specifications.

The fines committee called a meeting after a three-week break, with Michael Slater in the hot-seat as chairman. Slats turned out to be a tyrant with the extra powers bestowed on him, and handed out a series of hefty penalties for the various misdemeanours that have been committed recently. His fellow committee member, Merv, copped the harshest fine — five pounds for throwing the nurf soccer ball onto the Lord's playing field during the Test match. The new Daktari owner is Wayne Holdsworth. He was the man deemed a near-certainty to receive it when we gathered at Kingsford-Smith Airport before the tour began, and hasn't let his supporters down.

Lynette and I had a quiet evening away from everyone else, at a local Chinese restaurant. Spending a bit of time together is something we find very hard to do on a long cricket tour.

My roomie is once again Maysie. His trademark snore appears to have changed slightly, and now sounds more like a lion attacking its prey rather than the previous chainsaw melody which flowed from his nostrils. He has proved, once again, that he is a man of many hidden talents.

DAY 67 (June 30)

THE MORNING papers were full of the Martin McCague controversy. McCague played all his cricket in Australia, and even went to the Australian Cricket Academy in Adelaide, before deciding to use his birthplace as a means of making himself available to play cricket for England. And now he's in their third Test squad, and will, in all likelihood, make the final XI

The general feeling in the Australian team is one of disbelief at the reasons he has put forward for leaving Australian cricket. He claims he was treated poorly and should have had more of a chance for Western Australia. In fact, his statistics were very poor and he didn't deserve the opportunities he thought were owed to him.

The most interesting quotes came from his own family. His father was quoted as saying: "I hope he takes five wickets in both innings but that Australia wins by one run."

As a way of relaxing before a Test match, I generally like to go to the movies. It gives me a chance to clear my head and get away from all the hype, so this afternoon Lynette and I went to the cinema to watch *Fire in the Sky* — a true story about a man who gets abducted by aliens.

The team meeting tonight was fairly brief, with most importance being placed upon the need for no-one becoming complacent. It was also stressed that this Test represented a chance to retain the Ashes. There are two changes to the twelve from Lord's — Brendon Julian and Paul Reiffel are in for Craig McDermott and Damien Martyn.

As is the norm before a Test, the team dined together, this time at an Italian restaurant selected by the "Clayton's" social committee. It turned out to be a good night. Everyone is looking forward to ending any chances of a Pom revival in the series.

THIRD TEST / McCague defends decision to switch sides and pull his weight for England

Don't call me traitor

PETER JOHNSON reports on a row that Australia claim takes gloss off Ashes battle

96

A treasured moment — meeting the Queen at Lord's.

Smith, caught Healy bowled Warne, in England's second innings of the third Test at Trent Bridge.

Allan Border waits for the ball to be returned from the Nottingham crowd during the third Test.

My brother Mark, on the putting surface at the beautiful Portmarnock course in Ireland.

A worried England captain Graham Gooch, on the final afternoon at Trent Bridge.

Brendon Julian and I leave the field after our match-saving partnership on the final afternoon of the third Test.

The Sheik of Tweak — Shane Warne.

THE THIRD TEST

DAY 68 (July 1)

YESTERDAY, in the quest for a peaceful night's sleep, I had purchased, at the suggestion of a local pharmacy owner, a set of wax earplugs reputed to "stop noise nuisances". I thought the term "noise nuisances" was something of an understatement in describing what was emanating from my roomie's nose, but I thought I'd give the plugs a go.

The good news was that I lost only one hour's sleep last night, but not as a result of the recommended wax earplugs. They, in fact, were generally more troublesome than the commotion from the adjoining bed and at one stage threatened to become embedded in my earhole.

Breakfast turned out to be a complete waste of time. The hot breakfast took 35 minutes to arrive, leaving about 30 seconds for consumption. Not even our quick bowlers could manage to throw it down that swiftly.

The mood on the bus on the way to the ground was relaxed. But at the same time everyone was a little apprehensive — you never really know what's in store before a Test. But one thing is for sure — someone will turn out to be a hero for his side and many will be playing for their positions by the time the next Test match arrives. Such is the nature of playing at the highest level, when so much is expected of everyone.

Paul Reiffel was made 12th man, which meant Brendon Julian made a return. We found ourselves in the field after Graham Gooch won the toss and decided to make full use of the seven specialist batsmen that his side now includes.

Lathwell, making his Test debut, and Atherton were dismissed in the morning session. Atherton claimed he was the victim of a dubious bat-pad decision, but we thought it was obvious to everyone except the batsman. His show of disapproval will no doubt start a storm of protest from the media over the umpires favouring the opposition team.

Robin Smith was particularly severe on anything overpitched and remained unbeaten

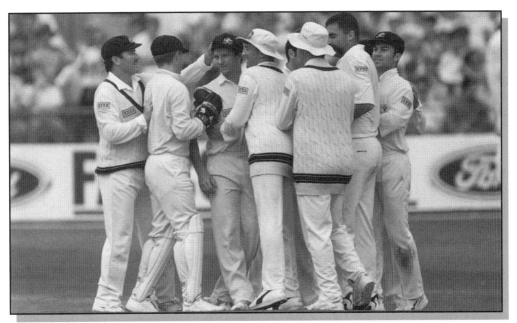

Celebrating my catch of Graham Thorpe in the English first innings. The other players are (left to right): Border, Healy, Warne, M. Waugh, May, Hughes and Slater.

on 50 at lunch. It was quite obvious that he was a danger man we needed to remove as soon as possible. Unfortunately our bowling after lunch was not as good as we have become accustomed to, but the roll of the dice went our way when Smith, on 86, was miraculously caught and bowled by Julian off a full toss. Soon after, Stewart mishit a long hop from Shane Warne straight to the cover-point fieldsman, Mark Waugh. These two dismissals completely changed the face of the game. England were suddenly 5 for 174, instead of three for around the same score, which I'm sure is what they thought they should have been.

Most of the wives are in attendance for this Test match, as well as a *60 Minutes* crew, who are a doing a story on Shane Warne. They'll be following him around for a couple of days trying to find out more about this potential superstar. I just hope they don't put him on too high a pedestal too early, because he'll quickly learn that many Australians put down their champions if they hit a lean spell. Warney has only just begun his career, and needs to be left to play his cricket with as few distractions as possible, at least until he feels comfortable in his surroundings. Being able to handle the media is very important these days. They can intrude into your personal life as well as your cricket results, and, if not handled properly, can affect the individual concerned greatly. Dealing with the media was the biggest and most difficult adjustment I had to make when first selected in the Test team, at the age of 20. Hopefully, Warney is better prepared to handle it than I was.

The new-look England side showed more resolve than some of the teams we have encountered here in the past, and, at the end of a tough day's play, had reached 6 for 276. Hussain has looked confident from ball one, and is 50 not out at the close.

Our best bowlers were once again Hughes and Warne, who took three and two wickets respectively.

Another Indian restaurant gained my patronage tonight, and the food was so good, I'm beginning to think Tubs and Maysie might not be as silly as they look. I was accompanied by Lynette and the Healys and by the end of the night, my tastebuds were beginning to like the spices of the sub-continent, just as my two teammates have been constantly been telling me they would.

DAY 69 (July 2)

FOR THE second day in a row the ground was at full capacity. The weather was perfect, and our first task was to finish off the English innings as quickly as possible.

The last four wickets fell for the addition of only 45 runs. Hussain finished with an impressive 71 and Merv, once again, turned in a courageous performance, claiming 5 for 92 off 31 overs. He was ably supported by Warne who took 3 for 74 off 40.

Taylor and Slater safely negotiated the 30 minutes to lunch. We hoped for a platform that would guarantee us a sizeable lead, so that we can apply some pressure on England in their second innings. But Slater fell victim to a dubious LBW decision. We wondered whether it had been brought about by the newspapers saying the English umpires are the only ones in the world who favour the opposition team. That sort of media talk only creates pressure on the umpires that isn't needed.

By the time the sandwiches and scones were laid out on the table in preparation for the tea interval, we were in a comfortable position, at 2 for 124. We saw the third session as vital, as it could have set up the match for either side. The last two hours began in great style for Australia, until Mark Waugh was caught three-quarters of the way to the boundary, trying to dispatch Peter Such over the long-on boundary.

Normally this dismissal would have brought AB to the crease, but he was suffering from acute hayfever and itchy eyes — basically crook — so I was elevated one position up the order, to number five. Hayfever is something that has affected a lot of our players over here, myself included, and daily medication is the only remedy. Luckily it's a condition that only seems to affect us in England.

Boon continued his mission to grind the opposition to the point of submission. He looks almost immovable, with his immaculate technique, backed up by unfaltering concentration, making him the scourge of the English fans. Unfortunately, my innings was short-lived. I was caught behind for 13, playing a lazy defensive prod that deserved what it got — a long and painful walk back to the dressing room. There were only 30 minutes of play left when I was out and during that time, England took another wicket, that of Healy, to change the nature of the game and put the contest back on level par.

At stumps the scoreboard read Australia 5 for 262, with Boon on 88, Julian on 5, and Border to come in next. Hopefully we can still gain a large first-innings lead.

They say playing sport at the top level can push anyone's character to the limits and expose any flaws you may have. Tonight I'm feeling depressed and sorry for myself, which I know is no good to anyone. But I feel as if I let myself and the team down today ... and there isn't much consolation in knowing that.

It's times like this when a player needs some sort of support, either from fellow players or family. Luckily Lynette is here, and spending a quiet evening with her put everything back in perspective. The only solution is to make sure that I work that little bit harder next time.

DAY 70 (July 3)

I WOKE up this morning in a state of panic, fearing my roomie must have passed away during the evening. There wasn't the slightest hint of a murmur coming from his bed throughout the night. However, there was a good reason for that. Maysie didn't sleep a wink, claiming he was too afraid to keep me awake with his snoring and, as a result, couldn't relax enough to fall asleep himself.

Down at the ground the boys were up in arms because all the kit bags had been tampered with. But there was no need to panic as it was purely a safety measure. Prince Andrew was visiting the game today and all bags had to be checked out by sniffer dogs in case of bombs being on the premises.

Thirty minutes after the resumption, Boonie helped himself to his sixth first-class hundred on the tour (and second consecutive Test hundred), but was out shortly afterwards. BJ was already back in the pavilion and the game hung in the balance. But, as everyone has come to expect, AB dug his heels in. He put on an invaluable partnership with Warney, who remained unbeaten on 35 when our innings was cruelly terminated by a dubious LBW on Tim May with the total at 373 — a very handy 52-run lead.

Lunch today was something I've never encountered before in a cricket match — sausages, onions and gravy with, inevitably, the typically English choice of french fries, mashed potatoes, boiled potatoes, baked potatoes or all of the above. This was followed by apple pie and ice cream, making for a brick-in-the-stomach type of feeling when we walked back onto the ground to resume play. Most players who are batting or are next in generally don't eat much at lunch, generally opting for a salad or just ice cream, with the same applying to bowlers who are required to bowl straight after the interval.

The much-talked-about new-look England side has been a considerably tougher proposition already, with a greater sense of urgency and commitment evident in their play. However, the day's final two hours went in our favour, thanks again to Hughes and Warne, who took two wickets each. Merv again showed us he has the ability to capture a wicket at a vital stage with a delivery that appears innocuous to the average viewer. It's brought about by the aura that the bowler generates — a power that Ian Botham always had at his disposal. Now Hughes has it.

By the end of the day's play we had the Poms on the ropes, and are ready to deliver the knock-out blow. They're 4 for 122 — only 70 runs ahead.

There is a rest day scheduled for tomorrow because, of all things, tradition has it that

Dinner at the Red Brick House Inn.

no cricket is played while the men's singles final is on at Wimbledon. So a large group of guys and partners decided to let off a bit of steam and head out for the night.

Cracker and Heals came up with a restaurant "two miles" from town that covered most taste sensations, ranging from Italian to French. Unfortunately for Cracker, he had a small misunderstanding with the owner about the exact location of the place, the Red Brick House Inn. It was actually 45 minutes away, on the brink of Sherwood Forest. Luckily six of the eight couples had team cars at their disposal. Unluckily for Cracker, Merv and his wife and Warney and his fiancee caught a cab. As the journey (and fare) mounted with each kilometre, Cracker must have realised he was a fair chance of spending the night in the forest with Robin Hood once the big fella got hold of him. But Merv was not the only irate Australian. As the various couples finally arrived, all immediately informed Heals and Cracker they would get their revenge sometime in the future.

However, it wasn't the distance that angered them. They had been followed by a freelance cameraman who tried to take snapshots every time they stopped at a set of lights. Invasion of your privacy over here is quite common, especially if you're a well-known personality. But this was far too extreme. Finally, at one set of lights, the gentleman was politely told that if he didn't quit he would not be able to walk comfortably because his camera would be lodged in a certain part of his anatomy.

Despite these early hassles, all the couples (Healys, Waughs, Julians, Holdsworths, Reiffels, Slaters, Hugheses and Warnes) had a great night. Warney and his girl Simone were adventurous, ordering french fries and sauce as their entrees — although it was not really surprising as neither touch any vegetables except potatoes.

DAY 71 (July 4)

THE ENGLISH tabloids have changed their plan of attack, and this morning preferred to stir up the apparent umpiring and appealing controversies rather than continue to bag their own team. The *Sunday Sport* virtually called us cheats — they think our appealing is unwarranted. Most of the other papers, plus the TV channels, ran stories suggesting the whole Australian team is on its last warning from match referee Clive Lloyd, because we've been putting too much pressure on the umpires.

This "warning" came as a shock, as none of our management were aware that Clive Lloyd had in fact any problems with our behaviour. We could only assume he had leaked his concerns to the press without informing us.

I spent most of today, the rest day, relaxing. My body is weary from the seemingly endless hours we have put in the field. We've been dictating games to the point where we have been batting for roughly about a third of each game and fielding for the rest in the quest for victory.

Seeing as we owed the day off to the fact that Wimbledon was on, it seemed only fair to watch the American, Pete Sampras, win the final in four sets. By the time I went to sleep tonight, the batteries felt recharged and I was ready to get back into the action tomorrow.

Three happy Australians. From left: Mark Taylor, Tim May and Shane Warne.

DAY 72 (July 5)

THE TEAM gathered at breakfast with the news of another player going down — Wayne Holdsworth announced his engagement to Sally. He joined Damien Martyn, Michael Slater and Shane Warne, all of whom have become engaged in the past six months. It leaves Brendon Julian and Matthew Hayden as the only single guys in the tour party.

Graham Gooch came out swinging this morning in the search of the knockout punch, or to at least put his side out of danger. He played a number of unusually high-risk shots, particularly off Tim May who was unlucky not to claim his wicket. A series of miscued lofted drives landed fortunately (for the England captain) in open spaces. Gooch found himself a very determined partner in Graham Thorpe and, after the nightwatchman Caddick was dismissed, they safely negotiated the rest of the morning session to leave England at 5 for 210. The game was back to level par, and we realised the session after lunch would be a crucial one.

Surprisingly, after the break the two English batsmen seemed to change their aggressive policy and extended their partnership by only 54 runs, in probably the dullest two hours of play in the series so far. The one positive aspect to come out of the session for England was the emergence of Graham Thorpe as a Test-quality batsman. He has a good technique and temperament, and looked capable of playing a long innings.

England's cause was helped when Merv strained a groin muscle and had to leave the field. During the afternoon we were told he'll take no further part in the match, leaving our attack particularly thin, with a heavy workload falling on the spinners.

Our bowlers tired in the last session, and the English batsmen capitalised on some loose bowling, scoring 98 runs in the last session. Gooch reached another very good hundred, his second for the series — not a bad effort considering his 40th birthday is not far away. Thorpe continued his impressive performance, and needs only a further 12 runs tomorrow for a debut Test hundred.

Tonight we learned that the news on Merv is not as bad as expected, although it will take a couple of weeks of intensive physiotherapy for him to be fit enough to make the next Test, at Headingley. His injury was just one setback in a day of major disappointments. We felt at the start of the day that we needed only one or two early wickets to put us in a position to wrap up the series. But as it turned out, we might find ourselves battling to save the Test tomorrow.

It is apparent after the four days of this Test that we are going to have a much tougher time against this current crop of English players than we've had in the previous eight Tests we've played in England (six in 1989, two in 1993). There seems to be a greater pride in this team, and a willingness to back their own ability. And they even have a hint of arrogance about them, something that has been missing up until this match.

Tea tonight was at Pizzaland, with Lynette and friends we first met when I was playing for Nelson in the Lancashire League back in 1987.

DAY 73 (July 6)

THE TEAM made its way out onto the field with a feeling of deja vu this morning, and for a very good reason. Just as we were preparing to walk out, someone pointed out that, once the day's play began, we would have fielded at some stage of every day of the match, something which is quite unusual in a Test.

The hoped-for wrapping up of the English tail didn't eventuate. Instead, Thorpe and Hussain pummelled the attack for about 40 minutes, with Thorpe being unbeaten on 114 when Gooch's declaration finally came. Hussain, who had batted so well in the first innings, completed a fine double to be unbeaten on 47. We needed 371 runs to win in five-and-a-quarter hours — roughly four-and-a-half runs per over — a target that might have been realistic had we got off to a solid start. But our first priority was not to lose the Test.

The chase started in familiar fashion, with Slater and Taylor putting on 46 without appearing in too much trouble. But then, 10 minutes before lunch, Slats yorked himself off Such and was bowled. That dismissal appeared to make the win an unrealistic goal. That was especially so when, soon after the break, the new-look English attack accounted for Taylor through a poor bat-pad decision. Mark was quickly joined in the pavilion by Mark Waugh and Border, who both fell victim to an inspired spell of high-quality bowling from Caddick.

The crowd sensed an English victory, as for the first time in the series we were under real pressure. I made my way to the crease to join Boon in a battle not only for the team but for myself as well. But while I stayed alive at one end, two more wickets fell at the other. First, Boonie got a faint touch that went through to the keeper, and, in the last over before tea, Healy departed LBW to an inswinger from Ilott.

Mark Waugh, bowled by Caddick, on the eventful final day at Trent Bridge.

CRICKET — THIRD CORNHILL TEST / Lack of second spin-bowler proves decisive factor as Australians hold out to secure draw

Resurgent England run into brick wall

Christopher Martin-Jenkins

Such a good wicket... Australian opener Michael Slater is beaten comprehensively by the Essex spinner and bowled for 26 at Trent Bridge yesterday Picture: FRANK COPPI

ENGLAND stopped the rot and the Ashes are still at stake, but in the end the pitch was too good and the bowling not quite good enough. A seventh-wicket stand of 87 by Steve Waugh, whose Test place had been in some jeopardy, and the 22-year-old giant Brendon Julian, whose maiden Test fifty was scored with great aplomb off only 68 balls, combined to preserve the Australians' unbeaten record in first-class matches after England had taken six wickets before tea.

Five days ago, no doubt, England would have settled for the draw which keeps the series alive. Having come so close to a greater prize, however, the final act was an anti-climax after Graham Thorpe's 114 not out and his unbeaten stand of 115 with Nasser Hussain had set up the opportunity to go all out for the win.

Had it been achieved it would have reduced Australia's lead in the series to 2-1 with three matches still to play, but to have competed throughout the game and finished in the ascendant after seven successive defeats against four different countries represents a most welcome improvement by the reshaped England side.

Not since the Sydney Test of January 1991 have England come so close to beating Australia. It is 16 Tests now since they have done so. What they needed on the final day was a second spinner, to turn the ball away from the right-handers.

Peter Such, varying his trajectory hardly at all, despite the encouragement of luring Michael Slater down the pitch to miss an on-drive for the first wicket, generally turned the ball out of the rough or not at all.

Had either Ian Salisbury or Philip Tufnell been in the side to assist him, life would have been doubly difficult for a side in search only of a draw.

A fifth bowler would, however, have meant no seventh batsman and the contribution of Hussain at number seven was important, especially in the first innings after England had rejected the chance to bowl first at the only time in the game when the pitch suited seam bowling. England must beware of prejudging conditions at Headingley, where the fourth Test will start a fortnight tomorrow, but the chances are that they will again have to make do with only one spinner.

Setting Australia 371 to win in a minimum of 77 overs, England took only one wicket before lunch, and in such fast-scoring conditions — a placid pitch and a very rapid outfield — a repeat of Headingley 1948, when Australia scored 404 to win after Norman Yardley had declared on the last morning, was not out of the question.

Instead, on a bright and blustery afternoon, five more Australians were dismissed, three to Andrew Caddick in an 11-over spell of three for 16. Emphatically, the boot was on the other foot.

Such took a second wicket six overs after lunch when Taylor, who had looked extremely lucky not to be edged over his four to four to a straight, good-length ball by Martin McCague in only the third over, got an inside edge on to his pad and was caught in the gully. In the next three overs two more Australians came and went to Caddick.

Relishing a strong breeze from the north-west over his right shoulder, he first hurried Mark Waugh to bowl him off the inside edge, then angled a ball across Allan Border.

Drawn to play at first, he attempted to withdraw the bat but merely nudged a gentle catch to first slip.

Caddick followed up with the potentially crucial wicket of the hitherto immovable David Boon, who cut fiercely beneath a short ball which bounced higher than he had expected.

By tea, Ian Healy too had gone, lbw to an inswinger from Mark Ilott, and at 115 for six Australia were still 52 overs from safety, the atmosphere feverish.

Steve Waugh and Julian rose to the challenge admirably. Waugh needed some luck against Caddick outside his off stump but McCague, in his honest desire not to bowl wildly, might have tried more often to unsettle him with a rib-tickler.

Given the strong wind in his favour, he was less menacing than England hoped, but Julian's long reach and orthodox technique served him well and Waugh's stomach for a fight has never been in doubt. Gradually, on the brightest of evenings, they played the overs away, 30 of them in all, before Gooch shook hands on an honourable draw.

Thorpe's maiden Test hundred in his second innings for England had arrived with a bold hook in Julian's second over of the morning.

Already he had been lucky not to be run out after a misunderstanding with his partner, Nasser Hussain; now his top-edged hook flew rapidly towards Slater at long leg, bounced over his head and then across the rope. Thorpe's delight was every bit as evident and as spontaneous as Slater's had been at Lord's. He is the youngest England cricketer, and the first from Surrey, to have scored a hundred in his first Test since Peter May made one in his first game against South Africa at Leeds in 1951 at the age of 21.

He never saw his first ball but remembered George Geary's advice: "If in doubt, push out."

Thorpe is 23 and the 16th England player to make a century in his first Test against Australia. He keeps illustrious company with those who have made hundreds against Australia on their first Test appearance: W.G. Ranji, 'Tip' Foster, George Gunn and, most recently, the Nawab of Pataudi in 1932-33.

Against all-comers, the list is rather less auspicious and a reminder that this singular achievement is no guarantee of lasting success. After May, Arthur Milton in 1958, John Hampshire in 1969 and, most recently, Frank Hayes in 1973 are the only other examples.

Milton now scouts for England talent in the West Country, Hayes coaches at Felsted and Hampshire will be standing as an umpire before this Ashes series is over.

Thorpe has little in common in method with any of these, but his technique and temperament rendered irrelevant a first-class average of only 25 this season prior to this impeccable innings.

His durability will be tested afresh against the West Indies in the Caribbean this winter. He already has valuable experience there during the third of his four A tours for England. In four first-class matches he averaged 32.

Perhaps the batsman he most resembles is the most prolific of Surrey's left-handers, John Edrich.

On such a good pitch, and against this relatively depleted Australian attack, he was seldom beaten, but he has the same ability to remain quite unaffected by the drama of any previous delivery, whether it has beaten his outside edge or been despatched for four; and he has that priceless Edrich capacity for using the pace of the ball to run it through the gully or glance it to long-leg.

This is a worker; an accumulator of quality, a true Test batsman in the making.

Hussain played no less well, adding 31 of the 60 added yesterday morning in only 10 overs, with a selection of what greengrocers might call "choicest" off-side strokes.

What a change it was to see the Australians chasing the leather round a grassy outfield, a transformation symbolised by little David Boon scurrying in front of the boundary rope instead of hovering expectantly at short-leg.

After 40 minutes Gooch felt safe in making an excellent declaration, one which, given a good start, did not put the match wholly out of Australia's reach.

Thorpe is true Test batsman in the making

FULL SCOREBOARD Page 32

At the final interval we were in grave danger of losing, and the dressing room atmosphere was tense and nervous.

The Englishmen had 32 overs remaining in which to create a marvellous victory. Conversely, BJ and I had the chance to prove our mettle under the pressure of trying to save a Test match. The first 30 minutes of play after the break proved as tough as any Test match cricket I've encountered. But we managed to survive, and as each over was safely negotiated, we could see the Englishmen drop their heads, as if acknowledging they could no longer win the game.

This acceptance of the situation to me typifies the difference between the two sides at the moment. We believe we can win under any situation, whereas the Englishmen don't know how to win. It's been so long since they tasted success.

Today was the first time I've batted with BJ for any length of time, and I found we immediately struck up a good rapport out in the middle. We backed each other up with positive comments to the extent where, at one stage, the two of us were actually saying more than the eleven members of the opposition.

After the 31st over of the session, Gooch finally realised the game had run its course. We had finally saved a match on the last day, something we have struggled with in other Test series of recent times.

The feeling in the room after the match was one of relief at saving the match, especially after we had looked down and out at tea time. But we were also disappointed, particularly as we had the game at our mercy coming into Day 4. Full credit must go to the English team for fighting back and nearly forcing a victory.

The end of a Test match is a time for the team to get together to let off some steam after five days of intense pressure. The usual consequence of such an evening is a hangover and I won't be surprised when the panadeine is handed out on the bus the tomorrow morning.

TO LEEDS VIA DUBLIN

DAY 74 (July 7)

WITH LIVERS working overtime, and sunglasses the order of the day for everyone, we boarded the bus for our next destination — Stone, in Staffordshire, where we play the Minor Counties tomorrow.

Worrying news quickly filtered through the bus with the reminder that we were to stop at Burton-on-Trent along the way, at a brewery, for a luncheon with XXXX executives, followed by a guided tour of the premises. There would, of course, be several obligatory lagers. Just what we needed!

However, lunch was safely and successfully negotiated, but the remainder of my journey on the bus was rather uncomfortable. Being somewhat weary I used the floor as a makeshift bed, and was tossed from pillar to post. After reaching the safety of the hotel, I spent the rest of the afternoon in the "batcave" with the curtains drawn extremely tight, blocking any penetrating sunrays.

Later, most of us visited the local cinema-city, only 200 metres from the hotel, to see either *Assassin* or *Cliffhanger*. The lollyshop in the complex gained our enthusiastic patronage, and chaotic scenes ensued, with snakes, bananas and fudges being thrown about, and the place ending up in something of a mess. It was time to make a quick getaway, with a large bag of sweets tucked under each arm, plus a couple of drinks for good measure.

Cracker Holdsworth, after scoring his first runs of the tour, against the Minor Counties. He finished with a grand total of five, as indicated by Ian Healy.

DAY 75 (July 8)

THE SQUAD for the game against Minor Counties was reduced to 15 when Merv travelled down to London with our physio to receive specialist treatment on his troublesome groin — a move which will hopefully allow him to recuperate away from the scrutiny of the media.

A very good crowd was in attendance today, at a typically undulating minor-league ground. It seemed every one of the 3000 supporters was armed with an autograph book, which is something we have come to expect at every ground we play at. The warm-up for us in these sort of fixtures is very laid-back — consisting of a perusal of the wicket, a few catches (three or four), some throw-downs, followed by a cup of tea and, for a few of the lads, a visit to the Ladbrokes tent.

This morning Junior rushed back to the rooms in a state of excitement, as the local bookie had rated us a generous 14/1 chance of scoring 200 runs in the first session (two-and-a-quarter hours), on a ground the size of a postage stamp. On hearing the news, most of the batsmen dived into their bags searching for their wallets. But we were disappointed to learn of a subsequent development — the bookie would only let us on for a total of 30 pounds. As it turned out the bookie did the right thing by us as we stumbled to be 6 for 130 at lunch, with the keen-as-mustard Minor Counties players pulling off some great catches to back up some useful bowling, and give themselves a sniff of an historic victory.

Mark Taylor and Paul Reiffel added some respectability to our total by each scoring 50s and we ended up on 230 — which we reckoned was enough. The two highlights of our innings were Ziggy being the first player to secure Plucka for a second time (to the amusement of the Aussie players, who appealed in tandem with the Minor Counties' opening bowler on a fine edge through to the keeper) and Cracker collecting his first runs on tour — a square cut for four that saw him carry on as if he'd scored the winner in an FA Cup Final with 30 seconds left to play.

The freezing cold weather was the convenient theory put forward by our fieldsmen after we had spilled two catches in the first three overs. But their top order didn't hang around long anyway, with Reiffel and Holdsworth each taking wickets in what could be the beginning of a showdown between them for a Test spot.

With the game safely in our keeping, Tails decided to roll his arm over, in the quest of the two wickets he needs to win a bet he and I have had with Patrick Keane (an English journalist). Patrick gave us odds of 5-1 — and Tails put 20 pounds on it and I had 50.

There was great jubilation when Taylor enticed their number nine down the wicket, and craftily darted the ball down the legside for Ziggy to whip the bails off. It was a glorious piece of cricket — at least in the eyes of Tails and myself. Pistol then spoiled the party by taking the wicket of their last batsman, capping off a great game for him — 50 not out and five wickets — but Tails and I weren't happy. I'd never before seen a man chastised for taking a wicket, especially his fifth in an innings, but on this occasion, Pistol copped a serve from both of us for delaying our victory over the pressman.

The good news is that the bet is for the whole tour. The pressure is now on Tails, as the search for his second and cash-claiming wicket will have to be continued against a first-class side. For a bowler of his quality he is heading into uncharted territory.

Quite a few of the guys gathered at the local pool hall in the evening, where Warney paraded around the table as if he was Walter Lindrum. While the rest of us went to school in our youth, Warney obviously fine-tuned his craft behind the cue instead.

The last thing I did tonight was pack my bags for Ireland, which was when I realised my blazer and trousers have been left behind at Southampton. Luckily the manager has a spare pair of strides which will get me through.

DAY 76 (July 9)

A HEFTY penalty is in order for the management at our next fines meeting. This morning we checked our luggage into Aer Lingus a full two-and-a-quarter hours before the flight — leaving us all that time to twiddle our thumbs in the airport lounge, instead of being between the sheets back at the hotel.

The 45-minute flight, under the guidance of Captain Howard Hughes (Spruce Goose), went smoothly until we made our approach to Dublin through thick clouds. At that point the Fokker was thrown about considerably by the turbulence, which caused Tubs to break out in a cold sweat, while BJ was looking like the grim reaper in the aisle seat, his head bowed between his legs.

The usual comforting comments came thick and fast from the boys, who offered all sorts of remedies for the travel sickness — from anchovy pizzas to fish milkshakes — all of which were surprisingly turned down. The plane finally touched down after a nasty stomach-churning last 10 minutes and the team immediately headed to the hotel, to check in and get changed for a round of golf at the sixth-highest rated course in the British Isles — Portmarnock.

At this famous course, the first five holes were negotiated with a fair degree of skill by the trio of S. Waugh, Martyn and Warne. Then a severe thunderstorm, complete with hail, sent us scurrying to a nearby bunker shelter which was already packed with locals by the time we reached it. Obviously their knowledge of the weather was far greater than ours. The sky looked as if the end of the world was at hand and hail had blanketed the greens and fairways. But the locals calmly declared: "We'll be back on in five minutes."

And, of course, they were right. But the interruption had affected our finely-tuned games, and from that point the XXXX balls began to stray off the beautifully manicured fairways and into the thick heather, never to be seen again.

Another light storm came, but didn't deter us and we soldiered on. The grips and our clothes became soaked, it became almost impossible to hang on to the clubs, and soon the dozen or so balls in my bag dwindled to a handful. The distinct possibility loomed that there would be none at all by the end of nine holes. The initial keenness at the first tee had diminished to such an extent that the bar increasingly looked a far more enticing proposition than the prospect of trampling through the rough in wet and freezing conditions for another nine holes. So a round that had promised so much early on was terminated — in favour of a pint of Guinness and some toasted sandwiches.

DAY 77 (July 10)

THE PREPARATION of some of the team members for the one-day game against Ireland left some slight room for improvement. For example, Tim May lost sight of the fact that cricket shoes and socks are a useful commodity when bowling and batting, while Matt Hayden neglected to bring any form of cricket shirt with him.

The serious business of warming-up for the fixture began with dealing with a horde of autograph collectors clamouring for good positions, followed by a chat with the groundsman, a visit to the tent where the locals were selling their home-made apple tarts — very tasty too — and then a couple of practice deliveries for the bowlers and throw-downs for the batsmen. Most importantly, the teams lined up to meet the local dignitaries before the traditional beginning — the visiting side batting first.

It was a day off for me, and I had planned a relaxing few hours; we have a very busy schedule ahead. Slater and Hayden once again tore the opposing attack apart before Slater went for 56. This brought in Mark Waugh who promptly picked up where Slater had left off. When Mark eventually departed, the Irish celebrated, but if they had have known what the next overs would bring, they would have gladly spilt the simple catch Junior offered.

Skipper Border made his way to the crease to generous applause from the crowd of about 3000 keen cricket followers — and proceeded to pulverise the attack, smashing a century off 46 balls in 35 minutes! The highlights of his spectacular knock were the five consecutive sixes he hit, all of which went right out of the ground. Unfortunately, the record-equalling sixth six was averted by the bowler who tossed in a wide delivery that AB only just managed to slice for a couple — much to the displeasure of the crowd, who had worked themselves into a state of near frenzy.

While AB was going crazy at one end, Hayden was marching to another century at the other — again proving to everyone how much this guy loves batting and scoring runs against any type of opposition; it's a trait very important in an ambitious batsman.

AB put the Irish bowlers out of their misery after 49 overs, with the total at 3-361. The Irish innings then got off to a poor start with the loss of three quick wickets to an attack comprised of Holdsworth, Julian and Reiffel — who are in a three-way tug-of-war for Test positions at Headingley, a renowned seamer's paradise.

Afternoon tea featured the largest gathering of cakes, sandwiches and pies ever to grace a dining-room table — most of which, sadly, was left untouched thanks

TOUR MATCH

Brilliant Border gives the Irish a fine exhibition

By Charles Randall in Dublin

THE conclusion at Clontarf's pretty ground on Saturday was a fairly narrow one-day win to the Australians by 272 runs — the green "baggy" versus the green saggy.

Irish eyes will not be smiling, though, if Ireland's women cannot close that gap they meet Australia in their World Cup, which starts in England next week.

The prospect of those Australian baggy caps on show in Dublin for the first time since 1977 attracted a crowd of about 2,500 inside the privet hedges of Clontarf.

The two teams were introduced to Mary Robinson, Ireland's president, in a dignified start that was soon forgotten as the Australians took command.

Allan Border narrowly failed to hit six sixes in an over for the first time in his long career.

He blamed the delay in retrieving the ball for "stuffing me up" when he aimed a mighty blow unsuccessfully at the last delivery.

The bowler was Angus Dunlop, who works in his family's textile business in Dublin. He almost became Border's favourite person as his first five off-breaks, oozing cunning and spin, disappeared out of the ground.

But Australia's captain had to be content with what he thought was his most rapid hundred, off 46 deliveries, in his innings of 111.

Border and Matthew Hayden, who hit 133 not out, put on 153 in 15 overs before the declaration arrived at 361 for three in the 50th over.

Justin Benson returned yesterday morning to county duty with Leicestershire having contributed embarrassingly little to Ireland's day. His four overs of seam cost 25 runs and, as opening bats-

Allan Border...putting on the batting style with six hits in Ireland

tamely to mid-wicket and was dismissed for one run.

Stephen Warke, a Belfast pensions advisor and Ireland's captain, was able to take a relaxed view, especially in the week that Ireland had been admitted to the ICC Trophy tournament in Kenya.

He said: "Really this was an exhibition game and not part of our build-up for Kenya. We're getting more professional in our attitude and will improve, I'm sure."

Irish cricket, on the march with the sponsorship of Allied Irish Bank, has much to be proud of in its long history — even before the dismissal of the West Indies for 25 in Derry in 1969.

That nine-wicket Irish victory was an exhibition that went wrong, while Saturday's 272-run defeat was a game that went right. They would understand that in

111

The Australians enjoy the delights of the local catering at the hurling. The tourists are (left to right): Tim May, Brendon Julian (behind May), Ian Healy, Wayne Holdsworth, Michael Slater and Paul Reiffel.

to our physio Errol Alcott, who watched over the boys like a hawk. With the game safely in our keeping, the mood of the afternoon became somewhat relaxed, and Slater and Hayden graced the bowling crease with their finely-tuned actions.

Hayden threw his Adonis-like frame (so *he* says) at an Irish batsman and produced a delivery that leapt off the wicket and crashed into the startled batsman's helmet. This left the heavily-shaken Irishman at Hayden's mercy and he was duly dispatched by the menacing-looking part-time trundler.

Slater, not to be outdone, produced a display worthy of a man regarded as cannon fodder in the nets, and snared a wicket with his deceptive pace ... or lack of it. The Irish crumbled under the onslaught and were all out for 89. But the locals appeared to have enjoyed both the occasion and the entertainment during the day.

The festivities continued at the conclusion of the game, with a band striking up in a marquee adjoining the ground. After listening to the music for a couple of hours, the lads decided they would provide some additional entertainment by performing a rendition of *Khe Sanh*. With the quartet of Slater, S.R. Waugh, Holdsworth and Reiffel — led by Slater, whose opening burst at the microphone was: "It's great to see you all here, we hope you're having a great time. We're now going to play one of our favourites, just for you ... let's do it, boys."

These couple of lines proved to be the highlight of the performance; the locals stood in silence, stunned — obviously because they didn't know the words, certainly not because of the quality of the singing — and the boys made a quick exit upon finishing, our tails between our legs. We think the act may need just a few minor adjustments before our next gig.

DAY 78 (July 11)

OUR LAST day in Ireland dawned with most of the lads sporting nasty hangovers. After overcoming a slow start, half the team opted for a game of golf and the rest trekked off to watch a provincial hurling final between Wexford and the reigning All-Ireland Champions, Kilkenny, at Croke Park.

I chose the latter option. I'd seen the game of hurling on TV before and its mix of skill and madness had held me captivated. To be able to actually attend a game was a nice fringe benefit of touring and playing sport at a high level. The Aussie contingent for the hurling consisted of May, Julian, Reiffel, Holdsworth, Healy, Mike Walsh (our scorer), Des Rundle (the team manager) and me, and we got into the spirit of the occasion by donning headgear and headbands in the two teams' colours.

In what was a compact, almost ancient stadium, the atmosphere was tremendous. The beginning of the match saw a player from each side squaring off, armed with their sticks (which look similar to hockey sticks except they have a larger head). The referee threw in a ball similar to a cricket ball, only slightly softer — and the mayhem commenced. At once there was a flurry of sticks and one of them promptly snapped in half, with one piece spinning through the air — an event which caught BJ by surprise. For a split second he thought it was an airborne limb!

The first five minutes of the game held us all spellbound, except for Maysie, who seemed to find the whole experience amusing, perhaps because of the element of madness. As the contest settled down, it became evident that great skill was required, with players taking one-handed catches, hitting the ball off-balance, kicking and palming the ball to teammates, and juggling the ball on the end of the stick while running.

The battle ended up in a 20-all draw, after Kilkenny scored a superb goal with only 10 seconds to go. To be there was a great experience.

Just when we thought our highly enjoyable trip to Ireland had gone off without a hitch, Marto couldn't find his passport and plane ticket when we reached the airport terminal for the trip back. Some quick talking by the newly-designated manager, Tim Zoehrer (Des Rundle stayed in Ireland for three-days' holiday), led to a replacement ticket; and luckily a passport isn't needed to leave Ireland. This minor crisis averted, the lads boarded the Fokker with some trepidation, and memories still fresh of the rough landing on arrival three days before.

The feeling among the team about our trip to Ireland is that the next Ashes Tour should consist of six Tests in Ireland, with a three-day trip to England thrown in. After a smooth flight and a safe touchdown at Manchester Airport, we were taken to Mottram Hall in preparation for a big XXXX golf day tomorrow.

With Slats at Dublin airport, after the hurling.

DAY 79 (July 12)

THIS MORNING presented the prospect of something pretty rare — a day without either training for or playing cricket. The whole team was instead required to play in the XXXX golf day, one of our official "scheduled" events on tour. The thought of a golf day is an enjoyable prospect for most of the guys, with the possible exception of Wayne Holdsworth. He can't see much value in trying to get a little white ball in a hole and then trying to repeat the deed time after time. His lack of enthusiasm may also have something to do with the fact that he possesses the worst golf swing I've ever laid eyes on. On the rare occasions he is lured to the course, Cracker usually spends most of his time with his head bowed, trying to find wayward tee shots that have ended up deep in the thick heather.

Each of the 17 Aussies joined three other partners, who had paid 500 pounds between them for the day — all of which goes to charity.

The three members of my group made Wayne Holdsworth look like a maestro with the club. Ball after ball was either missed completely or mis-hit into the rough, giving us no chance of snaring the silverware at the end of the day. My own game deteriorated badly after two or three reasonable holes and by the time we reach the halfway stage, a very telling statistic highlighted our poor showing to that point — we had lost more balls between us than stableford points accumulated!

After a drink and a bite to eat, we were determined to make amends for our rather slow start. Following an inspirational pep talk by our captain, the team was ready to make a charge at the leaders. These fleeting thoughts were quickly dismissed when the tee shots from the 10th resulted in:
- an air swing
- a topped drive into the thick bushes
- a long ball into an adjoining herd of Freisian cows
- a skied tee shot 50 metres down the middle of the fairway.

The last mentioned was possibly the best shot played between the four of us on the back nine as our golf went from bad to worse. The 19th hole did not come quickly enough.

The winners for the day were the members of Mark Waugh's group — but the highlight of the evening's dinner proved to be a quote from Wayne Holdsworth after the raffle was drawn for an autographed bat. The winner, having the choice of either an Australian or English bat, commented: "Seeing I'm playing with the Aussies, I think I'll take their bat."

At this Cracker observed sagely: "Good choice ... there aren't any Englishmen on the England bat anyway."

The evening coach trip to Derby took one-and-a-half hours, and we were very happy when we finally checked into the Breadsall Priory Hotel, a supposedly haunted residence set on an 18-hole golf course just outside the city. Tomorrow's game, a three-day match against Derbyshire, provided some fireworks back in '89, and could be lively again. My roomie, once again, is Maysie.

PS: The mystery surrounding Marto's passport was solved by a further inspection of his baggage. The offending item was safely tucked away in one of the side pockets of his suitcase!

Shane Warne practices at Derby

DAY 80 (July 13)

TODAY WE had the "pleasure" of playing at the Racecourse Ground in Derby, a venue that really does not inspire one to perform great deeds. There is such an absence of any atmosphere, because the crowd are so far from the play and need binoculars to get a decent look at the action. The place also has the capacity to bring on the initial stages of hypothermia. There's not a windbreak in sight, and the wind howls across the ground.

Having studied a wicket which looked as though it would suit the pacemen, AB won the toss and inserted the opposition. But it didn't take long at all before the advertising boards were receiving a pummelling at the hands of the local openers, Kim Barnett and Peter Bowler. The score raced to 71 without the slightest hint of a wicket before Pistol gave the team some sort of hope by enticing Bowler to edge one through to the keeper. Mildly inspired by this taste of success, we managed to send three more Derbyshire batsmen back to the pavilion, and have the locals four down for 160 at lunch.

Another treat awaited the boys on the dining room table; the lunch-time meal consisted of a jacket potato with bolognese sauce. The club is currently on the brink of bankruptcy — and this was obviously a cost-cutting measure.

After hoeing into this nutritious meal, it was time to get back to the task of dismissing the locals before the early stages of pneumonia took hold. Unfortunately the Derbyshire captain had different plans and the boundaries came thick and fast until rain saved us any more punishment with the score at 5 for 244, and two-and-a-half hours' play still scheduled. Some of our bowlers came in for harsh treatment, in particular Wayne Holdsworth, whose return from 15 overs was one wicket for 113 runs. The term given to such a feat (a bowler conceding 100 runs or more) is known as "getting a sidecar", and lately Cracker has been putting together quite a collection.

Quote of the day came from Mark Waugh. After taking a catch at second slip, he was heard to observe: "I've *never* dropped a catch while wearing my sunglasses."

Next over, of course, the obvious happened and he grassed a difficult chance, much to the slips cordon's amusement ... and the bowler's annoyance.

The team departed from the ground at 5.30pm after play was officially abandoned. Tonight some of the guys were locked into a XXXX function — but five of us had the chance to see INXS live at Leicester, an hour down the motorway.

The keen music aficionados of the team — Warne, Boon, Julian, Reiffel and S. Waugh — ended up meeting the members of the band, and discovered they're all big cricket followers. They wanted to talk sport; we wanted to talk music. The concert ended up being a great night for all of us, except when lead singer Michael Hutchence announced that we were in the audience — a fact that went down like a lead balloon with the mob. A chorus of instantaneous booing broke out in the concert hall.

With Tim Farriss (left) and Kirk Pengilly of INXS.

DAY 81 (July 14)

CRACKER TODAY brought off the biggest comeback since Lazarus — capturing four wickets for four runs in the morning session, to make his figures quite respectable. He polished off the Derbyshire innings very quickly, and along the way achieved a feat not performed by an Australian tourist since 1912 — a hat-trick — although the third victim was extremely unlucky to be given out caught behind. The ball actually deflected off his boot, and the appeal was only a token gesture on Cracker's behalf.

Paul Reiffel finished with four wickets and was undoubtedly our best bowler. He should find himself in the starting line-up for the Fourth Test at Headingley — with the likelihood that the wicket there should suit him perfectly.

During the Derbyshire innings, there were quite a few confrontations between opposing players, with neither side totally to blame. The ill-feeling that was evident in the '89 clash certainly resurfaced — adding some spice to the contest.

As anticipated, Derbyshire pace bowlers, Devon Malcolm and Simon Base, used all of the wicket in their desire to either take wickets or to do some physical damage to the batsmen. But they didn't realise our top three batsmen, Hayden, Slater and M. Waugh, are rather partial to the cut and hook shots and consequently the run rate was maintained at around six an over.

Hayden departed for a well-compiled 40, just as Slater was shifting into top gear. Slats was absolutely murdering the short stuff being dished up to him, and cruised to another highly-watchable hundred. M. Waugh joined in on the festivities, and was closing in on his 50 when the tea break saved the home attack from further embarrassment.

Once again, rain played a part in the game. Another downpour caused the last session to be abandoned after 30 minutes, with Slater on 133 and Waugh on 60. Malcolm, the English Test hopeful, had figures of 0-85 from 12 overs, while his new-ball partner, Base, fared no better. His return from 10 overs was 0-85.

With the top-order batting so well and the weather causing time losses in most games, I feel as if I haven't had a decent bat for ages. I'm becoming frustrated at the lack of opportunities, but on the positive side it is making me hungrier for success. I just have to wait for a chance.

I needed to get rid of some excess energy, so I took to the hotel's gym where Merv, with the help of Errol Alcott, was busy trying to get fit for the next Test which begins in about a week's time. At this stage he is probably a 50-per-cent chance of making it.

Later on, Warney and I headed into town in search of an Italian meal. After being told the wrong directions at least half-a-dozen times, we ended up locating one — but only after 40 minutes of driving around in circles.

Worse was to follow for Warney when, to his horror, he located a few mushrooms — a vegetable that makes him heave just by looking at it — in his spaghetti bolognese. In order to get a replacement dish, Warney told the waitress he was allergic to mushrooms, which worked, and an alternative meal was duly served.

Wayne in hat-trick world

by HAYDN MacKENZIE

AUSSIE paceman Wayne Holdsworth claimed a hat-trick in an astonishing eight-ball spell of 4-0 at Derby yesterday to boost his hopes of a Test debut.

Holdsworth wiped out the Derbyshire tail-end and said: "I've never taken a hat-trick before, except off my sister in the backyard, and she used to whack me around a bit as well."

It was the first Australian hat-trick since Merv Hughes struck at Perth in 1988 and the 24-year-old will hope it is a change of fortune in a disappointing tour so far.

Michael Slater reached 1,000 runs on the tour on his way to an unbeaten 133 and top of the tourists' run-makers as the Aussies raced to 268-1 off just 44 overs.

● Dutchman Adrianus Van Troost will not be eligible for England's Test team until 1998.

The Somerset fast bowler's hopes of having his qualification period cut from seven years to four have been dashed by Lord's.

"I think it's a disappointing decision," said England manager Keith Fletcher.

"Under International Cricket Council rules he could have been available in 1995 and I think four years is long enough to serve."

Brendon Julian bowling at Derby. The batsman is the Derbyshire captain, Kim Barnett.

DAY 82 (July 15)

I DREW the curtains this morning to find the sky a charcoal-grey colour. Steady rain was falling and there was quite obviously no chance of play — I'll have to wait again before I get an opportunity in the middle.

Down at the ground, the umpires decided to wait until 12.30pm before calling the game off. In the meantime, all the coffins were packed and the cards came out. The guys played a game of 1-2-3 drop. The key to this game is having the ability to bluff the other players, which happens after you have a quick look at your cards, then hold them in front of your body and, after the count of three, you either hold them or drop them. The winner is the person holding the highest cards or best hands. The bets became larger and larger, and a scuffle nearly broke out after Mark Waugh claimed to have a winner with a straight. His only opposition, Shane Warne, was quick to point out that 7, 8, 9, 10, Ace, wasn't quite a winner, which led to a set of cards flying out the window ... and the cash ending up in Warney's pocket.

When the game was finally called off, the lads boarded the team bus, which now has an extra passenger — a large photo of Craig McDermott plastered over the dashboard. The squad is now back to full strength.

The trip to Durham, situated in the north-east of England, is one of our longest hauls on the motorway during the entire tour. Videos fill in the time for us, with *Sleeping with the Enemy* showing in the front-section of the bus and *Rambo* in the back.

After we finally arrived at the Royal Country Hotel, I headed straight for the hairdresser, as I was about three weeks overdue for a haircut, and then to the hotel pool for a swim and spa.

Lynette also made her way to Durham, via a two-hour train trip from Nelson, in Lancashire, to Hull where she caught up with Helen Healy. They then drove for three hours to Durham, but couldn't find accommodation due to a "Tall Ship" festival at Newcastle. Eventually they found two rooms at the local university.

An Ashes campaign can become a testing time not only for the players but also for the wives and girlfriends. You get to spend very little time, together due to cricket commitments and the fact that the players' partners can't stay in the same hotel as the players. Luckily for Heals and me, our wives have been through it all before, are very patient with us, and take care of themselves completely in their travel and accommodation arrangements. This has made it easy for us to concentrate on our cricket.

Tea tonight was at another American-style eatery called Littlejohns, which, most importantly, served ice-cream cones, and therefore gave Emma Healy the opportunity to plaster the stuff all over her face, something she accomplished with ease.

DAY 83 (July 16)

JUST FOR a change it was pouring rain when we made our way down to the ground at Durham University. There we caught up with Dean Jones, who is currently coaching their Second XI. There was no training, so it was back to the hotel room to watch the British Open golf, and to get Hooter to have a look at my neck and back. I think I've put something out of place after yet another poor night's sleep.

Rather than sit in my room watching TV all day and emptying out the mini-bar fridge, I took the available option and headed out to the golf course with 10 of the squad. Teams were formed, with myself and Heals taking on Warney and Junior for a maximum purse of 20 pounds each.

The game began poorly, with balls flying into the rough never to be seen again, for everyone except Heals, who played the first five holes like a man inspired. But even with Heals' play, the quartet approached the sixth tee with the game still on level terms. The sixth hole bordered on a paddock full of pollen-carrying plants and bushes, which sent the Waugh brothers and Warney into bouts of uncontrollable sneezing and coughing, accompanied by watery eyes and noses. I was suffering, and developed a nasty-looking rash on my neck which became increasingly unsightly as it worsened into hives by the time another tee shot scattered the wildlife on the ninth hole. With the fairways strewn with phlegm from three blithering messes, the golf turned out to be a very ordinary affair. But the contest remained on an even keel.

The back nine holes produced some reasonable efforts and, as the boys assembled on the 18th hole, the duo of Healy and Steve Waugh appeared destined for a one-hole victory and a 20-pound windfall each. But the thought of taking Warney's cash proved too much of a distraction, as I let fly with a monstrous drive (all of 300 yards!) which unfortunately crossed three fairways on its travels and clattered into some heavy timber. Another tee shot was required. But then Heals, under pressure, produced a drive that safely found the fairway.

As the group made its way to the putting surface, the outcome rested on Warney, who needed two putts to draw and three to lose. Showing signs of cracking under pressure, his four-metre putt was only partly negotiated, and he was left with a bit more than a metre for a draw. That crucial putt was made that little bit tougher by a barrage of sledging from the opposition, but the biggest export since Kylie came through for his team to rescue a draw.

Back in the clubhouse, tales of the day's play were exchanged and, not surprisingly, Jonesy comes out with the quote of the day. The incident in question came about on a par five, where Jonesy pulled out a massive drive, followed it up with a super iron-shot, and capped it off by sinking the putt for a glorious eagle. He was obviously feeling pretty pleased with himself, and prepared to take the remainder of the course by storm. As he teed his ball up at the next hole, he spun around to his playing partners and exclaimed: "This is my lucky eagle ball and it's going to travel around the world with me from now on!"

The ball, now obviously doomed, sliced off the clubface, and will now not be making the trek from continent to continent that Jonesy had in mind for it.

Back at the hotel, I found a pile of messages, which, upon opening, discovered were all Warney's. It's just a continuation of the nightmare that all the hotels have had sorting out our mail and messages.

DAY 84 (July 17)

THE WEATHER had cleared sufficiently to make a full day's play possible, and a surprisingly large crowd was on hand to witness one of the all-time greats, Ian Botham, play his last first-class game.

The amount of media present today was enormous, with even Australia's Channel 7 here (they are putting together a story on Merv), as well as Sky TV who are doing a story on the side, and in particular Allan Border.

Durham won the toss, decided to bat on a good-looking strip and immediately took to our opening bowlers. They posted 0-71 off the first 10 overs, but the onslaught was slowed by the introduction of Paul Reiffel into the attack. But even with Reiffel's good form, the former English Test opener, Wayne Larkins, continued to score freely and went to lunch on 87 not out, and with his side very pleased with the 2-160 scoreline.

The middle session held very little joy for the Aussie boys, as all the Durham batsmen played aggressively. Just as he had done throughout his career, Botham took on the bowling, being particularly harsh on Holdsworth, who wasn't enjoying one of his better days. In fact at one stage, Wayne was heard to say to himself when running in to bowl at Botham: "C'mon Crack, where's this one going to go now?"

Botham's cameo innings came to an end when he tried to smash another one over the infield, but miscued and was caught at point, giving me only my second first-class wicket on tour. When a player of Botham's stature walks from the crease for the last time, it is a sad day for cricket. Great players only come along once or twice in a lifetime, and I feel privileged to have played against him.

The day ended with a wicket and a declaration by Durham at 8-385. Towards the end of the day, with all the front-line bowlers tiring, Matt Hayden used a rare bowling opportunity to snare his initial first-class wicket. But that wicket didn't come until after Tubs dropped a hot chance off his bowling, something I'm sure Matt will remind him of for the rest of his career.

After spending six-and-a-half hours chasing leather to the fence came just what I needed — a XXXX function at Middlesborough, 30 minutes' drive away, with Merv, AB and BJ. The function turned out to be another "stinker", with about 60 people turning up to a social club. But the night was somewhat saved by the host, who changed his normal routine and proceeded to take the mickey out of everyone present, giving us a couple of laughs.

With Ian Botham and Allan Border.

MERV'S DIET — (Selected at

Day One

Breakfast:
Two cups of coffee
One bowl of Special K, muesli and milk
Two slices of bread
One cup of tea
One apple
One banana
One plum
One peach

Lunch:
One glass of orange cordial
One steak, corn, potato and mixed salad
One large fries (McDonald's)
One McChicken sandwich
One medium coke
One cherry/custard pie

Dinner:
(at Planet Hollywood)
Nachos
One mixed fajita
One chocolate mousse

Cocktail Drinks:
Six beers
One Terminator
One Planet of the Apes
Three Beetlejuices
Two Sambucas
Six more beers

random)

Day Two

Breakfast:
Two slices of toast
One cup of tea
One bowl of muesli and milk
One pint of water

Lunch:
One ham-and-salad roll
One chicken-avocado-and-coleslaw roll
One Diet Coke
One jam donut

Dinner:
(Team dinner)
Four Diet Pepsi
One-and-a-half strawberry milkshakes
Chicken wings
Prawns, mussels and crab claws
Garlic bread
Two pieces of chicken
One-and-a-half racks of ribs
Fries
Chilli con carne
Corn and coleslaw
Two cappuccinos
One Diet Coke
One infant
And some cutlery

DAY 85 (July 18)

WITH THE wicket being a batsman's paradise and the boundaries short, as well as Durham being at the bottom of the County Championship table, we were all expecting to boost our tour averages and aggregates by the time we had all batted here. But, as is usual with cricket, you have to expect the unexpected, and Durham cut a swathe through our top order to have us 7-113 by the time the roast beef and Yorkshire pudding were ready to be served. Most of the dismissed batsmen fell to poor shots, probably as a result of being a little complacent and not concentrating fully.

As is so often the case, Heals proved to be the team's saviour. He and Paul Reiffel added some respectability to our score by putting on a century stand, while the rest of the team was glued to the TV, following the fortunes of Greg Norman in the British Open golf (which he finally won, to end our day on a sweet note). Our innings was terminated when Wayne Holdsworth tried to dazzle the crowd with one of his now famous back-foot drives, but mistimed the shot to give the bowler a simple caught-and-bowled chance. Heals was left unbeaten on 70 and the team short of the follow-on target, which meant we had to bat again to save the match. But with the first defeat of the tour looming, the boys knuckled down to the task, and, with Boon and Hayden at the helm, stumps were drawn with Australia 1-80 in the second innings.

My health hasn't been 100 per cent since Manchester and the local doctor advised me to have a chest X-ray to see if there is a virus present. Fortunately, the X-ray doesn't reveal anything major, and the conclusion reached is that my problem is a combination of hayfever, bronchitis and a mild chest cold, which requires a course of antibiotics.

Back at the hotel tonight, there was a bit of commotion centring on the third-floor lift. Merv and Wayne Holdsworth were stuck between the second and third levels, with the doors slightly ajar and a few of the lads heckling at them from above. The hotel management finally rescued the boys from their perilous location, and a reason was sought as to how the situation came to be. As it turns out, the confined space of a lift wasn't an ideal place for Merv to overwhelm Cracker or, as Merv would have put it, "share one of his normal bodily functions" by producing a "horse and cart". The result had Cracker frantically attempting to pull apart the doors in search of some breathable air — which caused a malfunction in the system and an immediate shutdown of the lift.

Opposite page: The producers of the Yorkshire Post fourth Test Preview, published on July 19, were kind enough to put me on the front cover.

TEST MATCH
SPECIAL

CRUNCH TIME FOR GOOCH...

ENGLAND V AUSTRALIA
LIVE FROM HEADINGLEY

YORKSHIRE POST

Free with Sports Monday

DAY 86 (July 19)

WHEN MENACING clouds hovered this morning, the general consensus among the players was that they'd produce a large amount of precipitation. Maysie did his bit to aid the cause by leaving tickets at the gate for three of his close friends, Mr D. Luge (deluge), Mr F. Flood (flash flood), and Mr R. L. Downpour (rather large downpour), in the hope they'd all turn up today. With Maysie's quota of three tickets being taken up, there was one very disappointed person, who is normally left a ticket by Tim at any venue, all over the world, wherever Tim plays — his name being Ferris Bueller, a man Maysie idolises and aspires to.

With steady rain falling and both teams assuming the game would be called off, Beefy Botham emptied the contents of a couple of bottles of Sauvignon Blanc, in recognition of the end of his career. But the celebrations were halted by the unwelcome news that rain has stopped falling and play would begin in 15 minutes.

Boon and Hayden cashed in on what we term "the teddy bears' picnic", a phrase used when the opposition is struggling or using part-time bowlers that allow easy runs. Both batsmen made hundreds. With the game "dead", Cracker was promoted to the coveted number-four position, and AB offered him 50 pounds if he reached 20. Meanwhile, back in the change rooms, Merv had the lads in fits of laughter as he ran through the diary he has kept of his diet on each day of the tour. So far his intake of food has not been unlike that of a white pointer shark, with a rather large thirst to boot!

Cracker had his chance to lighten AB's wallet, but after a flurry of sparkling boundaries, he momentarily entertained thoughts of actually trying to play as if he knows what he's doing with that lump of wood in his hands, and was caught at cover attempting an impersonation of Victor Trumper's cover drive. With the termination of Cracker's cameo display, I made my way to the wicket with 20 minutes left and the game having deteriorated to the state where Botham was wicketkeeping without pads or gloves, and one of the Durham fieldsmen had positioned himself among the crowd on the hill in preparation for another six off one of the part-time bowlers.

This unique position led to one of the greatest pieces of fielding ever seen, after the next ball, to Matt Hayden, was mis-hit as he attempted another six. The ball still appeared destined to reach the fence until the Durham fielder, Phil Bainbridge, dodged a couple of deck chairs on his way down the hill, took a mighty leap over the fence followed by a commando roll, and then clutched the ball in his hands and averted the boundary, to the tumultuous applause of the stunned crowd.

Play was stopped 30 minutes before the scheduled finishing time, with Hayden having continued his excellent county-cricket form to end up with 151 to his name. I was a nervous six not out. Botham received a standing ovation from everyone at the ground, a fitting tribute to the great player he has been.

We had another quick getaway, and the bus made its way to Headingley in Leeds in preparation for (hopefully) our Ashes-clinching Test match.

DAY 87 (July 20)

I DIDN'T get a bad night's sleep last night, considering Maysie was in the close vicinity to my bed. But an early-morning call from the *Australian Women's Weekly* woke me, to ask a few questions about National Stamp Collecting Month which I'm helping to promote in October. The conversation brought uncontrollable laughter from my roomie, especially when I informed the interviewer of my days as a collector in my youth. At one stage the discussion had to be halted, and May sent to the toilet to regain some composure, so I wouldn't completely stuff up the interview.

This move turned out to be disastrous, as the confines of the toilet only amplified the noise, and the giggling continued unabated. The interview concluded with the question: "What was your favourite stamp?"

I replied that I didn't really have a favourite one, at which time Maysie lost it, bursting out of the toilet with uncontrollable laughter and tears running down his face, pleading for no more.

Simmo gathered the team in the dressing room at the ground and expressed his concerns over our poor play and lack of intensity during the past couple of weeks. He stressed the need for us to lift our overall attitude if we are going to play well in the upcoming match. We were joined at training by Mike Whitney, who is over here doing commentary for Channel 9. Whit is a man who can lift his team-mates just by his presence. He epitomises the spirit of Australian cricket — always having a go and never giving in under any circumstances.

Personally, today's training session was one of the best I've had all tour. I spent at least half an hour batting during the two net sessions I managed to have, and concentrated on trying to get my feet moving which has been a problem of late. Another encouraging sign was that Merv appears to be something like 80-90 per cent fit, a tribute to the long hours Errol has spent trying to speed up the recovery process of his groin strain. Without our physio's guidance, Merv would definitely have been ruled out of the Test.

The much-talked-about Headingley wicket, a reputed seamer's paradise and batsman's nightmare, appears to be nothing like that at all. The playing strip looks like being a good batting wicket that should turn later — the surface is already dry with some cracks beginning to form.

The afternoon was spent in the hotel's gym doing a few exercises with Wayne Holdsworth. We then jumped into the spa and remained there for the next two hours. Most of the lads had a reasonably quiet night — the heavy schedule has taken its toll — and the boys need to re-charge the batteries over the next two days before the most important match of the tour begins on Thursday.

Lynette and Helen Healy would have by now spent their first day in Venice on their seven-day tour of Italy, a trip that allows them some time away from the cricket. It can be very tiring and sometimes boring for them to continually follow the team around and watch cricket day in and day out.

DAY 88 (July 21)

WE HAD another solid training session today, with the only scare being a slight groin strain to Brendon Julian, which has probably ended his chances of selection. But, even with this setback, the team has a great feel to it at the moment. Everyone believes that the English team may have received too many compliments about their last Test performance. We're all looking forward to crushing their newly-gained reputations.

Quite a few of the guys took to the golf course as their way of relaxing before the Test, while others went shopping in town, but for S. Waugh the sheets looked the most inviting option of all.

The routine before a Test match remained the same, with a team meeting scheduled at 6.30pm. We went through their batting line-up, trying to pinpoint any weaknesses, and then had a chat about their bowlers and what we might expect from them. But, as everyone knows, the best formula for success is line-and-length bowling backed up by enthusiastic fielding, to go with aggressive batting and a high level of concentration.

Our starting line-up hasn't been finalised as yet, but the XII is the same as for the previous Test except Reiffel has come in for Julian. The reason for not naming the 12th man is that the hierarchy wants to have one final look at the wicket before settling on a combination that will exploit the prevailing conditions.

The social committee, which has come under increasing pressure to smarten up their act, located a venue for tonight's pre-match dinner at an Italian restaurant called "Bibi's". To everyone's surprise, the boys came up trumps, with the evening turning out to be a runaway success. Without doubt, the highlight was the 480-pounds bill, creating a new record for the manager, courtesy of the Australian Cricket Board, to pay.

A colourful, but miserable scene at Headingley during the fourth Test.

Two moments from my best innings of the series, when I scored 157 not out, and put on an unbroken 322 with Allan Border, in the fourth Test. Opposite page: A square-cut to the boundary. This page: Acknowledging the Aussie dressing room after reaching my hundred.

AB with Paul Reiffel, Australia's bowling success story at Headingley.

Alec Stewart asks for a second serve of some Merv advice, after the English keeper had reached 50 on the fourth day of the fourth Test.

Atherton, stumped Healy bowled May, in England's second innings at Headingley.

The Australian captain reacts to a half-chance at Leeds.

Above: The Ashes are in safe hands.
Below: Bob Simpson, Merv Hughes and Allan Border watch Ian Healy open AB's prize for being the fourth Test's man of the match.

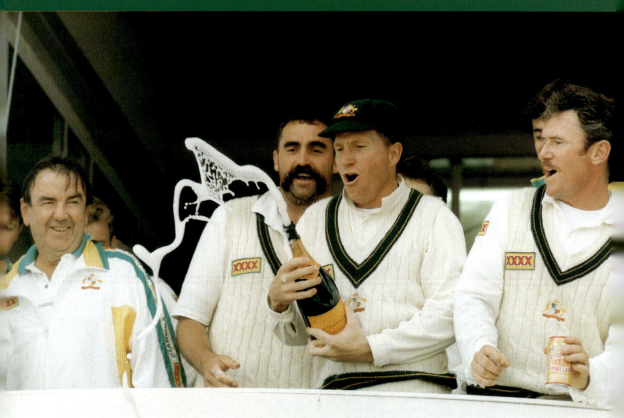

THE FOURTH TEST

DAY 89 (July 22)

WE ARRIVED at Headingley at 9.10am, and as soon as the bus entered the ground you could feel the excitement grow as the players thought of wrapping up the Ashes. The ground holds particularly fond memories for me, as I scored my first Test hundred here four years ago. Just being back here made me feel more relaxed and confident than is normally the case.

AB won an all-important toss, which meant we had the opportunity to score a large total on a good-looking wicket. Hopefully, after a couple of days, the wicket should aid our spinners in their quest for turn and uneven bounce. Surprisingly, the English selectors left out their only spinner, Peter Such, and went into the game with four seam bowlers. It appeared as if they were hoping the wicket would play as it has in the past, but the strip that has been prepared is devoid of green grass and will more than likely turn as the game goes on.

Taylor and Slater got us away to our now customary solid start. Slater in particular was very severe on anything over-pitched, while Taylor looked as solid as a rock, until the Englishmen got their initial breakthrough just before lunch with the total on 86. Debutant quick bowler, Martin Bicknell, trapped Taylor leg-before-wicket to the delight of the capacity crowd. But even with that setback, the atmosphere in the viewing room remained very relaxed, with guys reading papers, doing the crosswords, or just "cooling out" down in the dressing room, which is located at the back of the grandstand.

Upon the resumption of play, Slater, to everyone's shock, actually missed a ball and was bowled, playing across the line. But Mark Waugh once again kept the momentum going with Boon and the two of them saw us safely through to tea, with the total on 209.

In the final session Boonie continued to grind out another large total, but Mark, after a quickfire 52, has a lapse in concentration and let go a delivery that clipped the top of his off stump. Border strode to the wicket looking confident and extremely determined. Being next in, and with 90 minutes of play left, I would normally have felt extremely nervous, but by watching the two guys out in the middle, and realising how determined they were, I'm wasn't nervous at all. I knew they'd be there at the end of the day.

Sure enough, we finished at 3-307, with Boonie unbeaten on 102 (his 50th first-class century, 17th in Tests, and 8th on tour) and AB on 38. The day couldn't have gone better and the foundations are there for us to build up a match-winning total when play resumes tomorrow.

With a capacity crowd such as there was today, there is bound to be a rowdy element among them. After play, as Tim Zoehrer tried to board the bus which was parked outside the ground, he was manhandled by three thugs who gave him a working over with a mixture of upper cuts and jabs until our bus driver and Damien Martyn stepped in to stop the abuse. Ziggy is okay, but is now beginning to wonder whether he is cursed.

During the last week the following has happened to him:
• The *Yorkshire Post* previewed our team with pen pictures of everyone, including the now-absent Craig McDermott, except Ziggy, who was nowhere to be seen.
• Then came a scene where 200 fan letters were handed to the players, and Ziggy, thinking they were being distributed in alphabetical order, waited patiently — but alas no mail.
• Next came the team dinner, where everyone was happily tucking into their main course, while Ziggy was re-ordering his forgotten meal.
• And finally, during warm-ups, a stray cover drive found its way through a hole in the net and collected Ziggy flush on the ankle, which saw him hobble off to the change rooms in search of ice ... and a future Oscar, courtesy of the way the limp slowly disappeared as Ziggy got closer to the grandstand.

DAY 90 (July 23)

TYPICALLY GREY skies greeted the players as the teams made their way onto the ground for the second day's play. Boon was dismissed shortly after play began for a magnificent 107, and I made my way to the wicket under similar circumstances to four years ago, with 300 on the board and about 30 minutes having been completed of the second day. My innings also began in similar fashion to '89, with a couple of streaky shots and a few play-and-misses. But I felt confident and in control. By the time lunch was taken, AB had reached 75, I was 37, and Australia were in a great position. AB was committed to crushing the enemy.

Batting with Border makes you concentrate that little bit extra because you can see how much it means to him to give his wicket away. You play accordingly as anything less than 100 per cent concentration is not expected or accepted.

When he reached what was his 26th Test hundred, he immediately reminded me that we had a long way to go and to keep playing ball to ball, but at the same time aggressively. My total progressed smoothly until I reached the 90s, which have proved a bit of a stumbling block in the past. I wasn't helped by the rain which caused us to leave the ground twice, with my score on 93 and then 98. There were a few nervous moments on the field and in the change rooms, but, after a seemingly endless wait, I finally make the magic three figures. As in the past, the feeling of great satisfaction and pride engulfed me — as well as the relief of not getting out so close to a century.

With so many tough times in Test cricket, it is important to capitalise on your good times, so I set my sights on getting a big hundred. When play was halted for the day we are 4-613, with Border on 175 and S. Waugh on 144, a position we would never have dreamed of at the start of the day. When we returned to the rooms, all the guys passed on their congratulations, while AB and I collapsed into our chairs to relax after six hours of concentration.

Most of the English bowlers copped a mauling, and McCague left the ground midway through the day with back problems and his figures reading 0-113, at which time an Aussie journalist apparently quipped: "His working visa must have run out."

After having a successful day you are required to make yourself available for newspaper and television interviews before you have a real chance to celebrate or relax. Later in the evening, Lynette called from Venice and was pleased I had scored a hundred, but disappointed she had missed it. The first message of congratulations I received was from Dean Jones, who called to say well done, a nice gesture considering how tough it must be for "Lege" to watch from the sidelines, when he is so used to being there himself.

Congratulations from Paul Reiffel after the close of play on day two.

DAY 91 (July 24)

WE DECIDED to bat on for about 40 minutes this morning in order to, in AB's words, "cause further mental and physical disintegration". In fact, the declaration eventually came after 58 minutes, after Border had reached the summit for any Test-match batsman — a double century. The total was 4-653, the highest first-class score ever achieved at Headingley, with our unbroken partnership being halted at 332 runs, the seventh-highest ever in Tests for Australia.

Cricket can be a cruel game sometimes, as Mark Lathwell found out immediately after fielding for 13 hours straight. He nicked the second ball he faced and walked off to contemplate the turn of fate he had fallen victim to. But Robin Smith then made his intentions clear as he murdered the first ball he faced to the point boundary, nearly tearing a hole in the advertising boards. I doubt if there has ever been a more ferocious striker of the ball than Smith. He uses his solid frame and three-pound bat, which has a four-leaf clover stuck on the back of it for luck, to scare the bowlers on occasions, and regularly terrify the close-in fielders.

Atherton and Smith safely negotiated the remaining time before lunch to have England at 1-38. However, the middle session of the day went marginally our way, with two wickets to us and 96 runs to England, and was highlighted by yet another caught-and-bowled by May, who continues to grow in stature in the field. He even managed to halt the progress of a ball with his left hand at one stage!

Atherton and Gooch both reached half-centuries, before Reiffel was brought back into the attack. With the aid of the slope and the breeze, he found an extra yard of pace which unsettled the English opener. Eventually Atherton departed in the same fashion as Mark Waugh had the day before, letting one go, to follow up their 99 runs apiece at Lords. This dismissal signalled a middle-order collapse, as Reiffel claimed four wickets in 30 balls for only 17 runs (he finished the day with figures of 5-60). Not bad for a bowler the former England batsman, Geoff Boycott, said "can't bowl" in his weekly column.

England staggered to 195 for 7 at stumps. The day was clearly won by us again and everyone is especially pleased for Pistol, as it has been a tough tour for him, with very little luck — until today. It was great to see him get the rewards for all his hard work.

Back at the hotel, I headed straight into the spa. I felt about 60 years old out there today after my long innings.

A rare awkward moment for AB at Headingley, as he narrowly escapes being hit by a shot from Nasser Hussain.

DAY 92 (July 25)

THE TABLOID papers never seem to stop causing controversy, and this Test match has fallen victim to one of their devious schemes. During the first three days the *Mail on Sunday* used "directional microphones" to try and pick up conversations between players, and players and umpires, out on the field, and, in this morning's edition, actually reported a conversation between Paul Reiffel and umpire Harold (Dickie) Bird. Luckily for both the player and the umpire nothing controversial was said, but the thought of a private conversation being made public is outrageous. The TCCB has recognised this and issued a warning to the guilty paper to stop using the microphones or be banned from all future international matches.

Our squad was back to full strength today, after the return of BJ, who has been crook for the past week with a virus. He was sorely missed by his army of adoring fans, who are currently enjoying their school holidays.

The vital last three wickets were taken for the addition of only five runs off 29 balls, after Merv had tested out the available bounce in the wicket. He had Caddick and Bicknell both caught fending off the "chin music". The England total of 200 left them with a massive job of either batting for two full days or scoring more than 453 runs to save the game.

Some lost confidence and pride was restored when they batted a second time, and the scoreboard showed England at 37 without loss at lunch. They looked certain to make us earn our wickets more so than we did in the first innings, and the next session's play was typically tough Test match cricket, with neither side giving an inch. Only 79 runs were added, for the loss of Lathwell's wicket, a player who has looked a little out of his depth, technique-wise, at this stage. But he does have plenty of talent at his disposal.

With both May and Warne bowling a high percentage of overs in this match, it was only a matter of time before the "third umpire" was needed to adjudicate on a stumping chance. The third ump sits in a room by himself at the ground and has access to every possible camera angle needed to give a decision on a 'close call'. He communicates with the umpires in the middle through a two-way radio, who then gives the batsman out or not out. This method obviously sees the correct decision being made but far too much time is taken to reach the verdict. The batsman is left feeling like he is about to be executed, as he wanders around the wicket hoping for a reprieve.

The first to be sentenced to the confines of the dressing room was Michael Atherton, who was out by literally an inch. The second victim was Graham Gooch, whose fate was surely known before the bad news arrived for him. The other wicket to fall before stumps was Smith, out LBW to Reiffel not offering a short. Unbelievably, this was only the second time in his past 17 Test innings that a spinner hasn't got him out.

It was another great day for Australian cricket, and England are now on the ropes at 4-238. The only thing that will stop the knockout punch from being delivered tomorrow is the rain.

Back at the hotel, I spent half an hour doing a few weights and some stretching, followed by a relax in the spa.

DAY 93 (July 26)

WHEN I woke up this morning I was horrified to find out it was only 7.30am. It must have been the thought of winning a Test series or perhaps the excitement of knowing tonight would be celebration time that had me awake so early.

When play was about to start, our worst nightmares appeared about to be realised, as patchy rain was coming down. However, it ceased just before the scheduled starting time arrived, and play began on time. The first half hour went England's way, with Stewart extremely lucky to escape being given out caught behind off Hughes, probably the first mistake these two extremely good umpires, Nigel Plews and Dickie Bird, have made between them. But then Reiffel took the vital first wicket of the day, having Thorpe caught at first slip by Taylor. Two balls later, Pistol enticed Stewart to cut at a ball too close to his stumps, and saw Mark Waugh, at second slip, hold on to a miraculous one-handed catch. The ball was already two feet past Junior when he grabbed it. They say catches win matches, and I'm sure this one squeezed the last bit of life out of England.

Merv claimed his 200th Test wicket shortly afterwards, only the seventh Australian ever to achieve the feat. With the "big fella" in a celebratory mood, the next batsman, Bicknell, obviously expected a "rib tickler" first up. He found out too late he had chosen the wrong option, as he ducked an attempted yorker and was plumb LBW — a dismissal he won't want his grandkids to ever see.

With the lunch-time score at 8-279, all the guys packed their gear away to save it from being drenched in champagne and beer when we returned after the final wicket. The Cold Chisel CD was placed next to the "ghetto blaster", in readiness for *Khe Sanh* to be played. It's a song which blares out after each Australian victory.

After lunch, the team made its way out of the dressing room and onto the field with

The Test and Ashes have just been won, and the team waits for the presentations. Missing is Allan Border, preparing to go on the balcony and collect the winner's cheque and the man-of-the-match award. At back (left to right): Hayden, Reiffel, Martyn, M. Waugh, Tony Smith (baggage handler), Julian, Zoehrer, Des Rundle (manager), Warne, Holdsworth, S. Waugh. Front: Boon, Taylor, Slater, Hughes, May, Simpson.

Status Quo's *Down Down Deeper and Down* playing — a song that symbolised our hopes for the England side. The ninth wicket was taken shortly afterwards with probably the best ball of the Test — a Merv Hughes leg-cutter that crashed into McCague's off stump. With the rain clouds ever-present, we are all keen to wrap the game up as quickly as we could, and England's number 11 batsman, Mark Ilott, duly obliged by skying a ball off Tim May which I later found out was caught by AB. At the time the catch was taken, I was uprooting one of the stumps to keep as a souvenir of the occasion.

Immediately the celebrations began. All the guys congratulated each other and, at the same time, commiserated with the opposition, and in particular Gooch, who has shouldered most of the blame for their heavy defeats. It had just been announced to the press that he was stepping down from the captaincy, but would play on if selected. After the formalities of accepting the Ashes and responding to all our supporters from the players' balcony, it was back to our rooms for some real celebrating. What started out to be a tame affair turned ugly in a matter of seconds, after the press photographers asked for a bit of action, which came in the form of two cartons of XXXX being sprayed over everyone in the room within 30 seconds. After letting off steam for about 20 minutes, it was time for Boonie to lead us into the team song, which was sung with such pride and fervour on this occasion that it brought goosebumps to the skin.

Afterwards, all the players sat around in a circle and chatted. We were trying to take in what we have achieved and what it means not only to us but to everyone who supports cricket back in Australia. It's moments like these, when the camaraderie is so evident, that you wish time would stand still. These occasions only happen once or twice in a cricketer's lifetime.

The festivities continued back at the team hotel, where a room had been set aside for us, with the necessary amounts of food and drink available. As the night wore on the music got louder and the lads rowdier, and Merv was the victim of a mauling from the rest of the team as payback for all those years of torment he has inflicted on everyone.

Later on, the celebrations moved to a local nightclub, where the evening ended, after a chicken kebab dinner followed by a lift home in a police van for Tubs and me. We had been unable to track our hotel down and were wandering in a hazardous part of town.

MARK TAYLOR CAN'T BOWL!

DAY 94 (July 27)

I WOKE up feeling a little parched in the throat region, and promised myself I'd never drink again ... at least until we won again!

The 12 o'clock departure time for the bus proved to be far too elusive for Maysie and me. We preferred a later departure via one of the team cars, and arrived in Manchester around 3pm, after a meal of fish and chips at "Harry Ramsden's", somewhat of an institution in the north of England. The rest of the afternoon and evening was a very quiet affair, as we tried to recuperate in time for tomorrow's fixture against Lancashire. My only venture out of the room was a quest for a meal at the pub next door to the hotel.

DAY 95 (July 28)

SPECULATION WAS rife in this morning's papers as to who is going to be the next England captain. Atherton is the firm favourite, followed by Gatting and Stewart, with the outsiders being Kim Barnett, Martyn Moxon and Hugh Morris. If Atherton gets the nod, I believe it will be too early for him, as he is just cementing his own position in the side. And, from playing against him, I don't know whether he will be able to inspire the other players around him, although captaincy may bring out qualities in him that aren't evident now.

Down at the ground, play was unable to begin until 12 o'clock due to the wicket-square being wet from constant rain over the past week. However, the strip for our match was bone dry. Taylor went out to toss with his good health and well-being under threat if he returned with any news other than we were batting. Fortunately there was good news for Tubs' wife and kid, as the coin landed kindly for him. The dressing room erupted, with all the bowlers suddenly enjoying a new lease of life as they realised they would get at least a day's rest before they were required to participate.

The opening combination of Hayden and Taylor safely negotiated the remaining time before lunch. Matt had acquired a new nickname overnight, after the lads went to see *Jurassic Park*. They quickly recognised the similarity between a dinosaur's body and Matt's, in that they have a huge torso with a not so large melon — hence the new nickname, "Jurassic". I watched the next two sessions of cricket from the comfort of the change rooms, where Warney made an assault on the world record for the most plates of french fries in a day, with plate five being devoured shortly before tea. The scoreline at the end of the day showed Mark Taylor had helped himself to a century and Damien Martyn remained unbeaten on 70, with the total at 3-282.

I left the ground straight after the completion of play to meet Lynette at Nelson (40 minutes' drive away), and catch up with some friends from my Lancashire League days.

DAY 96 (July 29)

TO BREAK the monotony of doing the normal warm-up and stretching routine, a game of touch football was organised between the Julios and Nerds. But we Nerds were one player short, as well as having Boonie, who was unable to stretch out because of a sore knee, and the game turned into a one-sided affair. Our team did more miles than the Leyland Brothers, and ended up being thrashed 6-2. So much for a pleasant change — I was absolutely knackered for the start of the day, which found us fielding after an overnight declaration.

The morning session turned out to be a frustrating one with the ball continually beating the bat, which prompted a comment from our 12th man, Brendon Julian, that "they couldn't nick a TV in the Los Angeles riots". By the time tea was taken, Lancashire had progressed to 7-220, and a whisper was about that they intended to declare about 20 minutes after the interval.

Tubs saw this situation as the opportunity to capture his second wicket on tour and claim his winnings off his tormentor (Patrick Keane, journalist), who had inflamed the situation by positioning a large banner on the grandstand stating in bold print: "MARK TAYLOR CAN'T BOWL". With Tubs set to win 100 pounds, and myself 250 pounds, the unthinkable happened. A Taylor long hop was smacked to cover where I initially went the wrong way, and ended up spilling the chance — to the disbelief of Tubs and the mirth of Patrick, who couldn't hide his joy from the sidelines, and handed out a bevy of abuse at the missed opportunity. My distress over not winning the bet will pale into insignificance compared with the castigation I'll receive from Tubs for the rest of my playing days, or at least until he claims his initial first-class wicket — an unlikely feat.

To cap the day off, I lost my wicket for 17 with 10 minutes of play remaining, after an attempted cover drive deflected the ball back onto my stumps. At stumps, Lancashire were 85 runs in arrears with eight of our second-innings wickets in hand. Tomorrow promises to be an interesting day's play.

Being an international cricketer is never dull.

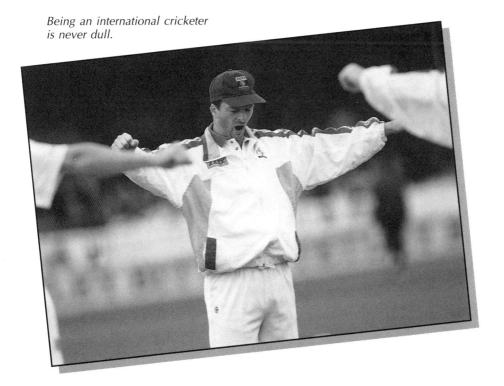

DAY 97 (July 30)

SIMMO RAN the team through a fielding drill this morning which was of a high quality, but unfortunately during the routine Tubs, in trying to pick a ball up on the run, slipped and fell heavily, doing damage to his knee and leaving some nasty divots in the turf.

Our batting performance in the morning session turned out to be, with the exception of Hayden's 78, one of our worst efforts on tour. We finished at 8 declared for 194, leaving the home team to chase 228 runs off 62 overs.

When we arrived on the field, I noticed the "Mark Taylor Can't Bowl" sign had been replaced by a "Steve Waugh Can't Catch" sign. I suspect it was erected by Taylor overnight, as a backlash to yesterday's debacle.

The locals then came out blazing, with John Crawley in particular looking as good a player as we have come across in England on this tour. At tea, Lancashire were 1-105, and, after the break, it soon became apparent we needed some sort of miracle to avoid our first first-class loss of the tour.

Then, for a short while, the Lancashire innings resembled a Queensland run chase as a couple of quick wickets fell. But they eventually regained their composure to record a memorable (for them) victory, and the crowd behaved as if they'd just won the World Cup and the Ashes all in one. The result has left a nasty taste in our mouths, but in the long run it may be good for us, just as a reminder that we can't afford to relax.

Luckily for myself, I won't be around when the interview I did for the *Manchester Evening News* comes out tomorrow, as I said at lunch-time we were sure things and no chance of losing today!

Having played the last six games in a row, it is my turn for a game off, so I'm leaving the guys for three days. They are making the long drive to Neath, in South Wales, tonight as another game starts in the morning. Lynette and I have decided to spend the next three days in London. Predictably, we became lost after missing the turnoff for the M6 on our way south, which extended the journey by an hour.

DAY 98 (July 31)

AS EXPECTED, Lancashire grabbed the headlines this morning, even relegating the appointment of the new England captain, Michael Atherton, to the inside back page.

We spent a lazy morning wandering around town doing some window shopping and not thinking about cricket, which made for a nice change. Upon returning to the room, I couldn't help but check on the team's progress at Neath and found out that Boonie has recorded yet another century, his ninth on tour, which equals Bill Lawry's feat of 1961 and leaves him four short of the immortal Don Bradman's 13 centuries from only 26 innings in 1938. Mark Waugh obviously had some fun as well in compiling a rapid 152 not out, including eight sixes, as the team approached 400 runs shortly after tea.

With Maysie and Tubs out of town, they'll never know that Lynette and I went to the Bombay Brasserie for dinner. The Indian cuisine has gradually grown on me to the point I'm actually enjoying it, but there's no way I can admit it to those two. They'd never let me have a moment's peace after all the abuse I've given them over the years about the amount of time they spend in Indian restaurants.

DAY 99 (August 1)

THE CHANCE of another sleep-in was not missed, especially as the day in store for me revolved around a bit of sight-seeing. First stop was Speaker's Corner in Hyde Park, where anyone who has something important to say or preach can do so, just by standing on a soap box and putting his or her point of view across to the large crowds that gather there every Sunday.

From there we walked in the park, where the Poms were having a day out in the sun, with deck chairs available at 50 pence if you want to work on your suntan while you laze about. Next stop was Bayswater Road, where artists display their works and are pretty successful judging by the amount of cash the Japanese tour parties seemed to be throwing about.

The sight-seeing tour came to a grinding halt as lunch was sought, and McDonald's came to the rescue. This was the end of my hunger and my tour of London. The evening was spent at the team's regular haunt on the '89 Ashes tour, the Break for the Border Mexican restaurant, which came up trumps again with a great feed.

DAY 100 (August 2)

THE BIG news of the day was undoubtedly the naming of the next English Test XII. Three changes have been made, and the new members are Devon Malcolm, Steve Watkin and Matthew Maynard, all fine choices who will add some aggression and fire to the side. The unfortunate three are Lathwell, Caddick and McCague, with Caddick the unluckiest. I feel he has great potential, but lacked guidance in the first four Tests and would thrive under a new regime. However, probably the unluckiest omission of all remains Graeme Hick, who we felt was just running into form when he was dropped. I'm sure he'll be a much better player when he returns to international cricket in the near future.

A lack of exercise over the past week has seen me pile on a few excess kilos, so during the day I spent some time in the gym trying to burn some calories off.

Glamorgan skid as Warne hits brakes

By GRAHAM CLUTTON

GLAMORGAN failed in their bid to become only the second side this summer to inflict defeat on the Australian tourists yesterday.

But the ebullient Welsh county managed to force a draw against the Aussies, who tomorrow travel to Edgbaston for the fifth instalment of their Ashes battle with England.

Having been set a realistic target of 287 in 59 overs, the Welsh county slipped to 96-4 and then abandoned the run-chase as the Aussies warmed up for Thursday's Test with a much more polished bowling display.

The tourists had bowled without too much passion, and subsequently without too much success, in the first innings as Glamorgan reached 363-8 declared on Saturday evening and Sunday.

But with the Tetley Bitter prize money up for grabs yesterday afternoon, they performed with much greater aplomb, and denied the Welsh county any real chance of emulating Lancashire's victory at Old Trafford last week.

Glamorgan's hopes of carving out a victory with a side which included two teenage debutants rested on the shoulders of Matthew Maynard, recalled to the England squad.

Problems

But the 27-year-old run-reaper, who had spent the morning basking in the glow of his Test recall, was unable to provide a repeat of his first innings century.

Having made 36 in 55 balls, a modest tally in his book, he was comprehensively bowled by Wayne Holdsworth. And with his dismissal at 92-3 went any realistic chance of a Glamorgan victory.

Glamorgan's problems had begun as early as the third over when skipper Hugh Morris (2) flashed at a wide delivery from Holdsworth and found David Boon waiting at gully.

And with the score stuck on eight, fellow opener James Williams (6) gave Boon another gully catch, this time off the bowling of Merv Hughes.

Maynard and Adrian Dale did provide some entertainment during their 84-run third-wicket partnership.

However, the bowling arrival of leg-spinner Shane Warne at 60-2 off 12 overs slowed things down, and the ensuing 10 overs produced just 18 runs.

With overs obviously an important consideration, Maynard set about upping the rate, and he paid the ultimate cost when playing around a straight delivery from Holdsworth that knocked back his middle stump.

Dale then edged a near unplayable delivery from Warne to wicket-keeper Ian Healy, and suddenly Glamorgan were staring straight down the barrel of another Aussie win.

But with the wicket getting slower and lower, David Hemp and Anthony Cottey eased the danger for an hour before the former shouldered arms to Warne and found himself bowled for 16.

And after Cottey had reached 38, he top-edged a sweep off Allan Border straight into the hands of square leg.

That was the last wicket to fall, however, and Glamorgan will feel relatively pleased that a side minus five first-choice players achieved what England have managed only once in four attempts so far this summer.

When the rain came to curtail proceedings in the final hour, Glamorgan had mustered 169-6 and had denied the Aussies another success.

GLAMORGAN v AUSTRALIA
Neath Match Drawn
Overnight: Australia 414-4 dec (M E Waugh 152 no, D C Boon 120, M J Slater 72) & 146-4. Glamorgan 363-8 dec (M P Maynard 132, P A Cottey 96; S K Warne 4-67)

Australia Second Innings Cont
P R Reiffel c & b Thomas............32
M G Hughes b Dale.....................71
A R Border b Dale......................23
M E Waugh not out......................2
D C Boon not out........................2
Extras lbl..................................5
Total 7 wkts dec......................225
Fall: 1-37 2-45 3-65 4-100 5-176 6-213 7-231
Bowling: Thomas 18-2-95-3 Bastien 10-0-31-0 Dale 9-0-41-2 Croft 12-2-46-1 Phelps 3-0-17-0

Glamorgan Second Innings
J R A Williams c Boon b Hughes.....6
H Morris c Boon b Holdsworth.......2
A Dale c Healy b Warne..............31
M P Maynard b Holdsworth..........36
P A Cottey c Martyn b Border.......38
D L Hemp b Warne....................16
R D B Croft not out...................11
C P Metson not out....................7
Extras b1 lb12 w1 nb8................22
Total 6 wkts............................169
Fall: 1-8 2-8 3-92 4-96 5-132 6-159
Bowling: Hughes 7-3-22-1 Holdsworth 12-2-45-2 Reiffel 10-1-34-0 Warne 17-3-44-2 Border 5-3-12-1

HUGHES HEAVE-HO: Merv Hughes despatches another delivery out of the ground during his big-hitting innings at the Gnoll *Picture by TREVOR WATERS*

DAY 101 (August 3)

WHEN I arrived at Edgbaston today and inspected the Test wicket, I couldn't believe our luck. It looked to be one of the driest wickets I've seen, which should suit our spinners and not their attack of four pacemen and one spinner. I can't wait to see England manager Keith Fletcher's face when he takes a look at the prepared strip, as he has been whingeing all week in the papers about groundsmen preparing wickets to suit our bowlers and not the home attack. On this occasion they haven't let him down. I'm sure England will be forced to call in another spinner to their squad to make the most of the conditions. The two most obvious candidates are Phil Tufnell and Ian Salisbury.

The team had a fairly relaxed training session, with everyone looking in good touch, especially Slats, who is hitting the ball so well. I put the question to Paul Reiffel: "Has this bloke (Slats) got any weaknesses?"

To which he replied: "Yeah, alcohol!"

A fair answer if you saw his batting at Lancashire after the Headingley Test celebrations.

The only serious worries in the camp are May, who has a slight tear in the hamstring which will hopefully be stable enough to allow him to play (he'll be vital to our success here), and Julian, who aggravated his groin strain while fielding at Glamorgan. The other minor worries are Taylor, whose leg strain looks like being nearly 100 per cent by match day, and Hughes, who has a groin strain and various other ailments from non-stop cricket. But I'm sure the big fella would have to be hospitalised to miss a Test match.

Back in the dressing room, all the guys made sure they were sitting in exactly the same positions as we were when we won the second one-day international here two months ago — just for good luck and a touch of superstition.

One of the benefits of being on such a tour is the chance to play at top-class golf courses and today we've been invited to play at The Belfry, the venue of next month's Ryder Cup (a bi-annual classic between the best golfers from Europe and the United States). After my previous two efforts on the golf course, I was close to disposing of my sticks, but today's effort has renewed my enthusiasm for the game. Heals and I turned in a blinder to fleece the club pro and his partner of their pride and cash.

The highlight for me was at the par four 18th hole. I had mishit my tee shot, and been told by the pro I couldn't reach the green from there and to lay up short of the water. Upon reaching the ball, I found it was lying in a divot hole on a sloping lie. With Heals out of the hole after finding the drink three times, the opposition lying in a good position, and the cash for the back nine holes up for grabs, Heals dared me to go for the green with a three wood. The key to my decision was the fact that Heals was prepared to drop his daks and reveal the birthday suit if my ball ended up on the green! With that added encouragement, the ball whistled off the club and immediately Heals reached for his fly. The ball sailed into the heart of the green and the rest of the story is for me to know and you to find out!

I had to rush back to the hotel as dinner had been organised with Dad, who is over here to watch Mark and me play in a Test together overseas. It would be nice if we could both make some runs here to make his journey worthwhile as this is the only Test he will get to see before going back to his newsagency at home. Dad is probably our biggest supporter, although he can be a little one-eyed when he watches the cricket. It would be great if we could both score hundreds, although that's probably hoping for a bit much as Dad believes he's a jinx whenever he watches us play.

DAY 102 (August 4)

IT MADE a nice change to have a roomie (Slats) who doesn't snore loudly, as it gave me a chance to get a decent night's sleep. The morning's paper revealed that England has called up John Emburey into their team, which is somewhat of a shock as he is just two weeks away from his 41st birthday. His selection hardly enforces the new youth policy the English selectors have promised.

Training was more intense today, as is the norm the day before a Test. There were quite a few spectators there to watch the net session and get some autographs. One of the more demanding spectators wanted a photo of Merv, and requested him to smile, to which Merv replied: "Why, is it raining?"

Practice confirmed that our injury worries have subsided with Maysie almost certain to play even though he's not quite 100 per cent. His presence will be vital to the outcome of the game.

The afternoon was spent with Lynette, who is staying at a hotel only 100 metres away from ours. The girls aren't allowed to stay with the team until the next match.

The pre-match team meeting took place at 6.30pm. The emphasis was put on the need for us not to relax at all and push even harder for victory, because if the two team's positions were reversed the Poms would be trying to crush us in the same manner we are attempting to do to them now. The team is the same XII as last Test, with Zoehrer on standby for May if he pulls up sore tomorrow morning. Everyone left the meeting in high spirits, with the feeling among the team being that we are going to win the series 5-0 and go home the most successful team ever to tour the United Kingdom.

The social committee, obviously encouraged by their fine choice at the last team dinner, once again did some searching and came up trumps with an American-style eatery that not only provided excellent food but an extensive range of cocktails which were sampled by the lads and given the seal of approval.

Allan Border, preparing for the fifth Test of the summer, at Edgbaston.

THE FIFTH TEST

DAY 103 (August 5)

AS BOTH sides inspected the wicket upon arriving at the ground, it was obvious, just from talking to some of the English bowlers, that they already had a negative attitude about the way the wicket would play and were almost expecting to cop a hiding. Maysie made himself available, a great boost for us, as I'm sure he and Warney will have a major impact on the outcome of the game.

The choice of ball for the Test was once again undecided. The English team changed their minds and wanted to use Reader balls instead of Duke balls, while our bowlers have gone off Readers and now prefer Duke balls. A toss of the coin was needed to decide the outcome, and when AB called correctly and nominated the Dukes, we felt we had another slight psychological edge before the game gets under way.

The second toss of the morning was won by Mike Atherton, who elected to bat on a wicket that should suit the batsmen for the first couple of days. Gooch, back opening and always a vital wicket, was taken early by Reiffel, who is bowling with confidence and rhythm, a bowler's two most important elements. Smith was next to go, courtesy of an off-cutter from Mark Waugh, and then Maynard, in his return to Test cricket, was caught in close off May's bowling for 0, which handed the initiative to us. The lunchtime total of 3-93 was definitely a score we would have accepted before the game started.

After lunch, Atherton continued to lead from the front, and appeared set for a big one. He teamed up with Alec Stewart, who, for the first time this series, looked as if he'd decided to play with a positive attitude. Runs were coming quickly, especially from the leg-spinner, until Stewart departed, caught-and-bowled to Warney in a "soft" dismissal that swung the balance back in our favour. This wicket was particularly important, as it ended a spell where, for the first time in the series, two of England's batsmen had got on top of Warney. There had been a stage where you could see their confidence increasing as each ball was negotiated.

The next two English wickets fell in the space of three balls, with Reiffel bowling Atherton for 72 and Hussain for three, the latter falling to one of the deliveries of the series — a superb leg-cutter that clipped the top of the off stump and must have almost prompted Geoff Boycott to give some praise to the skills of a bowler.

Some people, including myself, doubted the selection of John Emburey before the game, but in the next two-and-a-half hours of play he changed my mind. He was one of the few English batsmen this series who put a high price on his wicket and he made us work extremely hard to get him out, something we couldn't manage today. The wickets that did fall before stumps were Thorpe, who played very well until he flashed needlessly at a wide ball and was held by the ever-dependable and much underrated Healy, and Bicknell and Such, who fell to Reiffel in consecutive balls to give him another five-wicket haul. Pistol's was an outstanding performance considering he didn't play a lot of cricket up until the last Test.

Heals is a man who comes out with some great one-liners during the day's play, such as "let's see if we can't get one (a wicket) before stumps," when we have three-and-a-half hours of play left, or, using reverse psychology, "come on lads, they've got us right where they want us", and his most renowned line, "c'mon the emus!" The emu is a symbol we have adopted as the team's.

The end of day one saw England at 9-276, which represents a great day for us. But we must capitalise with our batting and score in excess of 400.

Dinner was at one of the popular fast-food chain outlets, Pizza Hut, which has been frequented by all of the players on more than one occasion this tour, and possesses two of the most important pre-requisites of a meal — speed and cheapness.

The old and the new. England captain Mike Atherton, and his predecessor Graham Gooch, at Edgbaston.

DAY 104 (August 6)

UNDER OMINOUS looking skies, the last English wicket fell to Reiffel, giving him six wickets, the first Australian ever to achieve this feat at Edgbaston. However, we were soon in trouble, and for only the second time this series, found ourselves under pressure. By lunch we had lost Slater for 22 and Boon for 0, both falling victim to the turning ball, on a wicket that was consistently suggesting there will be a result before the five days are up.

After lunch the atmosphere in the dressing room became a little edgy. Taylor was run out, after momentarily believing he was Carl Lewis and falling victim to the third umpire by a few centimetres. AB followed shortly afterwards, caught at first slip off a turning ball from Such, bringing me to the wicket with the crowd and English team sensing a victory.

The third delivery I faced may have been the turning point of the match. I danced down the wicket to Such, but yorked myself and gave Stewart a stumping chance. We would have been five wickets down and 196 runs behind, but such is the nature of the game that when you are down you never seem to make the most of these types of opportunities. The ball bounced out of Stewart's gloves — giving me a reprieve I didn't expect.

From that point a much-needed partnership between the two Waughs began to take shape. Mark was the more dominant partner, striking the ball nicely, while I endeavoured to locate the middle of the bat — something that eluded me for the first two hours of my innings. But, at that stage of the game, occupation of the crease was vital, and by tea-time we had consolidated our position to be 4-153. The game was back on an even keel, with the last session crucial to both sides.

The England side today decided to try a new tactic to unsettle the batsmen in the form of sledging. It was something, to be quite truthful, that I enjoyed, as it made me more determined to be there at the end of the day.

Mark continued in an aggressive mood after tea and brought up his century, to the delight of Dad who is sitting in the Members' Stand. This surely ended the notion that he jinxes us every time he watches us play. The only problem that arose in our partnership was our running between the wickets. We were involved in two mid-wicket collisions — so much for the theory that we have ESP!

Having said that, I couldn't believe it when Mark was caught behind square, off Ilott,

The English fieldsman celebrate the fall of the Australian captain, caught at slip by Hussain off Such, as our score slumps to 4-80 in reply to England's 276. But the next Australian wicket would not fall until the total was 233.

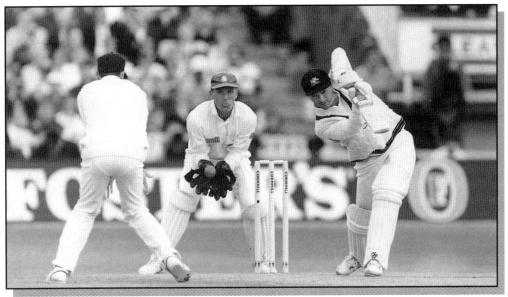

Ever watchful during my crucial partnership with Mark. The keeper is Alec Stewart.

with 15 minutes to go to stumps. I had a premonition the ball before that he was going to get out that way, which ended a superb innings and a 153-run partnership, our first century stand in Test cricket.

The last quarter hour was safely negotiated by Heals and me. By stumps, I'd been in the middle for almost four hours. It certainly wasn't my most fluent innings, but I was extremely happy with my concentration which has sometimes been a problem for me.

After concentrating for so long, I felt like nothing more than grabbing a quick feed with Lynette, which turned out to be Italian — with a surprise. Directly behind my seat was Martin Bicknell, a guy with whom I had shared quite an in-depth conversation in the middle, earlier in the day.

149

DAY 105 (August 7)

I SPENT a restless night, thinking about my job today, which was to try and get a big score for myself, and to make sure the team gained a substantial lead.

However, my overnight total had only increased by two, to 59, when I was the victim of one of the worst decisions of my Test career, and probably the most frustrating. I was given out, caught behind, but didn't get near the ball. I had spent four hours yesterday working hard to get the team into a good position, and suddenly the game was in the balance again.

However, Healy and Hughes, two of the hard men of the side, came together for a crucial stand. Healy played an innings of class, reaching 80 in quick time before falling with two minutes to go before lunch. Hughes was then unbeaten on 34, and the lead was 94, which could prove to be match-winning. After the break, vital contributions from our tail of Reiffel, Warne and May, all of whom are more than useful players, enabled us to have a 132-run advantage. With the prospect of the wicket suiting our spin bowlers over the next couple of days, we have another victory in our sights.

Such ended up being the pick of the English bowlers, taking 3 for 90 off 52.5 overs. But I felt both he and Emburey bowled too straight and didn't make use of the rough outside the line of the off stump. Consequently the ball didn't turn as much as it could have.

Gooch and Atherton began cautiously, before the latter was caught bat-pad. This was an important breakthrough, as Atherton has held the English innings together quite a few times this series. Smith then struggled through to stumps, but still seems unable to find the technique necessary to combat the turning ball. Gooch, England's best player of spin, remains at the other end, but, if he is dismissed early tomorrow, we should win comfortably. Even though England are 1-89 at stumps, there is no sign of panic in the camp. The feeling is that if we can get that early wicket, the others will come a lot easier.

After a quiet evening meal with Dad, I was greeted, upon entering my room, with the now customary pile of mail and messages addressed to Mark Waugh and Shane Warne. One in particular epitomised the continual mix-ups we have encountered, as it was sent to my room with Mark's name on it, and contained a message for Warney from his fiancee.

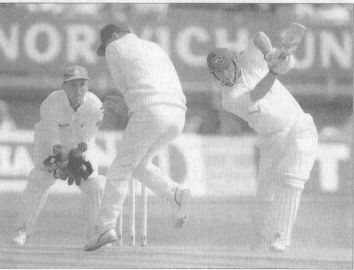

As Australia counter-attack fiercely, Atherton's men are plunged back into the old familiar trouble

Healy piles on England agony

Vic Marks at Edgbaston

Beefing it up: Thorpe leaps for safety as the belligerent Healy, watched by Stewart, blasts a drive. / Photograph by Adrian Murrell

Hughes, bowled Bicknell, but only after his stand with Ian Healy had given Australia a significant first-innings lead.

DAY 106 (August 8)

THE MOST important session of the game began well for us. Robin Smith was given out LBW to Warney after not being able to pick his "flipper" — a ball that comes out of the front of the hand and skids low. The decision appeared to be a fortunate one for us, as the ball looked as if it might have missed the off stump, but at least it put Smithy out of his misery. He still has no idea how to combat our spinners, a major factor in the scorelines of the series.

Worse was to follow for England, as Warney produced a phenomenal delivery to Gooch. This one landed almost two feet wide of the leg stump and was not even considered threatening by Gooch, who watched it pass by then spin back almost at right angles to clip the top of the leg stump. That one ball must have shattered the confidence of the remaining English batsmen, who had just seen the demise of their best batsman to a truly freakish delivery.

I must admit I was very glad to see the end of Smith and Gooch, as the position of silly mid-on, which I was occupying, is a terrifying experience when they are about. They both possess bats that weigh over three pounds (the average weight of a bat is two pound, eight ounces), hit the ball as hard as any player in the world, and continually intimidate you with shots that threaten to pulverise your body if you are in their flight path.

Gooch has been the linch-pin of the English side all tour. As soon as he has been dismissed, the Englishmen have tended to lose their way. On this occasion his fall precipitated a middle-order collapse, with Maynard, Stewart and Hussain all falling before lunch to some superb bowling from May and Warne which was backed up by a team going in for the kill. The only stumbling block for the session proved to be a fruit platter thrown by a disgruntled spectator. It showered the head of Tim May, positioned on the deep mid-wicket fence, which delighted the crowd, especially after it became obvious that a Granny Smith had found his forehead.

Graham Thorpe and John Emburey dug in after lunch, and showed some fight in a determined partnership that frustrated us to the tune of 104 invaluable runs stretching over 200 minutes of play. But, after Emburey's dismissal, the remaining batsmen fell quickly. Merv once again terrified Peter Such with the short delivery, a ball which will undoubtedly cause him sleepless nights during the forthcoming West Indies tour, while May and Warne continued to bowl magnificently in tandem, a performance that will be talked about in years to come. Their figures read: May — 48.2 overs, 5 for 89; Warne — 49 overs, 5 for 82.

We were left with a target of 120, with the rain our only danger, and Taylor and Slater reduced the chase to 111 by stumps.

The most interesting statistic of the day comes from our XXXX representative, who informed the lads we have now consumed or spilt an average of 900 cans per player. Not bad considering a few of the guys aren't great beer drinkers!!

Above: Ian Healy rushes to congratulate Shane Warne after the remarkable dismissal of Graham Gooch, bowled by a leg-break that pitched at least two feet wide of the leg stump, and left the English press lamenting the likely loss of the fifth Test.

Atherton needs a miracle now

By DAVID LLOYD
Press Association

THE loser's speech, carried as an item of standard equipment by England captains these days, was still in Mike Atherton's back pocket last night.

But, barring severe weather interference or a cricketing miracle of 1981 proportions, new skipper Atherton is only a few hours away from his first inquest appearance.

Graham Gooch knew the lines off by heart well before he quit at Headingley a fortnight ago.

And it is hard to imagine Atherton coming up with anything much different to, "Australia outplayed us — again."

But for some spirited afternoon resistance from Graham Thorpe and John Emburey, the fifth Cornhill Test at Edgbaston would be done and dusted by now.

As it is, Australia are left needing another 111 runs with all their second innings wickets in hand to make the series score 4-0.

That would equal the thrashing they handed out here in 1989. And only a supreme England optimist would bet much money against them going one better by winning at The Oval as well.

Add Australia's 3-0 triumph in 1990-91, and the Ashes 'contest' has become one of sport's least competitive events. Even Cambridge win the Boat Race occasionally.

England's last Test victory against the old enemy came 19 matches, and nearly seven years, ago. Not that defeats are inflicted only by Australia, of course.

In 10 Tests against four different opponents during the past 12 months, England have lost nine and drawn the other.

Any realistic hopes of that dismal record being repaired, effectively disappeared in the space of 13 pre-lunch overs when five wickets fell for just 21 runs.

England, having resumed 43 behind on 89 for one, were torn apart by spinners Shane Warne and Tim May.

Robin Smith's departure was only a matter of time. If possible, he looked even less comfortable than on Saturday evening, and fell lbw to Warne during the morning's ninth over.

It seemed as though the ball would have missed off-stump, but umpire John Hampshire's decision was a kind one on humanitarian grounds.

Matthew Maynard avoided a 'pair', but made only ten before he edged a forward defensive shot against May.

But the real killer blow came courtesy of another Warne wonder ball. If Mike Gatting is still suffering nightmares over that outrageous delivery at Old Trafford during the first Test, Gooch can now sympathise.

Having added only four to his overnight 44, the opener was left bewildered as Warne, going round the wicket, spun a ball back from nearly two feet outside leg-stump to hit the inside of middle.

Alec Stewart (5) soon followed, adjudged lbw to Warne, while Nasser Hussain (0) prodded May — via pad and bat — to silly point.

At that stage, with England still seven runs away from avoiding an innings defeat, the Birmingham faithful were dreading a result before lunch. Their gratitude to Thorpe and Emburey grew and grew during a 200-minute alliance for the seventh wicket which put to shame those earlier efforts.

Incredibly, it was the longest partnership in time terms that England had managed this series, and only their fifth century stand.

It finally came to an end on 104 when Allan Border, after a brief flirtation with his pacemen, recalled the spinners.

May's first ball concluded Emburey's valiant 37, Healy snapping up an edge. Two deliveries later, Martin Bicknell fell into the pad-bat trap.

And, with the score still 229, Thorpe — having made a fine 60 in nearly four hours — slogged at Warne and was comfortably stumped.

That gave Warne his 29th victim of the series, equalling Clarrie Grimmett's record Ashes haul for leg-spinners in 1930. But it was fitting that May should finish with five wickets as well in this innings, and he made sure of that by bowling last man Mark Ilott.

For the fourth time in ten attempts this summer, England had failed to total 300.

SCOREBOARD

ENGLAND v AUSTRALIA
Edgbaston
Overnight: England 276 (M A Atherton 72, J E Emburey 55 no; P R Reiffel 6-71) & 89-1. Australia 408 (M E Waugh 137, I A Healy 80, S R Waugh 59)

England Second Innings Cont
G A Gooch b Warne	48
*R A Smith lbw b Warne	19
M P Maynard c Healy b May	10
A J Stewart lbw b Warne	5
G P Thorpe st Healy b Warne	60
N Hussain c S R Waugh b May	0
J E Emburey c Healy b May	37
M P Bicknell c S R Waugh b May	0
P M Such not out	7
M C Ilott b May	15
Extras b11 lb9 nb2	22
Total	251

Fall: 1-60 2-104 3-115 4-115 5-124 6-125 7-229 8-229 9-229
Bowling: Hughes 18- 7- 24- 0 Reiffel 11-2- 30- 0 May 48.2- 15- 89- 5 Warne 49- 23-89- 5 Border 2- 1- 1- 0 M E Waugh 5- 2- 5- 0

Australia Second Innings
M J Slater not out	7
M A Taylor not out	2
Extras	0
Total 0 wkt	9

Bowling: Bicknell 2- 0- 6- 0 Such 3- 1- 3- 0
Emburey 1- 1- 0- 0

BOWLED OVER: Wicketkeeper Ian Healy celebrates England opener Graham Gooch's dismissal at Edgbaston, bowled behind his legs by Shane Warne for 48

DAY 107 (August 9)

I COULDN'T believe my eyes when I opened the curtains this morning. It looked as if the end of the world was about to happen. Leaden skies were all around, heavy rain was falling, and the prospect of play today appeared very slim.

Down at the ground, the Botham Test at Headingley in 1981 was being played on the BBC for the 105th time this season, obviously in the faint hope that it might inspire the Englishmen to perform similar deeds today. But rain was not to be their saviour, as the weather improved dramatically in the two hours between getting up and arriving at the ground, and play began on time to our great relief.

Early on it appeared the Botham miracle might have lifted the English. Taylor and Slater were out for the addition of only three runs, which sent a minor scare through our camp. However, this was our only moment of worry for the day, as Boon and Mark Waugh professionally set about the target and accomplished it with ease, 15 minutes after lunch. In the process, they posted a century stand, which they have achieved in every Test so far in the series, another milestone for the side.

But the biggest milestone of all awaits us at the final Test at The Oval, where we will have the opportunity to become the first Australian touring team to ever defeat England 5-0 in a Test series.

With England now 4-0 down after five Tests, and their whole cricket system being scrutinised in an effort to come up with some answers to their poor form in recent times, the chairman of the England cricket selection committee, Ted Dexter, announced today that he was stepping down from that position at the end of the current series. He blamed public pressure and a vote of no confidence from many of the county clubs' chairmen.

The celebrations in our room were rather subdued compared to Headingley, probably because victory today was a formality. The team is looking ahead to sixth Test, where it will be mayhem if we win. However, the bus trip to London tonight saw the party atmosphere start to engulf us, as the alcohol began to flow freely, and the frivolity continued unabated until the bus pulled into the Westbury. With the girls now able to stay in the same hotel, everyone met at the local watering hole, the Windmill, where the festivities continued until the early hours of the morning. It seems certain there will be some nasty hangovers in the morning.

PLAYING FROM MEMORY

DAY 108 (August 10)

A LOUD knock on the door this morning, followed by the arrival of the breakfast trolley, woke me from a semi-comatose state. I felt as if I'd had five minutes sleep after being run over by a Mack truck. More bad news soon arrived, as Lynette informed me that today was the sponsor's golf day and the bus was due to leave in 30 minutes — surely not enough time to make the sort of recovery needed to survive 18 holes of golf. The only consolation I had came when I entered the bus and realised AB was in an even more delicate state, as was Maysie, who looked rather pale.

The 45-minute journey was negotiated without the bus having to pull off the road for any emergencies. But the speed humps on the road leading to the clubhouse proved to be my undoing, and my condition rapidly disintegrated to the point where I had to leap out of the bus and hide in the members' toilets until I regained my composure.

The idea of the sponsor's day is for players to join forces with three representatives from the sponsor to form a team, with the sponsor's people always desperate to put up a good showing. So I was not surprised that my group didn't look all that pleased when I rocked up to the first hole with two bottles of water in my bag and no colour in my face. My first shot was a worry — it must have been about five years since my previous air swing but the odds on a repeat were quite short. However, the toe of the club made contact with the ball and it scurried off into the rough, giving me the necessary confidence to manage a bogey five.

Amazingly, after five holes of playing by memory, I was level par and the team was tearing the course apart. A much-needed pit-stop occurred after nine holes, where the hot dogs were a welcome sight. Merv set the early pace with a meagre six being downed in the five-minute break, but Warney was not far behind, with five "sauce" rolls being his impressive tally!

As the afternoon progressed our team remained consistent and by the time the round was over we had managed to run equal-first, with two other teams, in a performance nothing short of miraculous. The evening presentation was preceded by a formal dinner, where Merv, Matt Hayden and I embarked on a food frenzy, with three starters each and extra portions of main meals and sweets, all of which seemed to have the other guests stunned. They obviously thought we were all fit and trim sportsmen on strict diets. My golf team ended up running third on a count back and my prize was a carton of XXXX — just what I needed!

The bus trip to Kent tonight was much more subdued than the previous evening, and most of the occupants were fast asleep as we made our way onto the motorways we've been travelling on for the past three-and-a-half months.

DAY 109 (August 11)

THE GIRLS, who are now allowed to stay with us in the team hotels, have scored the "booby prize" first up with the worst location and amenities we have encountered on tour. On one side of the hotel is continuous traffic noise, which sounds as if they're about to drive their cars into your room. On the other is the loading docks for trucks to deliver their goods to a nearby department store. These deliveries start at 6.30am.

And then there is the decor in the rooms, which would have been very trendy in the '60s. Pink-and-purple bath tiles and orange carpet isn't my idea of good colour co-ordination!

Today was the first day of our three-day match against Kent, at the Canterbury ground, which is famous all over the world because of its huge oak tree situated on the playing surface inside the boundary fence. The toss was won by Taylor, who once again saved himself from the nasty injuries that would have resulted if we had found ourselves in the field first up.

Unexpectedly, Slater went early, and was soon followed by Hayden, but not before Matt had become the first Australian to score 1,000 runs on an Ashes tour without playing in a Test match. This feat proved once again that he is destined to become a permanent fixture in the side once he gets his chance.

I batted at number four, and while my innings was beginning slowly Taylor was scoring freely at the other end, until he mistimed a pull shot and departed for 78. As has often been the case on tour, the wicket was extremely slow and it was not easy to play aggressive shots, particularly as the Kent bowlers were concentrating on a negative line, wide of the off stump, to a ring field.

Martyn and I decided to try and bat out the rest of the day and test our powers of concentration, rather than play a reckless shot out of frustration. This was a tactic that seemed to bore even our own team, who all disappeared from the viewing balcony and went inside to swap cricketing stories and pass the time away.

Marto and I saw out the last four hours of play. I finished on a very satisfying 111 and Martyn was 56.

Dinner was spent with the Zoehrers, Julians and Warnes at an Italian restaurant. All the wives and girlfriends have got to know each other pretty well now, as they've all been travelling around with each other for the past couple of weeks.

The Australian players' wives and girlfriends outside the Ritz in London.

DAY 110 (August 12)

I MET dad for breakfast. Today was his last day before going back to Australia, although he wishes he could stay longer as he's had a great time seeing us both score centuries.

Our strategy was to score quickly this morning and then declare to try and set up a game later on. I lost my wicket trying to hit their quickest bowler out of the ground — not a real smart tactic — but Martyn and Heals carried on until we declared at 4-391. In the process, Marto scored his fourth century for the tour, another great performance from a guy who hasn't had the opportunity to play a Test in the current series.

Before taking the field, Tim Zoehrer seemed pretty pleased with the fact that his gloves had come up looking brand new with the aid of some boot polish. But he was brought down to earth by Ian Healy, who, in a reference to Ziggy's lack of cricket, asked: "How did you get them dirty in the first place?"

Being part of the group of players that haven't played Tests means you sometimes need a thick skin. Today our scorer, Mike Walsh, informed Ziggy that if he had a bad day behind stumps he was in danger of letting more byes through than he has scored runs on tour. The current statistics shows 32 byes and 51 runs.

The score at the end of the day was Kent 2-114, with Warney and myself each taking a wicket. This increases my tally for the tour to an impressive three first-class scalps. But, much more importantly, Wayne Holdsworth produced his best spell of bowling on tour so far. With The Oval Test only a week away, and the possibility of the pitch there suiting the quicker bowlers, the remainder of this match could be significant for Holdsworth, as he may be needed in the Test.

I spent a quiet night at home, as I've picked up the flu for the second time on this tour and am not feeling well.

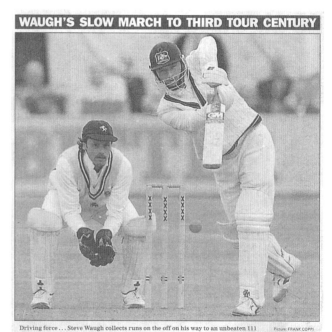

Driving force... Steve Waugh collects runs on the off on his way to an unbeaten 111   Picture: FRANK COPPI

DAY 111 (August 13)

IN ORDER to create a chance for a result, Kent declared at their overnight tally, and we batted long enough to post a second-innings score of 0-34 (thanks to Warne and Julian), before leaving Kent the task of scoring 311 off the remaining 85 overs for victory. As Julian is still hampered by his groin injury, I was given the chance to bowl a few overs, which turned out to be the best I've sent down all tour. The ball was moving around, and I ended up capturing 2-9 off five overs — it was time to open up the champagne!

Today was one of the very few days of the tour when the sun was shining *and* it wasn't windy. Such weather allows you to get into the game more than does a freezing-cold day with no crowd or atmosphere, and probably explains our good performance up until tea, when we had Kent six down and around 150 runs behind.

Two more batsmen fell quickly after the break, and Tubs quickly realised that here was his last chance to try and snare that elusive second wicket and accompanying reward. He decided to give himself a bowl before it was too late.

Tubby's bowling is best described as right-arm "nude nuts", meaning he thinks he's bowling leg spin but he's putting nothing on the ball to make it turn. His first three deliveries appeared so innocuous that the batsman could have kept them out wearing a blindfold, but perhaps it was this lack of talent coming from the fingertips of Taylor that led to the batsman's downfall. The fourth delivery was met with an arrogant-looking sweep shot which, to the delight of Taylor, saw the ball skid past bat and pad and crash into the leg-stump.

To Patrick Keane's credit, he immediately handed the cash to our 12th man, Paul Reiffel, who, to make the occasion even sweeter for both of us, relayed the money directly out to us on the field. The unfortunate batsman, Richard Davis, must now have developed an inferiority complex. It was he, in the corresponding match in 1989, who suffered the ignominy of being the first man Tim May ever hit for six. That event caused Dean Jones to lose 600 pounds to Tim Zoehrer, who had backed Maysie to hit a six at the odds of 10-1.

After the excitement of Taylor's wicket, the next dismissal — the match winner — was a complete anti-climax. As the lads made their way off the field there was some concern shown, as the door entrance to the dressing room was only about five-feet wide and it was doubtful as to whether Tubs' head would fit through it.

As soon as the guys had showered and packed, we headed for the motorway. The first pit stop allowed everyone to embark on a fast-food frenzy, and crisps, chocolates, drinks and ice-creams by the truckloads were scoffed as we got back on the road to our second-last destination. Such a diet did little for my ailing health. My cold has now definitely turned to flu, and when we arrived in Essex I went straight to bed.

DAY 112 (August 14)

LAST NIGHT was probably my worst night's sleep on tour. I felt as if someone had attached a vice to my head, and put pressure on my temples to go with a runny nose and sore throat. However, lady luck smiled upon me when I was named 13th man, with Warney 12th, which gave me three days to recover.

The highlights of the today's play against Essex were the centuries by the in-form batsmen, M. Waugh and Hayden. The only surprises were Slater being out without scoring and Boon not scoring a century. Australia ended up declaring with an hour to go, at 357 for 6, after once again making a mockery of a county attack. Essex were 1 for 60 at stumps, their reply being led by one of the most dedicated cricketers I've ever played against — Graham Gooch.

Despite the quality of the batting, I don't think the day will be remembered for the cricket, but for the diabolical meal that was served up at lunchtime. It was reputed to be chicken curry, but the chef must have been on work experience as the end product proved too tough an ask to digest.

After play, in order to avoid staying locked inside our hotel room all night, Lynette and I decided to join the Julians, Zoehrers, Simpsons and Warnes for a Chinese meal. The unusual eating habits of the Warnes are not particularly suited to the oriental cuisine, but Shane managing two bowls of prawn crackers and his fiancee some fried rice. They assured us later that this would be their last visit to this type of restaurant.

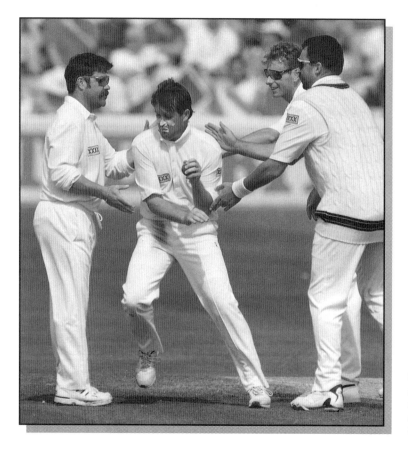

Tim Zoehrer, after taking a wicket at Essex, finds the congratulations from his team-mates a bit too enthusiastic.

David Boon, at practice before the fifth Test at Edgbaston.

Mark Waugh at Chelmsford, where in 1989 he scored a hundred for Essex against Australia. In 1993 he did the reverse, scoring 108 for Australia against his old teammates.

Wayne "Cracker" Holdsworth, as colourful as ever, at training before the fifth Test.

Mark Taylor, run out by a throw from Matthew Maynard, during the Australian top-order collapse on the second day at Edgbaston.

Two shots of Ian Healy, an important figure in Australia's Ashes victory. This page: A painful celebration with Shane Warne after Alec Stewart was caught and bowled by the Aussie spinner on the first day of the fifth Test. After Shane took the catch he ran down the pitch and jumped on Heals' foot. Opposite page: An attempted hook shot during his crucial innings of 80 in the same match that gave Australia a substantial first-innings.

Mark Waugh waits to be presented with the man-of-the-match award, after Australia had won the fifth Test to go four-up in the series.

DAY 113 (August 15)

THE ESSEX batsmen came out swinging in the morning session, with Gooch completing another half century in quick time and the incoming players helping to keep the four-runs-an-over scoring rate intact. Tim Zoehrer once again showed his tremendous all-round skills by taking three wickets with his leg spinners. He is an extremely good leggie, considering the lack of time he has to work on them.

One of the more unusual dismissals occurred when one of the Essex players was out, stumped Healy, bowled Zoehrer, which was probably the first time on an Ashes tour that two keepers have joined forces in this way.

Essex were dismissed mid afternoon, 89 runs behind. Border decided to give some of the lower-order batsmen a chance to score some runs, and changed the batting order around. But he did leave Slater, who is in need of a couple of runs, at the top of the innings. However, Slats, being a team man, realised the other guys need a hit more than he did and obliged by completing a pair for the match or, as the players say, picking up a "Mr Magoo" or the "googles".

Julian, relishing the opening role, tore Mark Ilott apart in a frenzied attack, striking 8 fours off 11 balls before being dismissed for 66, just when a hundred looked a formality. Merv then spared Slats from carrying "Plucka" around, as he too secured a duck — because he was the last man to do so, he must look after our mascot. At the end of the day our total was in a bit of a mess, but we still have Hayden, M.Waugh and Border to come, so our position is relatively safe.

After watching two full days of cricket, I'm beginning to appreciate how hard it must be for the guys who haven't played in all of the Tests over here. It can be a long, and sometimes frustrating and boring day when you have to watch, knowing you can't do anything about it. The five guys who have had to endure this on the current tour are Martyn, Hayden, Zoehrer, Holdsworth and Julian, all of whom have done a great job and never complained, putting them almost on a par with the '89 Ashes tour reserves of Moody, Rackemann, Campbell, Veletta, Zoehrer and May. Those guys were phenomenal in their support and attitude towards the guys who were playing in that memorable series.

DAY 114 (August 16)

DURING THE day, the England team for the final Test was announced, with Hick, Tufnell, Malcolm and Watkin in their squad, and Ilott, Smith and Emburey left out. As well, Angus Fraser is on standby for Bicknell. It is a team that looks to be more aggressive in nature than any they have previously chosen this summer.

Today is Lynette and my second wedding anniversary, and Simmo allowed me to leave the match at lunch-time and head to London before the rest of the team, who weren't scheduled to arrive until around 9pm.

We had dinner at a restaurant called Quaglinos, which is obviously very trendy and fashionable because only one or two items on the menu appeared edible. This was followed by *Miss Saigon*, which is playing at the Theatre Royal and turned out to be a great show.

Today has been one of the few times Lynette and I have been together to celebrate an occasion like this. I've been home for only two of Lynette's last nine birthdays (and only three of mine), as well as only having one Christmas Day at home in the last seven years. But such absences are one of the minuses that come with the job. Fortunately, they are far outweighed by all the plusses that accompany living the life of a Test cricketer.

The Australians with their replicas of the Ashes urn, which were presented to us by the people at the Westbury Hotel in London. Back (left to right): S. Waugh, Taylor, Rundle, Walsh, Hughes. Centre: Warne, Simpson, Slater, Martyn, Healy, Reiffel, M. Waugh, Alcott, Border. Front: Hayden, Zoehrer, Boon.

DAY 115 (August 17)

WITH ONLY five days of cricket left on the tour, and a chance to create history in front of us, the whole squad was reminded by Simmo and AB before training of the importance of finishing strongly and not thinking about going home until the Test is finished.

Slats, keen for some practice after his disastrous last outing, put on his gear and headed into the nets first up, only to find all the lads lining up in his net, keen for a bowl and claiming there were easy wickets to be had at his expense. Moments like these are only found in a team with good spirit, as they help bond the guys together and can relieve tension, by way of laughter, if someone is having a bad trot.

Practice was not as good as we would have liked, because the wickets were too much in favour of the bowlers. But at least they had a bit of pace in them which will be similar to the wicket the Test will be played on.

Back at the hotel, our trunks arrived and the nightmare process of packing all the gear we've accumulated over the past four months began. The hard part for me will be trying to fit it all in, a feat that could prove extremely difficult considering the mess that has engulfed my room.

The end of the tour is inevitably busy with cocktail parties and functions. Tonight a function was thrown by the Westbury Hotel, who, in a nice gesture, presented all the players with a replica of the Ashes urn. After the customary one or two drinks, we left for the Dog and Trumpet pub and my last XXXX function. This was the venue that saw some triumphant beer-sculling efforts by May, Waugh and Julian three months ago, but on this occasion the atmosphere was very subdued, and the closest we got to the XXXX was pulling a few pints for the locals. From there, Heals, Slats and I headed for our third appointment of the evening, a film night at the National Film Theatre, where previously unseen footage of highlights from past Ashes contests, dating back to the late 1800s, were shown. Watching players from different eras is something I enjoy, as you can see how they played in their day, and how they reacted to success and failure. Each additional piece of footage I've seen has given me a greater appreciation of their skill, and provided chances to see who has worn the baggy green cap before you. These old films offer some sort of link between the Australian players of today and all of those that have donned the baggy green in years gone by.

DAY 116 (August 18)

ROOM-SERVICE breakfast arrived at 8.30, which gave me enough time to actually enjoy my food, rather than having to go downstairs, wait 20 minutes before brekky arrived, and then scoff it down in time to make the bus.

Training was more intense today, and we are aided by a few net bowlers from the staff of the local side, in this case the Surrey second XI. Their contribution made it easier for the bowlers, as May and Hughes are still hampered by niggling injuries. All the Australian players appear in good form, and are looking forward to the Test and then the opportunity to go home after four-and-a-bit months of touring life.

I compiled a quick checklist this morning and realised I'd lost quite a few of my clothes in my travels. This fact, combined with the ability of laundromats to shrink and discolour the rest of my wardrobe, meant that the stage had been reached where shopping was a must. The afternoon was spent trudging around London in search of a bargain, but luckily an expert, in the form of Lynette, was on hand to lend some assistance to my plight.

An hour before the team meeting this evening, all the players congregated to get all personal tour memorabilia signed, such as stumps, posters, books and bats. The team meeting was brief, with the emphasis on forgetting the trip home, as it is only a week away, and on not giving the Poms a sniff of victory. We have to go in for the kill. Devon Malcolm was one player singled out for special attention, as he is the only strike bowler England have picked all summer. We can expect more hostility in this Test than we've previously encountered. The meeting ended on a humorous note, with news of the touring Australian press cricket match which was played yesterday. Two of our journalists suffered injuries. A torn hamstring to Malcolm Conn of *The Australian* brought muffled laughter from the squad, but best-received was the news of a top-edged hook shot from the blade of Jim Tucker (*Inside Edge* magazine) that led to six stitches being required in a nasty wound to his bottom lip. This will almost certainly save us all from the normal barrage of questions from him, at least until the swelling of his mouth subsides.

While the girls were happily enjoying their team dinner at the Hard Rock Cafe, the players' pre-match dinner was held at Casper's Restaurant, and once again ended up being an eating extravaganza. All the boys made sure the Australian Cricket Board was left with a hefty bill at the end of the evening.

The Australians stretch at training before the sixth Test.

THE SIXTH TEST

DAY 117 (August 19)

ENGLAND SUFFERED a setback in the warm-ups this morning when Graham Thorpe sustained a broken thumb after a ball from one of the net bowlers reared up from a length and struck him on the hand. With little time left before the start of the Test, a replacement, in the form of Mark Ramprakash of Middlesex, was summoned from nearby Lord's to take a place in the starting line-up.

The toss was won by England, who had also brought Angus Fraser in, and, as expected, they elected to bat on a very good-looking batting wicket. Hopefully, this will be a history-making Test victory for us, but, unfortunately, the first session turned out to be one of our worst exhibitions to date, with the bowlers either bowling too short a length or too full. Twenty fours were struck before lunch and the scoreboard read 1-115 off 27 overs.

Personally, it was a satisfying session, as I finally took my 50th Test wicket, having Gooch caught by Border. I must admit, when I first started playing Test cricket, I thought taking one wicket would be great, so 50 represents something of a milestone for me.

During the county game against Surrey here at The Oval, we all thought that the lunch-time meal couldn't be surpassed, but the pasta that graced our plates today made that effort pale into insignificance. It had the consistency and taste of Perkins Paste. But the situation was saved by some take-away sandwiches purchased from the canteen.

After lunch, Atherton became my second victim, falling LBW to a pretty useful outswinger. The champagne *will* be flowing tonight! Two more wickets fell in this session, that of Maynard, who was deceived by a Warne flipper (which meant Shane had taken the most wickets by a leg spinner for Australia in an Ashes series in England), and Hick, who departed 20 short of a century when it appeared a formality.

The scoring rate of the English was extremely quick. All their batsmen played shots from ball one, in an obvious change of strategy from what they had previously tried, and one that gained impressive results. However they would be disappointed that three of their top four batsmen made 50s, but none went on to make a hundred and really put the pressure on us.

For the first time this series, Merv appeared to be struggling. The opposition sensed this as well and, as a result, he went for more than four runs an over, which is very unusual for the big fella. The final two hours were a reflection of the way the day went, with the honours going back and forth and ending slightly in England's favour, at 7 for 353. The wickets were shared among our bowlers, but it was a day when it just didn't quite fall into place for us. Balls flew into gaps, a few catches were dropped, and a couple of decisions that could have gone our way didn't.

A quick getaway was required after play, as Lynette and I were due at the theatre, with Tim and Katherine May, to see *Five Guys Called Mo*. It was an entertaining and fun show, but at the same time worrying, as you were always a chance to be called on stage to dance. Maysie and I were not exactly blessed with rhythm at birth.

DAY 118 (August 20)

ANOTHER CLOUDLESS sky greeted the players (the third sunny day in a row). Our pre-play warm-ups involved a 20-25 minute stretch, followed by a quick fielding session, and then a bat and bowl if you felt you needed it. That left about 30 minutes to relax before play began.

The important task of wrapping up the England tail was achieved fairly quickly, for the addition of only 27 runs, with the previously unlucky Reiffel gaining the last two wickets. But when we batted, the impact of Devon Malcolm's selection was felt almost immediately. First he surprised Slater, having him caught in close trying to hook a ball that beat the batsman for pace and bounce. Then Boon was also undone by the unaccustomed bounce, being snapped up by Gooch at bat pad to leave us at 2-42 at lunch and under some pressure.

The English attack for this game boasts three very good Test match bowlers, and none better than Fraser, who has been out of Test cricket for 18 months after two operations to correct some hip problems. His type of bowling doesn't allow the batsman to relax at any stage, as he is always putting the ball in the danger area and making you play at most deliveries. This is an attribute that was sorely lacking from the English bowling in the first five Tests.

Steve Watkin is another bowler along those lines, with perhaps a yard more pace, and he, Fraser and Malcolm make up a very useful bowling combination, as was proved throughout the day.

The caterers at The Oval made the biggest comeback since Cracker's bowling spell at Derbyshire by providing one of the best lunches on tour, in the form of salmon, instead of the previously inedible concoctions that have been served up here.

Mark Waugh was out soon after lunch, to a steepling delivery from Fraser that found the edge, but Taylor and Border steadied the ship until five minutes before tea when Tubs became Malcolm's third victim, caught in the gully. This brought me to the wicket for one ball before the interval, which nearly decapitated me on its journey through to the keeper.

After tea, I was just beginning to feel comfortable when I missed a straight one from Fraser that sent me back to the pavilion for 20. In trying to work out why I missed it, I came up with two reasons. One, lack of concentration at the moment of delivery; and two, this must be one of the worst "sighting" grounds for a batsman. Spectators are seated in front of the sightscreen at one end, and the other end is bright white due to a reflection off painted steps which are situated next to the sightscreen.

With the English team having a good day, the crowd was extremely vocal and a real buzz surrounded the ground all day. It created an atmosphere you can only get at a Test match. The remainder of the final session continued in the favour of England, with only Heals putting up resistance. He was undefeated on 39 at the close of play. Tomorrow morning's session will be vital as we are still 141 runs behind with only two wickets left. A lead of more than 100 for England will be hard to make up in the fourth innings.

As the effects of the flu were still haunting me, I made do with a quick take-away meal and an early night in preparation for a day in the field tomorrow.

DAY 119 (August 21)

THE MORNING dawned to more blue sky and another warm day, which took the number of sunny days to about 10 for the entire tour. When we arrived at the dressing room there was a huge box full of confectionery, which had been sent by a guy who had had two bats signed by us, and was immediately set upon by the players. It's energy-sapping work out on the field and the sugar would help get us through.

When play began, Healy continued his one-man crusade against the English attack. He was nervously supported from the change rooms by Mike Whitney, who had backed Heals at 33-1 to be our top scorer in the first innings.

Whit returned to the commentary box with a winning ticket in his wallet, as Healy ended the innings unbeaten on 83, after one of his finest knocks. We were left only 77 behind, and still with a real chance of victory if we could bowl well. The star of the English bowlers was Fraser, who captured 5-87 off 26.4 overs, in a performance that will almost certainly earn him a spot in the England touring team to the West Indies to be announced in four weeks time.

Unfortunately our plan of taking early wickets didn't materialise, as Gooch and Atherton both gorged themselves on some wayward bowling that yielded 50 runs from the first nine overs and allowed Gooch to become the highest run scorer for England in Test cricket. He surpassed David Gower's total of 8,231 runs, a tremendous feat considering Gooch had spent three years out of Test matches because of a rebel tour of South Africa.

Yesterday's superb lunch was obviously some sort of hoax, as today's effort was back on a par with other previous efforts here. It was only digestible when combined with copious quantities of orange cordial to deceive the taste buds. While the players were doing it tough in the lunchroom, the same couldn't be said of the wives and girlfriends who were mixing with society's elite, downing tea and scones and living life to the full.

England, now sensing a chance of victory, followed Border's example in similar situations and consolidated their position in the middle session, losing only Atherton for the addition of 77 runs, and building a platform to launch an assault on us later. But, after tea, Hick was out, trying to slog May over the infield just when he looked set to go on to get a big score. Then Merv produced an inspired spell, just when he looked down and out. Calling on his inner strength, he produced a couple of superb overs, and kept us in the game by taking two wickets with consecutive deliveries.

Gooch then fell, six runs later, to another one of Warney's unplayable balls, and the game had turned completely on its head. At this point, England's lead was 263, with 5 wickets in hand, a position we wouldn't have thought possible 30 minutes before. A lot of lesser teams might have thrown the towel had they been faced with the situation we found ourselves in at tea, but that's what makes our side a real tough one to beat. We've got heart and fight, two qualities needed in a winning side.

If anything has let us down in the current game it has been our normally excellent catching, and possibly the turning point of the match came when Ramprakash was missed on 0. His departure would have made the score 6-186 with half an hour left. But credit must go to the English as they survived the remaining time to have a lead of 287 going into the fourth day.

We learned today that, as tipped earlier on in the tour, the people of Wagga Wagga will be hosting a ticker-tape parade through the city for the home-town boys, Slater and Taylor, in recognition of their centuries at Lord's and efforts on tour. This was a talking point when quite a few of the guys and girls ate at the Bombay Brasserie tonight, which has proved to be a bit of a favourite among the players, even though it generally exceeds the meal-allowance budgets.

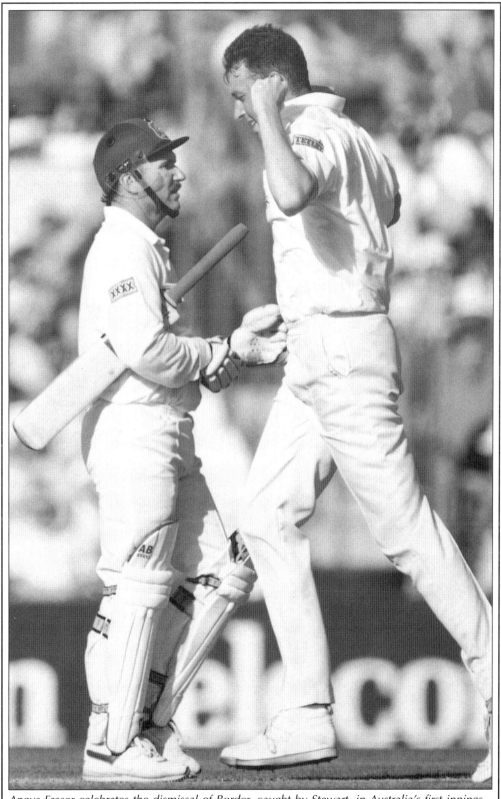
Angus Fraser celebrates the dismissal of Border, caught by Stewart, in Australia's first innings.

DAY 120 (August 22)

I KNEW it was too good to be true — four days without a hint of rain — but today compensated for that statistic. Constant rain fell, which delayed the start until lunch. In the meantime, more bats had to be signed and chocolate bars eaten, with the latter the players' first choice.

Play finally got underway at 1.25pm, but in real terms only 45 minutes' play was lost as the playing conditions state that, in the event of time being lost, we can play an extra hour to finish at seven o'clock instead of six. The cricket proved very frustrating. Every time we took a wicket the next pair would stay just long enough to keep the score mounting towards a very tough target. We couldn't steamroll their latter-order batsmen as we have been used to, and Mark Ramprakash made the most of his fortunate selection and missed chance by not only guiding the tail, but scoring 64, his highest tally to date in Tests.

Hughes, Reiffel and Warne each took three wickets, and during the innings another amazing stat for Warney was recorded — he bowled 439.5 overs, the most ever in an Ashes series, surpassing Clarrie Grimmett's 398.2 overs in 1928-9. The task for us to win is 391 runs, but our chances weren't helped by the rain and bad light that forced us off the field with only one run to our name. The last 90 minutes were lost, making our target of 390 in 6 hours tomorrow almost impossible.

There was relief for the bowlers at the end of the day — there is no more bowling to be done. I just hope everyone's mind is on the job tomorrow, as I'd hate the give the Poms a taste of victory — something they haven't known against us for the last seven years.

I had a quick feed tonight with Heals at the Break for the Border, where we discussed the tour and what lies ahead for the team over the next couple of years. In the near future we will no longer have the services of Allan Border, a player whose presence won't be fully appreciated until he's gone. But I'm sure with guys like Hayden and Martyn waiting in the wings, the prospects for Australia's cricket future look very bright indeed.

The virus I've had for the past couple of weeks has now been passed onto Lynette who isn't thrilled about it. She's been virtually bed-ridden for the past two days.

DAY 121 (August 23)

FOR THE first time on tour the team bus was caught up in a traffic jam on the way to a game. The problem occurred while crossing the Thames, and we didn't arrive at the ground until 20 minutes later than normal.

The morning began well for us, with the first 20 runs coming quickly. This promising start raised hopes of an Australian victory — we hoped to be in a position where we needed around 180 runs in the last session with six or seven wickets in hand. A tough ask but not impossible. But, unfortunately, we then lost three wickets in 15 balls, which wiped out any thoughts of victory and left survival as the only objective.

First to go was Slats, who was the victim of a very poor decision. He was followed immediately by Boonie who didn't offer a stroke and was adjudged LBW, in a line-ball decision which, unless someone else didn't trouble the scorers, guaranteed Plucka a new home in Launceston.

England were now growing in stature, and Malcolm produced a brute of a delivery that crashed into Tubs' ribs, sent him down on his knees, and shook him up enough to see him play on to his stumps in the next over. Watkin had now taken all three wickets to fall, but things then settled down, and M. Waugh and Border managed to halt the progress of the English bowlers by surviving until lunch.

It seemed like we're getting all our bad luck in one day, as AB was given out caught behind, second ball after lunch, even though it was quite obvious he had missed the ball. The noise must have come from his bat flicking his pad. When I arrived at the crease I was given every opportunity to sharpen up my ducking and weaving techniques, as Malcolm gave me a barrage of short-pitched stuff, just to make me feel welcome.

With the team in need of a stabilising partnership, I was surprised to see Mark out hooking, especially as there were two players waiting

The final wicket of the series — Warne lbw to Fraser.

for the hook shot on the boundary. I don't think Mark realised there was an extra man waiting for him to take the bait. Heals followed shortly after, also attempting to hook, so it was left to Merv and me to try and see out the remaining three hours — a tough ask but not impossible as the wicket was still playing superbly.

Just when things seemed under control, and with only 15 minutes to go until tea, big Devon Malcolm came back and produced a quick first-up yorker that swung in to trap me LBW and almost certainly hand the game to the Poms. Worse was to follow two overs later, when Merv became the third batsmen out from the hook shot. Such cricket suggested we didn't have our minds on the job. The hook is a high-risk shot and one we should have been avoiding in the circumstances.

Reiffel, Warne and May all stuck to the task valiantly, but the inevitable happened with half-an-hour's play left ... we finally lost to England. The loss has left a sour taste in our mouths and dampened the end-of-tour celebrations.

With the series over, all of the players from both sides got together for a drink and a chat. But not for long. Half the English team were on the motorway home before they had finished their beer, which was something we couldn't believe, especially as they had just won a Test match. They weren't even going out together to celebrate. This to me explains why we were a much tighter-knit group. We enjoy our victories together, and moments like these bond everyone together, in a link which are so important when times get tough.

Eventually we went back to the hotel, to get changed before heading out for our end-of-tour dinner at the Blue Print Cafe on the Thames. These proceedings started fairly sedately, until the alcohol had its desired effect on Cracker who then stole the show with his repertoire of songs and bad-taste jokes, most of which he'd learned off Merv during the tour.

Other highlights from the evening included Warney's famous Archie Arscholetorn joke and Maysie's legendary recollection of his 42 not out versus the West Indies. But the truth was that the evening was actually fairly tame, as everyone was still disappointed with today's loss on top of the fact we had now been away for over four months. A few of the guys are keen to get home.

WINDING DOWN

DAY 122 (August 24)

I WOKE up at 8.30 and couldn't get used to the fact that it wasn't a cricket day. We have all become so used to getting on the bus and making our way down to the ground. However, there was time for one more signing session, which occupied an hour. All our team photos had to be signed, and we had to cater for all the last-minute requests from friends, which surely took us to about 10,000 signatures for the tour.

Being the last day together, XXXX put on their end-of-tour dinner, which was in reality a thank you to the players, but also a function to decide the winning captain from the "Brain Strain" competition we have had to endure throughout the tour. Merv and Marto lined up for the title, with a CD player as the trophy on offer. There was never really any doubt who would win, as it came down to the last event which involved the respective wives and girlfriends having to dress their partners up in sports gear — with the most ridiculous looking one the winner after two minutes. The winner, of course, was Merv.

The end of the XXXX function signalled the official end of the tour, and everyone made their way back to the hotel to pack their coffins and trunks, which are being sent back by sea. I couldn't believe the amount of gear I had accumulated along the way, including autographed bats, and mementos, such as stumps and balls, that have special significance for me.

In looking back on the tour and trying to work out why we were so successful, it's impossible to pick out one reason. It was a combination of many factors. There was the way the younger members of the tour party fitted into the side so well; the pinpointing of the opposition's weaknesses by the coach and captain; the team spirit that pulled us through in tough times; and, most importantly, there was the will and desire for everyone to give 100 per cent in our quest to keep the opposition pinned down when we were on top. That last characteristic made us a tough side that thrived on success, and was something that intimidated the opposition. We sensed it making a gulf between the two sides which couldn't be filled.

I can only hope I'll be a part of the next Ashes campaign to England in 1997. This tour has left me with many friendships and memories that will last forever.

The "Brain-Strain" final reaches its inevitable conclusion.

Top: The final team dinner.
Above: Jack and Georgina Boon, with Emma Healy (in front).
Right: Stephen and Lynette Waugh.
Below: The Steve Waugh coffin, packed and ready to go home.

MEMORABLE MOMENTS

ALLAN BORDER

After I made a double-century at Headingley, I took the catch to clinch the series and then looked up to see that everyone had been diving for souvenir stumps even before the catch was taken!

The celebrations in the dressing rooms after the match rank with the best we've had.

MARK TAYLOR

- Scoring a hundred at Lord's.
- Taking my first first-class wicket at Canterbury.
- And, through that wicket, taking the cash off Patrick Keane — one of the journalists.

DAVID BOON

My top two memories would be making my first hundred in England, at Lord's in the second Test ... and the golfing tour to Ireland.

An Ashes tour always has many memorable moments — too many to mention.

MATTHEW HAYDEN

I think this question is always the toughest question to answer. Do you go for an entire event, an emotion, or a pinnacle of achievement created through ongoing dedication and commitment?

For me, this ongoing climb for a piece of memorabilia in Ashes history never eventuated. I'll therefore have to say that my most memorable moment on tour involved Slats, who punched hard in the Test series, and through the entire tour, not only on the field, but off as well. His climb has been perfect. His Test hundred at Lord's was a truly memorable moment — a moment of time which expressed something I so desperately want to achieve in the future. Hopefully, when I do reach that goal, it will be an event we are both involved in.

IAN HEALY

ON THE CRICKET FIELD: AB catching the last English wicket of the first Test with nine overs to go. I remember that day because it was important for me to have a good day behind the stumps, after making my first hundred the day before. I did keep well and knew we would we hard to beat from then on.

SOCIALLY: Michael Slater's excessive joy after winning the second Test at Lord's. He got so wrapped up in the team atmosphere, that he:

- Forgot to meet his fiancee in time before leaving the ground with the rest of us;
- Drove the porcelain bus prior to the team party (he had several attempts to start the bus);
- Was refused entry into a London nightclub, due to his friends' poor health, and just couldn't believe how they could survive financially without him in there!!

Thanks for the memory, Slats — "that's the way all Test victories should be celebrated, mate."

David Boon, after his hundred at Headingley.

Merv, with Merv the dog, before the first ball of the third Test.

WAYNE HOLDSWORTH
On a tour such as this it is very hard to pinpoint any one moment. If a tour goes successfully every moment is memorable and this tour was no exception.

Something I will always remember is the day I was selected to represent my country. This is a feeling that will only be bettered by selection in an Australian XI for a Test match. An Ashes Tour is a dream come true for any cricketer, and I will always cherish the moment I was chosen to go on this one.

My fondest memory of the tour itself would be the inspirational bowling of Merv Hughes. After Craig McDermott flew home with injury, the press said we would suffer in the bowling department. However, this was not the case. Innings after innings, Merv kept bowling and taking wickets, and showed just how much pride he has in representing his country. He did a fine job and showed why he is Australia's number-one bowler.

The heights Merv has reached in Test cricket are fantastic, and I hope that one day I too can reach these heights. I would love nothing more than to play my first Test with him in the side, bowling at the other end. Merv epitomises what wearing a baggy green cap means. He showed me and maybe one day I'll be able to show someone else!

MERV HUGHES
Three things stand out that I will remember for a long time:
- Shane Warne's first ball in Test cricket on English soil, which bowled Mike Gatting.
- The last ball of the fourth day, first Test, when I bowled Gatting.
- Tim May bowling to Ilott, and AB completing the catch which won the fourth Test, the series, and meant we had retained the Ashes.

BRENDON JULIAN
To pick one moment throughout this tour is impossible. Personally, I will never forget being selected to play for Australia, and scoring 56 not out at Trent Bridge to save a Test with Steve Waugh is something I'll remember!

This tour was especially memorable for the debut players, such as Michael Slater and Matthew Hayden, and the success they had. Also outstanding were the performances of Hughes, Warne, Reiffel, and the batsmen, who complemented each other. And, of course, Healy with his all-round talents. These things will be with me for the rest of my life.

DAMIEN MARTYN

The most memorable moments on tour were every Test we won, to keep the Ashes in Australia. To actually be on an Ashes tour, especially one in which the team did so well, is something I'll remember for the rest of my life — there's nothing like beating the POMMIES!

My best moment personally was my 50 at Lord's. It was good to get out there and have a go. My thanks go to AB for that one.

TIM MAY

In stark contrast to my Ashes tour in 1989, this tour provided quite a few memorable moments, including my five wickets at Edgbaston, the tandoori chicken marsala at Shimla Pinks in Birmingham, and the discovery of Sol beer.

However, top of my list would have to be our win at Lord's, not because we won or that I took a few wickets, but because my parents were there and able to share in the thrill of me playing at Lord's. They had travelled to England in '89, to hopefully see me play in a Test, but ended up going home pretty disappointed. For me to be able to make their trip worthwhile in '93 gave me the biggest thrill of my cricketing life.

CRAIG McDERMOTT

Two things stand out from my abbreviated stay in England:

I'd left for hospital soon after at tea on the first day of the Lord's Test, just as Boonie was going out to bat. He's a guy who's always supported me, and I knew how much getting a hundred in England meant to him.

As soon as I came to after my operation, around midnight after the second day's play, the first thing I thought of was how Boonie had gone. So I got on the phone, still high as a kite from the anaesthetic, and called him. He told me I sounded drunk (which I'm sure I did!) ... and that he'd reached his goal.

I'll also never forget Heals' first first-class hundred in the first Test at Old Trafford. It was a great moment for the team, and for Heals, whose been such an important member of the team, on and off the field, for the past few seasons.

One of my favourite memories of the tour — in the Trent Bridge dressing room after batting most of the afternoon to save the Test.

PAUL REIFFEL
The three days in Ireland, especially the party after the game, and the final of the hurling in Dublin the next day.

The fourth Test at Headingley, where we won the Ashes and I managed five wickets.

MICHAEL SLATER
There have been so many memorable moments on tour, but the one that stands out as the most memorable for me was playing the leg-glance during the second Test at Lord's that brought up my first Test hundred. To be lucky enough to have scored my first hundred at Lord's, "the home of cricket", in my second Test was a dream come true, and a moment that I will always cherish.

SHANE WARNE
- Being part of the team that retained the Ashes.
- Ian Healy stumping Graham Thorpe at Edgbaston.
- My first ball in Ashes cricket.
- The stand between AB and Tugga at Headingley.
- Paul Reiffel's bowling at Headingley.
- Merv's 200th Test wicket.

MARK WAUGH
Asking me what my most memorable moment on tour was is a real tough question — I find it very difficult to single out one particular moment as there are many special individual and team occurrences.

Michael Slater, man of the match at Lord's

The Australian cricketers with members of INXS. Back row: Dominic (XXXX rep), Shane Warne, Michael Hutchence, Simon (our bus driver), Paul Reiffel, Brendon Julian, Kirk Pengilly, Steve Waugh, Garry Gary Beers. Front: Andrew Farriss, David Boon, Tim Farriss, Jon Farriss.

I must say that scoring 99 at Lord's in the second Test was a day I won't forget too easily. A close second was a great visit to the FA Cup Final at Wembley, and, of course, there was that great moment when we retained the Ashes at Leeds.

STEVE WAUGH

The first thing that comes to mind is the sheer horror and shock on Mike Gatting's face when he was bowled by that first unplayable delivery bowled to him by Shane Warne. I'm sure plenty of their players carried the memory of that delivery with them throughout the series and, as a consequence, never really came to grips with Warney. He went on to be the major difference between the sides.

Other highlights for me were Slat's joy at scoring his debut hundred at Lord's, Heals' arrogant shot to score his first Test century, and Reiffel proving that determination and will-to-succeed will come through if you want it bad enough. I'll also remember the claiming of the Ashes at Headingley, on top of putting on 332 with Allan Border in a record partnership earlier in that Test.

TIM ZOEHRER

The first day of the Leeds Test, when, while trying to get onto the bus, I was mistaken by three Yorkshire boxers for a punching bag!

ERROL ALCOTT

- Merv Hughes losing four kilos one week ... and putting on six kilos the next.
- Craig McDermott begging me for relief of the pain he was suffering from his strangulated bowel, one hour before his emergency operation.
- Retaining the ASHES!

Celebrations at Headingley, featuring (left to right): Mark Taylor, Damien Martyn, Matthew Hayden, Michael Slater, Steve Waugh and Shane Warne.

MIKE WALSH
- Being involved in another great Ashes tour with great people.
- Scoring the Boon century at Lord's.
- Scoring the Holdsworth hat-trick at Derby.
- Watching Warne and May bowl during the tour.
- Watching Warne's first ball in Test cricket in England.
- Gatting, bowled Merv with the last ball of the fourth day, in the second innings of the first Test.
- Mark Waugh's one-day innings at Edgbaston.
- The batting of Slater, Hayden and Martyn during the tour.
... And just everything about the tour.

BOB SIMPSON

As coach and selector, my most pleasurable and memorable moments do not come in one precise package.

Selecting the team, and then helping to implement the thoughts behind the selections has been my greatest joy. When the selectors met early in the year to plan the 1993 Ashes party we were conscious of the need to make some changes that would infuse even more enthusiasm into the team.

Team selection is rather like tackling a jigsaw. Some parts (in the form of experienced, successful players) are easy to form, but filling in the gaps is generally a different matter. However, in 1993 these gaps proved a little easier to fill, as the newcomers fitted snugly into place. At Test level, Shane Warne, Michael Slater and Paul Reiffel have been outstanding successes, while Matt Hayden and Damien Martyn both did enough to win a Test berth in normal circumstances.

While the jigsaw of Test selection never seems to be totally finished, the newcomers and near-newcomers gave me my finest moments.

TOUR RECORD

TOUR SUMMARY

Date	Versus	Result
April 30	England Amateur XI	Australians won by 94 runs
May 2	Duchess of Norfolk's XI	Australians won by seven runs
May 3	Middlesex	Australians won by 69 runs
May 5-7	Worcestershire	Australians won by five wickets
May 8-10	Somerset	Australians won by 35 runs
May 13-15	Sussex	Match drawn
May 16	Northamptonshire	Northants won on run-rate
May 19	**England**	**Australia won by four runs**
May 21	**England**	**Australia won by six wickets**
May 23	**England**	**Australia won 19 runs**
May 25-27	Surrey	Australians won by 174 runs
May 29-31	Leicestershire	Australians won by 97 runs
June 3-7	**England**	**Australia won by 179 runs**
June 9-11	Warwickshire	Match drawn
June 12-14	Gloucestershire	Match drawn
June 17-21	**England**	**Australia won by an innings and 62 runs**
June 23-25	Combined Universities	Australians won by 166 runs
June 26-28	Hampshire	Match drawn
July 1-6	**England**	**Match drawn**
July 8	Minor Counties	Australians won by 58 runs
July 10	Ireland	Australians won by 272 runs
July 13-15	Derbyshire	Match drawn
July 17-19	Durham	Match drawn
July 22-26	**England**	**Australia won by an innings and 148 runs**
July 28-30	Lancashire	Lancashire won by five wickets
July 31-Aug 2	Glamorgan	Match drawn
Aug 5-9	**England**	**Australia won by eight wickets**
Aug 11-13	Kent	Australians won by 89 runs
Aug 14-16	Essex	Match drawn
Aug 19-23	England	England won by 161 runs

Matches	Played	Won	Lost	Drawn	Tied
Test matches	6	4	1	1	-
Three-day matches	15	6	1	8	-
#Limited-overs Internationals	3	3	-	-	-
#Other limited-overs matches	6	5	1	-	-

Non-first-class matches

Match One (April 30)

v England Amateur XI, at Radlett *(Australians won toss)*

AUSTRALIANS

MJ Slater c Evans b Van Lint	41
ML Hayden c Van Lint b Hackett	151
*MA Taylor c Dean b Hackett	53
DC Boon not out	24
ME Waugh not out	1
Extras (lb 13, w 5, nb 4)	22
Total (3 wkts, 55 overs)	**292**

Did Not Bat: DR Martyn, #TJ Zoehrer, SK Warne, CJ McDermott, BP Julian, WJ Holdsworth.

Fall of Wickets: 1-92, 2-221, 3-283.

Bowling: Arnold 11-2-51-0; Roshier 11-1-62-0; Hackett 10-2-74-2; Van Lint 11-0-49-1; Evans 11-2-40-0; Sharma 1-0-3-0.

ENGLAND AMATEUR XI

SJ Dean c Zoehrer b Holdsworth	48
#SV Waterton c Zoehrer b Julian	8
*MJ Roberts b Holdsworth	17
I Stokes c Zoehrer b Holdsworth	1
R Sharma c Zoehrer b Julian	11
M Hussain c Zoehrer b McDermott	39
PG Roshier c and b Julian	12
A Van Lint c Taylor b McDermott	3
RA Evans not out	12
KA Arnold c Holdsworth b Warne	5
NP Hackett b Warne	1
Extras (lb 5, w 18, nb 18)	41
Total (45.2 overs)	**198**

Fall of Wickets: 1-60, 2-82, 3-99, 4-102, 5-125, 6-149, 7-166, 8-183, 9-192, 10-198.

Bowling: McDermott 10-0-35-2; Holdsworth 8-3-28-3; Julian 11-2-60-3; Warne 9.2-1-41-2, Martyn 6-0-23-0; Taylor 1-0-6-0.

Umpires: JH Hampshire and B Dudleston

AUSTRALIANS WON BY 94 RUNS

*Captain
#Wicketkeeper

Match Two (May 2)

v the Duchess of Norfolk's XI, at Arundel *(Australians won toss)*

AUSTRALIANS

MJ Slater b Graveney	13
DC Boon c Parks b Headley	14
ME Waugh b Headley	6
DR Martyn c Garner b Botham	5
*AR Border b Botham	18
SR Waugh b Garner	59
#IA Healy not out	47
BP Julian c Cowdrey b Headley	20
PR Reiffel b Headley	9
SK Warne b Headley	0
Extras (lb 5, w 7)	12
Total (9 wkts, 50 overs)	**203**

Did Not Bat: WJ Holdsworth.

Fall of Wickets: 1-20, 2-27, 3-40, 4-42, 5-68, 6-150, 7-188, 8-203, 9-203.

Bowling: Garner 10-2-32-1; Headley 10-1-51-5; Graveney 10-2-32-1; Botham 10-1-29-2; Fleming 7-0-32-0; Greig 3-0-22-0.

DUCHESS OF NORFOLK'S XI

TR Ward run out	33
G Fowler c Healy b Julian	11
*PWG Parker lbw Holdsworth	77
GR Cowdrey c SR Waugh b ME Waugh	0
MV Fleming c Healy b ME Waugh	0
IT Botham b ME Waugh	13
IA Greig c Healy b ME Waugh	6
#RJ Parks c Healy b ME Waugh	1
DW Headley c ME Waugh b Julian	16
J Garner b Julian	8
DA Graveney not out	5
Extras (lb 12, w 12, nb 2)	26
Total (49.5 overs)	**196**

Fall of Wickets: 1-38, 2-66, 3-66, 4-66, 5-87, 6-112, 7-114, 8-162, 9-176, 10-196.

Bowling: Holdsworth 9.5-1-42-1; Julian 10-0-49-3; Reiffel 10-0-35-0; Warne 10-1-26-0; ME Waugh 10-2-32-5.

Umpires: DJ Constant and GI Burgess

AUSTRALIANS WON BY SEVEN RUNS

Match Three (May 3)

v **Middlesex**, at Lord's *(Australians won toss)*

AUSTRALIANS

MA Taylor b Feltham	7
ML Hayden c Roseberry b Fraser	122
MJ Slater run out	1
DR Martyn run out	66
*AR Border b Fraser	8
SR Waugh not out	19
#TJ Zoehrer not out	7
Extras (lb 7, w 6)	13
Total (5 wkts, 55 overs)	**243**

Did Not Bat: PR Reiffel, TBA May, CJ McDermott, WJ Holdsworth.

Fall of Wickets: 1-23, 2-28, 3-167, 4-187, 5-226.

Bowling: Feltham 8-4-19-1; Cowans 11-0-36-0; Emburey 11-4-37-0, Fraser 11-0-76-2; Weekes 7-1-31-0; Keech 7-0-37-0.

MIDDLESEX

M Keech b McDermott	0
MA Roseberry c Taylor b Martyn	47
MR Ramprakash lbw McDermott	0
JD Carr c Zoehrer b Martyn	3
*MW Gatting run out	32
PN Weekes c Zoehrer b Martyn	12
#KR Brown c Holdsworth b McDermott	24
MA Feltham b Reiffel	17
JE Emburey b Martyn	10
ARC Fraser not out	0
NG Cowans c Zoehrer b Holdsworth	0
Extras (lb 6, w 9, nb 14)	29
Total (48.1 overs)	**174**

Fall of Wickets: 1-5, 2-5, 3-14, 4-74, 5-103, 6-140, 7-145, 8-169, 9-173, 10-174.

Bowling: McDermott 11-2-51-3; Reiffel 8-3-23-2; Holdsworth 7.1-0-22-1; May 11-2-31-0; Martyn 11-1-41-3.

Umpires: VA Holder and RA White.

AUSTRALIANS WON BY 69 RUNS

Match Four (May 5-7)

v **Worcestershire, at Worcester** *(Australians won toss)*

AUSTRALIANS — First Innings

ML Hayden c Lampitt b Tolley	3
*MA Taylor c Rhodes b Illingworth	39
DC Boon lbw Radford	108
ME Waugh c Curtis b Tolley	7
DR Martyn c Lampitt b Illingworth	25
SR Waugh not out	49
#IA Healy c Hick b Newport	6
BP Julian c Weston b Newport	9
PR Reiffel b Lampitt	5
SK Warne b Lampitt	3
WJ Holdsworth c Weston b Newport	0
Extras (5 lb, 1 w, 2 nb)	8
Total	**262**

Fall of Wickets: 1-3, 2-104, 3-124, 4-170, 5-194, 6-212, 7-248, 8-253, 9-261, 10-262.

Bowling: Newport 22.5-6-59-3; Tolley 16-5-36-2; Radford 15-5-53-1; Lampitt 16-3-47-2; Illingworth 15-2-52-2; Weston 2-0-10-0.

Batting time: 315 minutes
Overs: 86.5

AUSTRALIANS — Second Innings

*MA Taylor c Lampitt b Radford	40
ML Hayden c Hick b Newport	96
DC Boon st Rhodes b Illingworth	106
ME Waugh run out	15
DR Martyn c Newport b Illingworth	3
SR Waugh not out	12
#IA Healy not out	1
Extras (4 lb, 8 w, 2 nb)	14
Total (5 wkts)	**287**

Fall of Wickets: 1-71, 2-252, 3-262, 4-273, 5-275.

Bowling: Newport 15-1-58-1; Tolley 9-2-40-0; Radford 7-1-56-1; Illingworth 12.5-1-70-2; Hick 6-0-33-0; Lampitt 5-0-26-0.

Batting Time: 228 minutes
Overs: 54.5

WORCESTERSHIRE — First Innings

*TS Curtis lbw Julian	1
WPC Weston c Martyn b Julian	17
GA Hick c Taylor b Reiffel	5
DB D'Olivera c Healy b Holdsworth	13
ACH Seymour c Healy b Julian	6
SR Lampitt lbw Reiffel	4
#SJ Rhodes c Healy b Reiffel	0
RK Illingworth c Taylor b Holdsworth	12
PJ Newport run out	7
NV Radford c Healy b Holdsworth	4
CM Tolley not out	21
Extras (1 b, 5 lb, 3 w, 12 nb)	21
Total	**90**

Fall of Wickets: 1-1, 2-31, 3-35, 4-47, 5-55, 6-59, 7-59, 8-68, 9-82, 10-90.

Bowling: Holdsworth 7.5-3-15-3; Julian 13-6-31-3; Reiffel 10-5-21-3; ME Waugh 3-0-17-0.

Batting time: 147 minutes
Overs: 33.5

WORCESTERSHIRE — Second Innings

*T Curtis lbw Julian	67
P Weston c Taylor b Holdsworth	16
GA Hick lbw Holdsworth	187
D D'Oliveria b Warne	27
ACH Seymour not out	54
SR Lampitt not out	68
Extras (10 lb, 1 w, 28 nb)	39
Total (4 wkts, declared)	**458**

Fall of Wickets: 1-21, 2-189, 3-252, 4-337.

Bowling: Holdsworth 23-3-96-2; Reiffel 26-7-68-0; Julian 19-1-96-1; Warne 23-6-122-1; ME Waugh 15.1-2-59-0; Martyn 2-1-7-0.

Batting time: 441 minutes
Overs: 108.1

Umpires: R Palmer and BJ Meyer

AUSTRALIANS WON BY FIVE WICKETS

Match Five (May 8-10)

v **Somerset, at Taunton** *(Australians won toss)*

AUSTRALIANS — First Innings

MJ Slater c Lathwell b Kerr	122
MA Taylor c Lathwell b Van Troost	0
DC Boon c Parsons b Kerr	27
*AR Border c Burns b Van Troost	54
ME Waugh c Lathwell b Van Troost	68
SR Waugh c Burns b Caddick	38
#TJ Zoehrer b Van Troost	22
MG Hughes c Harden b Trump	36
TBA May not out	4
SK Warne st Burns b Trump	11
CJ McDermott c Follard b Kerr	23
Extras (4 b, 8 lb, 14 nb)	26
Total	**431**

Fall of Wickets: 1-0, 2-64, 3-187, 4-245, 5-305, 6-332, 7-381, 8-385, 9-396, 10-431.

Bowling: Caddick 22-1-90-1; Van Troost 18-2-89-4; Kerr 12.4-2-77-3; Hayhurst 14-4-50-0; Trump 22-3-101-2; Lathwell 2-0-12-0.

Batting Time: 326 minutes
Overs: 90.4

AUSTRALIANS — Second Innings

MA Taylor not out	18
MJ Slater not out	12
Extras (1 b, 1 lb, 8 nb)	10
Total (0 wkts, declared)	**40**

Bowling: Caddick 6-1-14-0; Van Troost 5-1-16-0; Kerr 0.3-0-8-0.
Batting time: 46 minutes
Overs: 11.3

SOMERSET — First Innings

AN Hayhurst not out	49
MN Lathwell c Zoehrer b McDermott	0
RJ Harden c Border b McDermott	7
*CJ Tavare c and b May	62
NA Folland lbw Warne	1
#ND Burns not out	7
Extras (7 lb, 18 nb)	25
Total (4 wkts, declared)	**151**

Did Not Bat: KA Parsons, JID Kerr, AR Caddick, AP Van Troost, HRJ Trump.
Fall of Wickets: 1-1, 2-19, 1-136, 4-137.
Bowling: McDermott 10-2-36-2; Hughes 15-3-63-0; ME Waugh 6-0-17-0; May 10-2-23-1; Warne 6-3-5-1.
Batting time: 181 minutes
Overs: 47

Umpires: KE Palmer and DR Shepherd
AUSTRALIANS WON BY 35 RUNS

SOMERSET — Second Innings

AN Hayhurst b Warne	89
MN Lathwell c Zoehrer b Hughes	15
RJ Harden c Boon b May	34
*CJ Tavare c Taylor b Warne	31
NA Folland st Zoehrer b Warne	32
#ND Burns run out	6
KA Parsons c McDermott b May	1
JID Kerr c Hughes b May	12
AR Caddick c McDermott b May	13
AP Van Troost c SR Waugh b Warne	8
HRJ Trump not out	0
Extras (b 17, lb 9, nb 18)	44
Total	**285**

Fall of Wickets: 1-37, 2-135, 3-187, 4-216, 5-231, 6-245, 7-253, 8-274, 9-284, 10-285.
Bowling: McDermott 14-0-72-0; Hughes 11-2-32-1; ME Waugh 1-0-3-0; May 23.3-5-75-4; Warne 28-6-77-4.
Batting Time: 284 minutes
Overs: 77.3

Match Six (May 13-15)

v Sussex, at Hove *(Sussex won toss)*

SUSSEX — First Innings

NJ Lenham c Healy b McDermott	11
CWJ Athey c Hayden b Julian	33
K Greenfield c Border b Julian	55
*AP Wells c Martyn b McDermott	93
MP Speight lbw Julian	0
CM Wells c Hayden b Hughes	6
#P Moores c Healy b Hughes	22
IDK Salisbury c Reiffel b Julian	59
ACS Pigott c Reiffel b Julian	5
AN Jones b Waugh	20
ESH Giddins not out	0
Extras (b 4, lb 12, w 3, nb 30)	49
Total	**353**

Fall of Wickets: 1-22, 2-76, 3-209, 4-209, 5-220, 6-244, 7-295, 8-322, 9-350, 10-353.

Bowling: McDermott 23-3-89-2; Hughes 16-3-58-2; Reiffel 21-2-58-0; Julian 22-5-63-5; May 17-3-53-0; Waugh 2.1-0-16-1.

Batting time: 409 minutes
Overs: 101.1

SUSSEX — Second innings

NJ Lenham b May	19
CWB Athey c Martyn b May	27
K Greenfield st Healy b May	3
MP Speight c Healy b Reiffel	0
CM Wells not out	4
#P Moores not out	5
Extras (6 b, 10 lb, 18 nb)	34
Total (4 wkts)	**92**

Fall of Wickets: 1-60, 2-75, 3-78, 4-78.

Bowling: McDermott 5-1-16-0; Julian 5-0-13-0; Hughes 10-3-19-0; May 14-6-19-3; Reiffel 5-1-9-1.

Batting time: 154 minutes
Overs: 39

AUSTRALIANS — First Innings

MJ Slater b Giddins	73
ML Hayden st Moores b Salisbury	66
DR Martyn c Giddins b CM Wells	136
*AR Border run out	33
SR Waugh st Moores b CM Wells	124
#IA Healy not out	24
BP Julian not out	16
Extras (1 b, 7 lb, 2 w, 8 nb)	18
Total (5 wkts, declared)	**490**

Did Not Bat: TBA May, MG Hughes, PR Reiffel, CJ McDermott.
Fall of Wickets: 1-115, 2-174, 3-237, 4-442, 5-451.
Bowling: Jones 18-1-90-0; Giddins 21-3-95-1; Pigott 25-4-73-0; Salisbury 33-1-116-1; CM Wells 18-0-67-2; Athey 8-0-41-0.
Batting time: 448 minutes
Overs: 123

Umpires: HD Bird and MJ Kitchen

MATCH DRAWN

Match Seven (May 18)

v **Northamptonshire, at Northampton** *(Northamptonshire won toss)*

NORTHAMPTONSHIRE

A Fordham lbw McDermott	101
NA Felton c ME Waugh b Reiffel	32
RJ Bailey not out	82
*AJ Lamb not out	37
Extras (12 lb, 5 w, 4 nb)	21
Total (2 wkts, 55 overs)	273

Did Not Bat: MB Loye, DJ Capel, AL Penberthy, #D Ripley, JP Taylor, A Walker, NGB Cook.

Fall of Wickets: 1-67, 2-203.

Bowling: McDermott 11-1-48-1; Hughes 9-0-52-0; SR Waugh 4-0-20-0; Reiffel 10-1-35-1; May 11-0-49-0; Border 7-0-40-0; ME Waugh 3-0-17-0.

AUSTRALIANS

MA Taylor not out	89
ME Waugh b Cook	74
DC Boon st Ripley b Bailey	12
*AR Border not out	3
Extras (3 b, 1 lb, 1 w)	5
Total (2 wkts, 39 overs)	183

Did Not Bat: SR Waugh, DR Martyn, #IA Healy, TBA May, MG Hughes, PR Reiffel, CJ McDermott.

Fall of Wickets: 1-144, 2-171.

Bowling: Taylor 7-0-26-0; Walker 5-0-17-0; Penberthy 6-0-32-0; Capel 5-0-35-0; Cook 8-0-34-1; Bailey 8-1-35-1.

Umpires: JH Harris and AA Jones

NORTHAMPTONSHIRE WON ON RUN-RATE

Match Eight (May 19)

The First Limited-Overs International, at Old Trafford *(England won toss)*

AUSTRALIA

ML Hayden c Stewart b Lewis	29
MA Taylor c Fairbrother b Illingworth	79
ME Waugh c Fairbrother b Jarvis	56
DC Boon c Fairbrother b Illingworth	2
*AR Border c Lewis b Illingworth	4
SR Waugh c and b Lewis	27
#IA Healy c Thorpe b Caddick	20
MG Hughes b Lewis	20
PR Reiffel run out	2
CJ McDermott not out	3
TBA May not out	1
Extras (1 b, 8 lb, 2 w, 4 nb)	15
Total (9 wkts, 55 overs)	258

Fall of Wickets: 1-60, 2-168, 3-171, 4-178, 5-186, 6-219, 7-237, 8-244, 9-254.

Bowling: Caddick 11-1-50-1; Pringle 10-3-36-0; Lewis 11-1-54-3; Jarvis 11-0-55-1; Illingworth 11-0-48-3; Hick 1-0-6-0.

ENGLAND

*GA Gooch c ME Waugh b McDermott	4
#AJ Stewart b Hughes	22
RA Smith c and b McDermott	9
GA Hick b Reiffel	85
NH Fairbrother c Reiffel b SR Waugh	59
GP Thorpe c Taylor b McDermott	31
CC Lewis run out	4
DR Pringle c Taylor b SR Waugh	6
RK Illingworth run out	12
PW Jarvis c Reiffel b SR Waugh	2
AR Caddick not out	1
Extras (8 lb, 9 w, 2 nb)	19
Total (54.5 overs)	254

Fall of Wickets: 1-11, 2-38, 3-44, 4-171, 5-194, 6-211, 7-227, 8-240, 9-247, 10-254.

Bowling: McDermott 11-2-38-3; Hughes 9.5-1-40-1; May 11-2-40-0; Reiffel 11-0-63-1; ME Waugh 2-0-12-0; SR Waugh 10-0-53-3.

Umpires: BJ Meyer and DR Shepherd
Man of the Match: CJ McDermott

AUSTRALIA WON BY 4 RUNS

Merv Hughes, as brave and belligerent as ever, at The Oval.

Shane Warne, bowling during the sixth Test. The umpire is Mervyn Kitchen.

Michael Slater, in trouble against Devon Malcolm at The Oval.

Gooch, caught Healy bowled Warne for 79, in England's second innings of the sixth Test, the innings in which he became his country's highest run-scorer in Test cricket.

The English captain, Mike Atherton, and his deputy, Alec Stewart, celebrate the final dismissal of the series.

AB shows The Oval crowd what it's all about.

Match Nine (May 21)

The Second Limited-Overs International, at Edgbaston *(Australia won toss)*

ENGLAND

*GA Gooch c Healy b McDermott	17
#AJ Stewart b McDermott	0
RA Smith not out	167
GA Hick c Healy b Reiffel	2
NH Fairbrother c Taylor b SR Waugh	23
GP Thorpe c Border b McDermott	36
CC Lewis not out	13
Extras (2 b, 4 lb, 2 w, 11 nb)	19
Total (5 wkts, 55 overs)	277

Did Not Bat: DR Pringle, DG Cork, PW Jarvis, AR Caddick.

Fall of Wickets: 1-3, 2-40, 3-55, 4-105, 5-247.

Bowling: McDermott 11-1-29-3; Hughes 11-2-51-0; Reiffel 11-0-70-1; May 11-0-45-0; SR Waugh 8-0-55-1; ME Waugh 3-0-21-0.

AUSTRALIA

MA Taylor b Lewis	26
ML Hayden b Jarvis	14
ME Waugh c Fairbrother b Lewis	113
DC Boon c Stewart b Pringle	21
*AR Border not out	86
SR Waugh not out	6
Extras (5 lb, 3 w, 6 nb)	14
Total (4 wkts, 53.3 overs)	280

Did Not Bat: #IA Healy, MG Hughes, PR Reiffel, CJ McDermott, TBA May.

Fall of Wickets: 1-28, 2-55, 3-95, 4-263.

Bowling: Caddick 11-1-43-0; Jarvis 10-1-51-1; Lewis 10.3-0-61-2; Pringle 11-0-63-1; Cork 11-1-57-0.

Umpires: MJ Kitchen and KE Palmer
Man of the Match: RA Smith

AUSTRALIA WON BY 6 WICKETS

Match 10 (May 23)

The Third Limited-Overs International, at Lord's *(England won toss)*

AUSTRALIA

ML Hayden c Stewart b Caddick	4
*MA Taylor c Stewart b Reeve	57
ME Waugh c Stewart b Caddick	14
DC Boon b Illingworth	73
DR Martyn not out	51
SR Waugh c Gooch b Caddick	8
#IA Healy not out	12
Extras (3 lb, 6 w, 2 nb)	11
Total (5 wkts, 55 overs)	**230**

Did Not Bat: BP Julian, MG Hughes, CJ McDermott, TBA May.

Fall of Wickets: 1-12, 2-31, 3-139, 4-193, 5-208.

Bowling: Jarvis 11-1-51-0; Caddick 11-3-39-3; Cork 9-2-24-0; Illingworth 11-0-46-1; Reeve 11-1-50-1; Hick 3-0-17-0.

ENGLAND

*GA Gooch c Hughes b May	42
#AJ Stewart c ME Waugh b Julian	74
RA Smith st Healy b May	6
GA Hick b Julian	7
NH Fairbrother c Boon b Julian	18
GP Thorpe c Healy b SR Waugh	22
DA Reeve run out	2
DG Cork b Hughes	11
RK Illingworth c Healy b Hughes	9
PW Jarvis c Hayden b McDermott	3
AR Caddick not out	2
Extras (6 lb, 8 w, 1 nb)	15
Total (53.1 overs)	**211**

Fall of Wickets: 1-96, 2-115, 3-129, 4-159, 5-160, 6-169, 7-195, 8-201, 9-208, 10-211.

Bowling: McDermott 10-1-35-1; Hughes 10.1-0-41-2; Julian 11-1-50-3; May 11-1-36-2; SR Waugh 11-0-43-1.

Umpires: HD Bird and R Palmer
Man of the Match: BP Julian

AUSTRALIA WON BY 19 RUNS

Match 11 (May 25-27)

v Surrey, at The Oval *(Surrey won toss)*

AUSTRALIANS — First Innings

ML Hayden c Kersey b Butcher	36
MJ Slater c Lynch b Benjamin	5
MA Taylor c Brown b Benjamin	7
ME Waugh lbw Thorpe	178
DR Martyn c Brown b Kendrick	84
#TJ Zoehrer c sub (Smith) b Thorpe	1
*AR Border c and b Kendrick	28
BP Julian c Lynch b Thorpe	27
PR Reiffel c Lynch b Thorpe	0
SK Warne not out	6
Extras (5 lb, 1 w)	6
Total (9 wkts, declared)	**378**

Did Not Bat: WJ Holdsworth
Fall of Wickets: 1-17, 2-35, 3-67, 4-304, 5-306, 6-329, 7-362, 8-363, 9-378.
Bowling: Benjamin 9-4-19-2; Murphy 20-1-66-0; Butcher 16-2-73-1; Kendrick 25-6-90-2; Boiling 12-1-85-0; Thorpe 13.3-4-40-4.
Batting time: 328 minutes *Overs:* 95.3

SURREY — First Innings

DJ Bicknell c Waugh b Holdsworth	15
*MA Lynch b Warne	48
GP Thorpe c Warne b Julian	3
AD Brown c Border b Reiffel	35
DM Ward c Martyn b Reiffel	9
MA Butcher lbw Warne	1
#G Kersey lbw Warne	4
NM Kendrick c Taylor b ME Waugh	41
J Boiling run out	19
JE Benjamin c Zoehrer b Holdsworth	4
AJ Murphy not out	24
Extras (2 b, 14 lb, 8 w, 4 nb)	28
Total	**231**

Fall of Wickets: 1-31, 2-37, 3-120, 4-122, 5-129, 6-135, 7-135, 8-196, 9-201, 10-231.
Bowling: Holdsworth 17-2-81-2; Julian 15-4-31-1; Warne 23.5-8-68-3; Reiffel 10-3-22-2; ME Waugh 5-2-13-1.
Batting time: 274 minutes
Overs: 70.5

AUSTRALIANS — Second Innings

MJ Slater c Lynch b Murphy	50
ML Hayden b Kendrick	33
MA Taylor c Bicknell b Murphy	80
#TJ Zoehrer c Thorpe b Murphy	4
BP Julian not out	0
Extras (4 lb)	4
Total (4 wkts, declared)	**171**

Fall of Wickets: 1-44, 2-152, 3-171, 4-171.
Bowling: Murphy 17.4-0-48-3; Thorpe 8-1-41-0; Kendrick 19-4-60-1; Boiling 4-1-8-0.
Batting time: 173 minutes *Overs:* 48.4

SURREY — Second Innings

DJ Bicknell c Zoehrer b Julian	8
*MA Lynch c Zoehrer b Reiffel	22
GP Thorpe c Zoehrer b Warne	23
AD Brown c Border b Reiffel	1
DM Ward c Zoehrer b Holdsworth	28
#G Kersey c Zoehrer b Julian	17
MA Butcher st Zoehrer b Warne	10
NM Kendrick c Zoehrer b Julian	5
J Boiling not out	5
JE Benjamin st Zoehrer b Warne	2
AJ Murphy c Holdsworth b Warne	5
Extras (2 b, 4 lb, 2 w, 10 nb)	18
Total	**144**

Fall of Wickets: 1-8, 2-42, 3-45, 4-73, 5-99, 6-116, 7-130, 8-131, 9-138, 10-144.
Bowling: Julian 12-4-30-3; Holdsworth 10-2-43-1; Reiffel 11-0-27-2; Warne 19.1-6-38-4.
Batting time: 207 minutes *Overs:* 52.1

Umpires: VA Holder and NT Plews

AUSTRALIANS WON BY 174 RUNS

Match 12 (May 29-31)

v Leicestershire, at Leicester *(Australians won toss)*

AUSTRALIANS — First Innings

ML Hayden c Nixon b Mullally	2
MJ Slater c and b Wells	91
DC Boon c Parsons b Wells	123
*AR Border not out	42
SR Waugh not out	44
Extras (6 b, 3 lb, 8 w, 4 nb)	21
Total (3 wkts, declared)	**323**

Did Not Bat: #IA Healy, BP Julian, SK Warne, MG Hughes, CJ McDermott, TBA May.

Fall of Wickets: 1-2, 2-216, 3-227.

Bowling: Mullally 26-5-65-1; Parsons 28-6-64-0; Wells 25-7-70-2; Pierson 23-6-82-0; Hepworth 5-0-33-0.

Batting time: 390 minutes
Overs: 107

AUSTRALIANS — Second Innings

ML Hayden c Whitaker b Pierson	15
#IA Healy c Mullally b Parsons	4
MJ Slater not out	50
BP Julian c Robinson b Pierson	5
SK Warne st Nixon b Wells	6
MG Hughes not out	5
Extras (3 lb)	3
Total (4 wkts, declared)	**88**

Fall of Wickets: 1-9, 2-54, 3-62, 4-70.

Bowling: Parsons 9-3-12-1; Wells 5-0-28-1; Pierson 7.5-0-45-2.

Batting time: 79 minutes
Overs: 21.5

LEICESTERSHIRE — First Innings

TJ Boon lbw May	32
*NE Briers b Julian	24
JJ Whitaker c Slater b May	18
PE Robinson c Healy b Warne	11
BF Smith b Warne	0
PN Hepworth not out	37
VJ Wells c Healy b May	17
#PA Nixon c Hayden b Warne	5
GJ Parsons not out	3
Extras (2 b, 8 lb, 1 w, 10 nb)	21
Total (7 wkts, declared)	**168**

Did Not Bat: AD Mullally, ARK Pierson.

Fall of Wickets: 1-59, 2-83, 3-104, 4-104, 5-104, 6-136, 7-149.

Bowling: McDermott 11-1-27-0; Hughes 9-2-19-0; May 24-7-62-3; Julian 10-2-19-1; Warne 12-5-31-3.

Batting time: 231 minutes
Overs: 66

LEICESTERSHIRE — Second Innings

TJ Boon lbw McDermott	11
*NE Briers c Boon b McDermott	12
JJ Whitaker c McDermott b Julian	18
PE Robinson b Warne	31
BF Smith lbw Warne	31
PN Hepworth run out	2
VJ Wells b Warne	9
#PA Nixon c SR Waugh b May	21
GJ Parsons b May	5
AD Mullally c Julian b May	0
ARK Pierson not out	0
Extras (6 nb)	6
Total	**146**

Fall of Wickets: 1-19, 2-26, 3-56, 4-84, 5-92, 6-111, 7-128, 8-146, 9-146, 10-146.

Bowling: McDermott 14-4-38-2; Hughes 8-1-21-0; Julian 6-0-21-1; May 13.3-3-39-3; Warne 13-3-27-3.

Batting time: 204 minutes
Overs: 54.3

Umpires: G Sharp and B Leadbeater

AUSTRALIANS WON BY 97 RUNS

THE FIRST TEST (June 3-7)

at Old Trafford *(England won toss)*

AUSTRALIA — First Innings

MA Taylor c and b Such	124
MJ Slater c Stewart b De Freitas	58
DC Boon c Lewis b Such	21
ME Waugh c and b Tufnell	6
*AR Border st Stewart b Such	17
SR Waugh b Such	3
#IA Healy c Such b Tufnell	12
BP Julian c Gatting b Such	0
MG Hughes c De Freitas b Such	2
SK Warne not out	15
CJ McDermott run out	8
Extras (8 b, 8 lb, 7 nb)	23
Total	**289**

Fall of Wickets: 1-128, 2-183, 3-221, 4-225, 5-232, 6-260, 7-264, 8-266, 9-267, 10-289.
Bowling: Caddick 15-4-38-0; De Freitas 23-8-46-1; Lewis 13-2-44-0; Such 33.3-9-67-6; Tufnell 28-5-78-2.
Batting time: 439 minutes *Overs:* 112.3

AUSTRALIA — Second Innings

MA Taylor lbw Such	9
MJ Slater c Caddick b Such	27
DC Boon c Gatting b De Freitas	93
ME Waugh b Tufnell	64
*AR Border c and b Caddick	31
SR Waugh not out	78
#IA Healy not out	102
Extras (6 b, 14 lb, 8 nb)	28
Total (5 wkts, declared)	**432**

Fall of Wickets: 1-23, 2-46, 3-155, 4-234, 5-252.
Bowling: Caddick 20-3-79-1; De Freitas 24-1-80-1; Such 31-6-78-2; Tufnell 37-4-112-1; Hick 9-1-20-0; Lewis 9-0-43-0.
Batting time: 528 minutes *Overs:* 130

ENGLAND — First Innings

*GA Gooch c Julian b Warne	65
MA Atherton c Healy b Hughes	19
MW Gatting b Warne	4
RA Smith c Taylor b Warne	4
GA Hick c Border b Hughes	34
#AJ Stewart b Julian	27
CC Lewis c Boon b Hughes	9
PAJ De Freitas lbw Julian	5
AR Caddick c Healy b Warne	7
PM Such not out	14
PCR Tufnell c Healy b Hughes	1
Extras (6b, 10 lb, 5 nb)	21
Total	**210**

Fall of Wickets: 1-71, 2-80, 3-84, 4-123, 5-148, 6-168, 7-178, 8-183, 9-203, 10-210.
Bowling: McDermott 18-2-50-0; Hughes 20.5-5-59-4; Julian 11-2-30-2; Warne 24-10-51-4; Border 1-0-4-0.
Batting time: 306 minutes *Overs:* 74.5

Umpires: HD Bird and KE Palmer
Man of the Match: SK Warne

ENGLAND — Second Innings

*GA Gooch handled the ball	133
MA Atherton c Taylor b Warne	25
MW Gatting b Hughes	23
RA Smith b Warne	18
GA Hick c Healy b Hughes	22
#AJ Stewart c Healy b Warne	11
CC Lewis c Taylor b Warne	43
PAJ De Freitas lbw Julian	7
AR Caddick c Warne b Hughes	25
PM Such c Border b Hughes	9
PCR Tufnell not out	0
Extras (11 lb, 1 w, 4 nb)	16
Total	**332**

Fall of Wickets: 1-73, 2-133, 3-171, 4-223, 5-230, 6-238, 7-260, 8-299, 9-331, 10-332.
Bowling: McDermott 30-9-76-0; Hughes 27.2-4-92-4; Warne 49-26-86-4; Julian 14-0-67-1.
Batting time: 481 minutes *Overs:* 120.2

AUSTRALIA WON BY 179 RUNS

Match 14 (June 9-11)

v Warwickshire, at Edgbaston *(Australians won toss)*

AUSTRALIANS — First Innings

ML Hayden lbw Munton	10
MJ Slater c Twose b Reeve	64
ME Waugh b Small	8
DR Martyn c Donald b Smith	116
*AR Border b Smith	66
#TJ Zoehrer c Twose b Smith	20
BP Julian c Ostler b Reeve	5
#IA Healy not out	1
Extras (1 b, 15 lb, 1 w, 10 nb)	27
Total (7 wkts, declared)	**317**

Did Not Bat: PR Reiffel, TBA May, WJ Holdsworth.
Fall of Wickets: 1-36, 2-53, 3-108, 4-255, 5-285, 6-293, 7-317.
Bowling: Donald 10-0-67-0; Small 13-3-40-1; Munton 20-4-57-1; Reeve 23-5-55-2; Smith 15.5-4-55-3; Twose 8-3-27-0.
Batting time: 330 minutes
Overs: 89.5

WARWICKSHIRE — First Innings

AJ Moles c Border b Reiffel	49
JD Ratcliffe c Zoehrer b Holdsworth	2
RG Twose b c ME Waugh b Julian	29
DP Ostler b May	5
*DA Reeve c Slater b May	23
TL Penney lbw Zoehrer	11
#M Burns run out	7
NMK Smith c Healy b May	0
GC Small not out	7
AA Donald not out	5
Extras (8 b, 11 lb, 1 w, 26 nb)	46
Total (8 wkts)	**184**

Did Not Bat: TA Munton.
Fall of Wickets: 1-12, 2-84, 3-107, 4-123, 5-149, 6-162, 7-162, 8-162.
Bowling: Holdsworth 9-0-34-1; Reiffel 14-8-30-1; Julian 11-2-40-1; May 23-5-58-3; Zoehrer 4-3-3-1.
Batting time: 238 minutes
Overs: 61

Umpires: JC Balderstone and GI Burgess

MATCH DRAWN
(No play was possible, due to rain, on June 11)

Match 15 (June 12-14)

v **Gloucestershire, at Bristol** *(Australians won toss)*

GLOUCESTERSHIRE — First Innings

BC Broad c Hayden b Warne	80
GD Hodgson lbw Hughes	16
MW Alleyne c Healy b Hughes	2
TH Hancock c Hayden b Warne	37
AJ Wright c Taylor b Warne	23
RI Dawson b Warne	1
#RC Russell c Martyn b Warne	26
RC Williams b May	2
AM Smith b Hughes	3
JM De La Pena b Hughes	0
*CA Walsh not out	4
Extras (3 b, 8 lb, 6 nb)	17
Total	**211**

Fall of Wickets: 1-57, 2-59, 3-134, 4-171, 5-172, 6-173, 7-182, 8-201, 9-204, 10-211.
Bowling: McDermott 18-4-45-0; Hughes 15-5-27-4; SR Waugh 5-0-24-0; Warne 28-9-61-5; ME Waugh 5-0-19-0; May 14-5-24-1.
Batting time: 300 minutes
Overs: 85

AUSTRALIANS — First Innings

ML Hayden c Hodgson b Walsh	57
*MA Taylor lbw De La Pena	12
DC Boon c Smith b De La Pena	70
ME Waugh c Wright b Walsh	66
#DR Martyn c Williams b De La Pena	51
SR Waugh c Hodgson b De La Pena	21
MG Hughes not out	46
SK Warne c Russell b Williams	17
CJ McDermott b Alleyne	11
TBA May lbw Alleyne	4
#IA Healy absent, injured	-
Extras (10 lb, 1 w, 34 nb)	45
Total	**400**

Fall of Wickets: 1-28, 2-149, 3-170, 4-270, 5-311, 6-319, 7-357, 8-370, 9-400.
Bowling: Walsh 15-5-50-2; De La Pena 20-2-77-4, Williams 24-2-115-1; Smith 19-1-85-0; Alleyne 8.2-0-55-2; Hancock 2-1-8-0.
Batting time: 349 minutes
Overs: 88.2

Umpires: NT Plews and GA Stickley

MATCH DRAWN
(No play was possible, due to rain, on June 14)

THE SECOND TEST (June 18-22)

at Lord's *(Australia won toss)*

AUSTRALIA — First Innings

MA Taylor st Stewart b Tufnell	111
MJ Slater c sub (BF Smith) b Lewis	152
DC Boon not out	164
ME Waugh b Tufnell	99
*AR Border b Lewis	77
SR Waugh not out	13
Extras (1 lb, 1 w, 14 nb)	16
Total (4 wkts, declared)	632

Did Not Bat: #IA Healy, MG Hughes, SK Warne, TBA May, CJ McDermott.
Fall of Wickets: 1-260, 2-277, 3-452, 4-591.
Bowling: Caddick 38-5-120-0; Foster 30-4-94-0; Such 36-6-90-0; Tufnell 39-3-129-2; Lewis 36-5-151-2; Gooch 9-1-26-0; Hick 8-3-21-0.
Batting time: 771 minutes
Overs: 196

ENGLAND — First Innings

*GA Gooch c May b Hughes	12
MA Atherton b Warne	80
MW Gatting b May	5
RA Smith st Healy b May	22
GA Hick c Healy b Hughes	20
#AJ Stewart lbw Hughes	3
CC Lewis lbw Warne	0
NA Foster c Border b Warne	16
AR Caddick c Healy b Hughes	21
PM Such c Taylor b Warne	7
PCR Tufnell not out	2
Extras (8 lb, 9 nb)	17
Total	205

Fall of Wickets: 1-33, 2-50, 3-84, 4-123, 5-131, 6-132, 7-167, 8-174, 9-189, 10-205.
Bowling: Hughes 20-5-52-4; ME Waugh 6-1-16-0; SR Waugh 4-1-5-0; May 31-12-64-2; Warne 35-12-57-4; Border 3-1-3-0.
Batting time: 330 minutes *Overs:* 99

ENGLAND — Second Innings

*GA Gooch c Healy b Warne	29
MA Atherton run out	99
MW Gatting lbw Warne	59
RA Smith c sub (ML Hayden) b May	5
GA Hick c Taylor b May	64
#AJ Stewart lbw May	62
CC Lewis st Healy b May	0
NA Foster c ME Waugh b Border	20
AR Caddick not out	0
PM Such b Warne	4
PCR Tufnell b Warne	0
Extras (10 b, 13 lb)	23
Total	365

Fall of Wickets: 1-71, 2-175, 3-180, 4-244, 5-304, 6-312, 7-361, 8-361, 9-365, 10-365.
Bowling: Hughes 31-9-75-0; ME Waugh 17-4-55-0; May 51-23-81-4; SR Waugh 2-0-13-0; Warne 48.5-17-102-4; Border 16-9-16-1.
Batting time: 550 minutes
Overs: 165.5

Umpires: MJ Kitchen and DR Shepherd
Video-replay official: JC Balderstone
Man of the Match: MJ Slater

AUSTRALIA WON BY AN INNINGS AND 62 RUNS

Match 17 (June 23-25)

v **Combined Universities, at Oxford** *(Combined Universities won toss)*

AUSTRALIANS — First Innings

ML Hayden c Windows b Gallian	98
MJ Slater c Gallian b Pearson	111
#DR Martyn not out	138
BP Julian b Hallett	1
#TJ Zoehrer c and b Hallett	4
SK Warne lbw Hallett	5
ME Waugh not out	29
Extras (2 b)	2
Total (5 wkts, declared)	**388**

Did Not Bat: *MA Taylor, TBA May, PR Reiffel, WJ Holdsworth.
Fall of Wickets: 1-189, 2-260, 3-261, 4-271, 5-283.
Bowling: Hallett 19-1-85-3; MacDonald 11-168-0; Gallian 13-0-62-1; Pearson 20-1-107-1; Snape 11-1-64-0.
Batting time: 270 minutes
Overs: 74

AUSTRALIANS — Second Innings

*MA Taylor c Shephard b MacDonald	57
ML Hayden c Montgomerie b MacDonald	18
ME Waugh b Snape	84
#TJ Zoehrer c Montgomerie b MacDonald	0
BP Julian c Wileman b MacDonald	18
SK Warne c Montgomerie b Snape	47
MJ Slater not out	3
Extras (4 lb, 2 w)	6
Total (6 wkts, declared)	**233**

Fall of Wickets: 1-31, 2-107, 3-107, 4-153, 5-208, 6-233.
Bowling: Hallett 7-1-26-0; MacDonald 23-1-80-4; Pearson 5-0-37-0; Gallian 7-0-37-0; Snape 8.5-1-49-2.
Batting time: 182 minutes
Overs: 50.5

COMB. UNIVERSITIES — First Innings

RR Montgomerie st Martyn b Warne	52
*JER Gallian lbw Holdsworth	1
RQ Cake c Julian b Warne	108
GBT Lovell st Zoehrer b Warne	20
JN Snape c ME Waugh b Holdsworth	18
MGN Windows b Reiffel	36
JR Wileman not out	15
#SF Shephard c ME Waugh b Julian	5
Extras (7 b, lb 12, w 1, nb 28)	48
Total (7 wkts, declared)	**298**

Did Not Bat: JC Hallett, RM Pearson, RH MacDonald
Fall of Wickets: 1-15, 2-94, 3-154, 4-207, 5-249, 6-285, 7-298.
Bowling: Holdsworth 21-5-52-2; Julian 16.5-2-67-1; Reiffel 15-5-43-1; Zoehrer 17-4-53-0; Warne 22-7-45-3; ME Waugh 5-2-19-0.
Batting time: 330 minutes
Overs: 96.5

COMB. UNIVERSITIES — Second Innings

RR Montgomerie b Julian	4
*JER Gallian c ME Waugh b Julian	16
RQ Cake c ME Waugh b Reiffel	16
GBT Lovell retired hurt	4
JN Snape lbw Julian	0
MGN Windows c Julian b Zoehrer	44
JR Wileman c Taylor b Warne	48
#SF Shephard lbw Warne	0
JC Hallett not out	6
RM Pearson c Taylor b Zoehrer	1
RH MacDonald c Waugh b Zoehrer	4
Extras (4 lb, 10 nb)	14
Total	**157**

Fall of Wickets: 1-25, 2-26, 3-30, 4-63, 5-138, 6-145, 7-146, 8-151, 9-157.
Bowling: Holdsworth 6-0-19-0; Julian 12-1-57-3; Reiffel 9-1-30-1; Zoehrer 11.3-7-16-3; Warne 12-6-21-2; Taylor 3-0-10-0.
Batting time: 191 minutes
Overs: 53.3

Umpires: DJ Constant and R Julian

AUSTRALIANS WON BY 166 RUNS

Match 18 (June 26-28)

v Hampshire, at Southampton *(Australians won toss)*

AUSTRALIANS — First Innings

ML Hayden c Nicholas b Shine	85
MA Taylor c Maru b Udal	49
DC Boon c Aymes b Maru	146
SR Waugh c Middleton b Udal	6
*AR Border c and b James	41
#DR Martyn c Middleton b James	6
#IA Healy lbw James	3
BP Julian not out	26
PR Reiffel not out	8
Extras (15 lb, 8 nb)	23
Total (7 wkts, declared)	**393**

Did Not Bat: TBA May, MG Hughes.
Fall of Wickets: 1-91, 2-225, 3-240, 4-319, 5-327, 6-345, 7-359.
Bowling: Shine 16-2-81-1; Connor 16-0-55-0; Udal 24-4-123-2; Maru 15-1-62-1; James 17-2-57-3.
Batting time: 326 minutes
Overs: 88

AUSTRALIANS — Second Innings

ML Hayden c Smith b Connor	115
#IA Healy lbw James	16
SR Waugh b Connor	0
BP Julian c Aymes b Udal	28
DR Martyn b Connor	13
*AR Border c Maru b Connor	3
MA Taylor c Aymes b Udal	24
MG Hughes not out	61
DC Boon not out	0
Extras (3 lb, 8 nb)	11
Total (7 wkts, declared)	**271**

Fall of Wickets: 1-37, 2-40, 3-96, 4-122, 5-132, 6-187, 7-268.
Bowling: Shine 2.4-0-8-0; Connor 19-3-77-4; James 11.2-3-22-1; Maru 15-3-57-0; Udal 17-3-94-2.
Batting time: 234 minutes
Overs: 65

HAMPSHIRE — First Innings

VP Terry lbw Hughes	2
TC Middleton c Hayden b Hughes	53
DI Gower c Martyn b Hughes	8
RA Smith c Hughes b May	191
*MCJ Nicholas b May	19
KD James not out	31
#AN Aymes not out	17
Extras (4 b, 2 lb, 3 w, 44 nb)	53
Total (5 wkts, declared)	**374**

Did Not Bat: SD Udal, RJ Maru, CA Connor, KJ Shine.
Fall of Wickets: 1-2, 2-28, 3-261, 4-317, 5-322.
Bowling: Hughes 18-2-60-3; Julian 19-1-95-0; May 15-2-63-2; Reiffel 15-1-76-0; SR Waugh 6-1-69-0; Border 7-0-45-0.
Batting time: 295 minutes
Overs: 78

Umpires: RA White & P Willey. (TE Jesty substituted for RA White on second day.)

HAMPSHIRE — Second Innings

TC Middleton c Taylor b Hughes	78
VP Terry run out	82
DI Gower not out	23
RA Smith c Healy b Hughes	0
*MCJ Nicholas b Border	12
KD James st Healy b May	1
SD Udal lbw May	0
#AN Aymes not out	8
Extras (3 b, 3 lb, 10 nb)	16
Total (6 wkts)	**220**

Fall of Wickets: 1-167, 2-178, 3-178, 4-199, 5-200, 6-200.
Bowling: Hughes 14-3-47-2; Julian 7-1-16-0; Reiffel 10-1-45-0; May 18-4-57-2; Border 15-3-49-1.
Batting time: 236 minutes
Overs: 64

MATCH DRAWN

THE THIRD TEST (June 1-6)

at Trent Bridge *(England won toss)*

ENGLAND — First Innings

MN Lathwell c Healy b Hughes	20
MA Atherton c Boon b Warne	11
RA Smith c and b Julian	86
#AJ Stewart c ME Waugh b Warne	25
*GA Gooch c Border b Hughes	38
GP Thorpe c SR Waugh b Hughes	6
N Hussain c Boon b Warne	71
AR Caddick lbw Hughes	15
MJ McCague c ME Waugh b Hughes	9
MC Ilott c Taylor b May	6
PM Such not out	0
Extras (5b, 23 lb, 4 w, 2 nb)	34
Total	**321**

Fall of Wickets: 1-28, 2-63, 3-153, 4-159, 5-174, 6-220, 7-290, 8-304, 9-321, 10-321.
Bowling: Hughes 31-7-92-5; Julian 24-3-84-1; Warne 40-17-74-3; May 14.4-7-31-1; SR Waugh 8-4-12-0; ME Waugh 1-1-0-0.
Batting time: 446 minutes
Overs: 118.4

ENGLAND — Second Innings

MN Lathwell lbw Warne	33
MA Atherton c Healy b Hughes	9
RA Smith c Healy b Warne	50
#AJ Stewart lbw Hughes	6
*GA Gooch c Taylor b Warne	120
AR Caddick c Boon b Julian	12
GP Thorpe not out	114
N Hussain not out	47
Extras (11 b, 11 lb, 9 nb)	31
Total (6 wkts, declared)	**422**

Fall of Wickets: 1-11, 2-100, 3-109, 4-117, 5-159, 6-309.
Bowling: Hughes 22-8-41-2; Julian 33-10-110-1; May 38-6-112-0; Warne 50-21-108-3; SR Waugh 1-0-3-0; Border 5-0-11-0; ME Waugh 6-3-15-0.
Batting time: 562 minutes
Overs: 155

AUSTRALIA — First Innings

MJ Slater lbw Caddick	40
MA Taylor c Stewart b McCague	28
DC Boon b McCague	101
ME Waugh c McCague b Such	70
SR Waugh c Stewart b McCague	13
#IA Healy c Thorpe b Ilott	9
BP Julian c Stewart b Ilott	5
*AR Border c Smith b Such	38
MG Hughes b Ilott	17
SK Warne not out	35
TBA May lbw McCague	1
Extras (4 b, 8 lb, 4 w)	16
Total	**373**

Fall of Wickets: 1-55, 2-74, 3-197, 4-239, 5-250, 6-262, 7-284, 8-311, 9-356, 10-373.
Bowling: McCague 32.3-5-121-4; Ilott 34-8-108-3; Such 20-7-51-2; Caddick 22-5-81-1.
Batting time: 471 minutes
Overs: 108.3

AUSTRALIA — Second Innings

MA Taylor c Atherton b Such	28
MJ Slater b Such	26
DC Boon c Stewart b Caddick	18
ME Waugh b Caddick	1
*AR Border c Thorpe b Caddick	2
SR Waugh not out	47
#IA Healy lbw Ilott	5
BP Julian not out	56
Extras (5 b, 5 lb, 4 w, 5 nb)	19
Total (6 wkts)	**202**

Fall of Wickets: 1-46, 2-74, 3-75, 4-81, 5-93, 6-115.
Bowling: McCague 19-6-58-0; Ilott 18-5-44-1; Such 23-6-58-2; Caddick 16-6-32-3.
Batting time: 314 minutes *Overs:* 76

Umpires: R Palmer and BJ Meyer
Video-replay official: B Dudleston
Man of the Match: GP Thorpe

MATCH DRAWN

Match 20 (July 8)

v Minor Counties, at Stone *(Minor Counties won toss)*

AUSTRALIANS

ML Hayden c Humphries b Newman	19
MJ Slater lbw Newman	1
DR Martyn c Humphries b Donohue	14
SR Waugh b Evans	22
*MA Taylor c Cockbain b Newman	53
IA Healy c Dean b Evans	16
#TJ Zoehrer c Humphries b Derrick	0
BP Julian b Smith	31
PR Reiffel not out	50
SK Warne c Dean b Smith	8
WJ Holdsworth c Derrick b Smith	5
Extras (8 lb, 3 w)	11
Total (54.3 overs)	230

Fall of Wickets: 1-1, 2-31, 3-37, 4-77, 5-97, 6-98, 7-138, 8-199, 9-219, 10-231.

Bowling: Newman 10-1-49-3; Donohue 11-0-43-1; Evans 11-1-48-2; Derrick 11-1-41-1; Smith 10.3-0-36-3; Adams 1-0-5-0.

MINOR COUNTIES

SJ Dean b Holdsworth	4
NR Gaywood c Zoehrer b Reiffel	14
NJ Adams c Zoehrer b Holdsworth	11
*I Cockbain c Zoehrer b Reiffel	70
MR Davies c Zoehrer b Reiffel	0
J Derrick st Zoehrer b Warne	16
#MI Humphries c SR Waugh b Holdsworth	21
PG Newman lbw Reiffel	9
RA Evans st Zoehrer b Taylor	5
K Donohue lbw Reiffel	0
A Smith not out	0
Extras (5 b, 10 lb, 3 w, 4 nb)	22
Total (48.3 overs)	172

Fall of Wickets: 1-4, 2-23, 3-47, 4-47, 5-104, 6-141, 7-157, 8-170, 9-170, 10-172.

Bowling: Holdsworth 11-3-44-3; Reiffel 9.3-3-28-5; Martyn 4-0-33-0; Julian 11-2-23-0; Warne 11-5-22-1; Taylor 2-1-7-1.

Umpires: DJ Halfyard and S Kuhlmann

AUSTRALIANS WON BY 58 RUNS

Match 21 (July 10)

v Ireland, at Clontarf *(Ireland won toss)*

AUSTRALIANS

MJ Slater b Curry	56
ML Hayden not out	133
ME Waugh c Curry b Harrison	26
*AR Border c McCrum b Moore	111
Extras (4 b, 5 lb, 26 nb)	35
Total (3 wkts, declared, 49 overs)	361

Did Not Bat: DR Martyn, #TJ Zoehrer, IA Healy, BP Julian, PR Reiffel, TBA May, WJ Holdsworth.

Fall of Wickets: 1-155, 2-208, 3-361.

Bowling: McCrum 8-1-46-0; Moore 9-0-66-1; Benson 4-0-25-0; Lewis 3-0-36-0; Curry 12-0-75-1; Harrison 12-0-72-1; Dunlop 1-0-32-0.

IRELAND

JDR Benson c Julian b Holdsworth	1
MP Rea lbw Holdsworth	11
*SJS Warke c Zoehrer b Holdsworth	4
DA Lewis b Reiffel	14
GD Harrison b Zoehrer	15
DJ Curry c Zoehrer b Reiffel	0
AR Dunlop c ME Waugh b Hayden	2
NG Doak c Healy b Slater	14
#RB Millar c Holdsworth b Zoehrer	9
P McCrum not out	2
ERP Moore c Healy b Zoehrer	0
Extras (6 b, 4 lb, 1 w, 6 nb)	17
Total (42 overs)	90

Fall of Wickets: 1-2, 2-19, 3-22, 4-39, 5-41, 6-59, 7-65, 8-85, 9-88, 10-90.

Bowling: Holdsworth 6-2-13-3; Julian 5-1-7-0; May 6-1-14-0; Reiffel 6-1-10-2; Zoehrer 10-4-23-3; Hayden 4-1-5-1; Slater 5-1-7-1.

Umpires: B Arlow and L Hogan

AUSTRALIANS WON BY 272 RUNS

Match 22 (July 13-15)

v **Derbyshire, at Derby** *(Australians won toss)*

DERBYSHIRE — First Innings

*KJ Barnett c Zoehrer b Reiffel	114
PD Bowler c Zoehrer b Reiffel	30
JE Morris c Warne b Julian	2
CJ Adams c Hayden b Reiffel	4
TJG O'Gorman c ME Waugh b Reiffel	6
DG Cork c Martyn b Holdsworth	56
FA Griffith b Holdsworth	41
MJ Vandrau c ME Waugh b Holdsworth	0
#KM Krikken c Zoehrer b Holdsworth	1
SJ Base c Zoehrer b Holdsworth	7
DE Malcolm not out	0
Extras (14 lb, 30 nb)	44
Total	**305**

Fall of Wickets: 1-71, 2-74, 3-91, 4-103, 5-201, 6-296, 7-296, 8-296, 9-304, 10-305.
Bowling: Holdsworth 22-3-117-5; Julian 19-3-71-1; Reiffel 21-3-82-4; Warne 10-5-20-0; SR Waugh 2-1-1-0.

Batting time: 317 minutes
Overs: 74

AUSTRALIANS — First Innings

ML Hayden c Vandrau b Cork	40
MJ Slater not out	133
ME Waugh not out	60
(Extras 3 lb, 2 w, 30 nb)	35
Total (1 wkt)	**286**

Did Not Bat: *AR Border, DR Martyn, SR Waugh, #TJ Zoehrer, BP Julian, PR Reiffel, SK Warne, WJ Holdsworth.
Fall of Wicket: 1-89.
Bowling: Malcolm 12-0-85-0; Cork 12-0-55-1; Base 10-1-85-0; Vandrau 7-1-27-0; Adams 3-0-13-0.
Batting time: 179 minutes
Overs: 44

Umpires: JH Harris and AA Jones

MATCH DRAWN
(No play was possible, due to rain, on July 15)

Match 23 (July 17-19)

v **Durham, at Durham University** *(Durham won toss)*

DURHAM — First Innings

G Fowler c Healy b Julian	41
W Larkins c Taylor b Holdsworth	151
PWG Parker c Martyn b Julian	2
S Hutton c Boon b Reiffel	47
P Bainbridge c Border b Holdsworth	3
IT Botham c Julian b SR Waugh	32
AC Cummins c Healy b Hayden	69
#CW Scott c and b May	5
PJ Berry not out	24
Extras (4 lb, 1 w, 6 nb)	11
Total (8 wkts, declared)	**385**

Did Not Bat: SJE Brown, *DA Graveney.
Fall of Wickets: 1-91, 2-95, 3-232, 4-246, 5-249, 6-296, 7-317, 8-385.
Bowling: Holdsworth 18-1-118-2; Julian 20-5-62-2; Reiffel 21-7-50-1; SR Waugh 14-3-50-1; May 16-4-63-1; Hayden 7.4-1-24-1; Martyn 6-1-14-0.
Batting time: 388 minutes
Overs: 102.4

AUSTRALIANS — First Innings

MA Taylor b Cummins	10
ML Hayden c Scott b Brown	7
DC Boon c Parker b Brown	27
SR Waugh c Scott b Brown	19
DR Martyn c Larkins b Brown	0
*AR Border run out	17
#IA Healy not out	70
BP Julian b Graveney	6
PR Reiffel c Scott b Brown	39
TBA May lbw Brown	0
WJ Holdsworth c and b Brown	5
Extras (4 b, 7 lb, 10 nb)	21
Total	**221**

Fall of Wickets: 1-8, 2-38, 3-66, 4-66, 5-83, 6-101, 7-113, 8-213, 9-213, 10-221.
Bowling: Cummins 18-4-62-1; Brown 22.4-1-70-7; Botham 6-2-21-0; Graveney 10-6-18-1; Bainbridge 5-0-27-0; Berry 4-0-12-0.
Batting time: 270 minutes
Overs: 65.4

AUSTRALIANS — Second Innings

ML Hayden not out	151
MA Taylor c Graveney b Cummins	1
DC Boon c Larkins b Berry	112
WJ Holdsworth c Parker b Berry	12
SR Waugh not out	6
Extras (3 b, 3 lb, 3 w, 4 nb)	13
Total (3 wkts)	**295**

Fall of Wickets: 1-10, 2-235, 3-251.
Bowling: Cummins 11-3-25-1; Brown 11-3-39-0; Bainbridge 11-1-51-0; Berry 14-1-91-2; Graveney 3-2-6-0; Botham 11-2-45-0; Parker 5-0-32-0.
Batting time: 253 minutes
Overs: 66

Umpires: JH Hampshire and DO Oslear.

MATCH DRAWN

THE FOURTH TEST (July 22-26)

at Headingley *(Australia won toss)*

AUSTRALIA - First Innings

MA Taylor lbw Bicknell	27
MJ Slater b Ilott	67
DC Boon lbw Ilott	107
ME Waugh b Ilott	52
*AR Border not out	200
SR Waugh not out	157
Extras (8 b, 22 lb, 4 w, 9 nb)	43
Total (4 wkts, declared)	**653**

Did Not Bat: #IA Healy, MG Hughes, PR Reiffel, SK Warne, TBA May.
Fall of Wickets: 1-86, 2-110, 3-216, 4-321.
Bowling: McCague 28-2-115-0; Ilott 51-11-161-3; Caddick 42-5-138-0; Bicknell 50-8-155-1; Gooch 16-5-40-0; Thorpe 6-1-14-0.
Batting time: 817 minutes
Overs: 193

ENGLAND — First Innings

MN Lathwell c Healy b Hughes	0
MA Atherton b Reiffel	55
RA Smith c and b May	23
#AJ Stewart c Slater b Reiffel	5
*GA Gooch lbw Reiffel	59
GP Thorpe c Healy b Reiffel	0
N Hussain b Reiffel	15
AR Caddick c ME Waugh b Hughes	9
MP Bicknell c Border b Hughes	12
MJ McCague c Taylor b Warne	0
MC Ilott not out	0
Extras (2 b, 3 lb, 17 nb)	22
Total	**200**

Fall of Wickets: 1-0, 2-43, 3-50, 4-158, 5-158, 6-169, 7-184, 8-195, 9-200, 10-200.
Bowling: Hughes 15.5-3-47-3; Reiffel 26-6-65-5; May 15-3-33-1; Warne 23-9-43-1; ME Waugh 3-0-7-0.
Batting time: 308 minutes *Overs:* 82.5

ENGLAND — Second Innings

MN Lathwell b May	25
MA Atherton st Healy b May	63
RA Smith lbw Reiffel	35
#AJ Stewart c ME Waugh b Reiffel	78
*GA Gooch st Healy b May	26
GP Thorpe c Taylor b Reiffel	13
N Hussain not out	18
AR Caddick lbw Hughes	12
MP Bicknell lbw Hughes	0
MJ McCague b Hughes	11
MC Ilott c Border b May	4
Extras (5 b, 3 lb, 1 w, 11 nb)	20
Total	**305**

Fall of Wickets: 1-60, 2-131, 3-149, 4-202, 5-256, 6-263, 7-279, 8-279, 9-295, 10-305.
Bowling: Hughes 30-10-79-3; Reiffel 28-8-87-3; Warne 40-16-63-0; May 27-6-65-4; ME Waugh 2-1-3-0.
Batting time: 468 minutes
Overs: 127

Umpires: HD Bird and NT Plews
Video-replay official: B Leadbeater
Man of the Match: AR Border

AUSTRALIA WON BY AN INNINGS AND 148 RUNS

Match 25 (July 28-30)

v Lancashire, at Old Trafford *(Australians won toss)*

AUSTRALIANS — First Innings

*MA Taylor c De Freitas b Barnett	122
ML Hayden lbw Martin	61
#DR Martyn not out	70
MJ Slater lbw Martin	20
ME Waugh not out	4
Extras (1 lb, 4 nb)	5
Total (3 wkts, declared)	282

Did Not Bat: SR Waugh, #TJ Zoehrer, SK Warne, MG Hughes, TBA May, WJ Holdsworth.
Fall of Wickets: 1-117, 2-243, 3-275.
Bowling: De Freitas 17-2-41-0; Martin 20-5-63-2; Watkinson 14-1-68-0; Barnett 20-1-87-1; Gallian 9-0-22-0.
Batting time: 302 minutes
Overs: 80

AUSTRALIANS — Second Innings

ML Hayden lbw Watkinson	79
MJ Slater c Hegg b De Freitas	3
SR Waugh b Martin	17
#TJ Zoehrer c Watkinson b De Freitas	9
ME Waugh b Barnett	21
#DR Martyn st Hegg b Barnett	38
SK Warne b Barnett	3
MG Hughes b Barnett	4
*MA Taylor not out	7
TBA May not out	0
Extras (1 lb, 12 nb)	13
Total (8 wkts, declared)	194

Fall of Wickets: 1-7, 2-47, 3-65, 4-104, 5-160, 6-169, 7-187, 8-188.
Bowling: De Freitas 14-4-46-2; Martin 12-2-36-1; Watkinson 8-1-28-1; Barnett 24-5-83-4.
Batting time: 219 minutes
Overs: 58

LANCASHIRE — First Innings

GD Mendis b Warne	29
JP Crawley run out	14
SP Titchard c Taylor b Hughes	2
NJ Speak c and b Warne	48
GD Lloyd b Hughes	44
JER Gallian not out	42
*M Watkinson c May b Holdsworth	15
PAJ De Freitas c Holdsworth b Warne	1
#WK Hegg not out	26
Extras (14 b, 1 lb, 4 w, 10 nb)	29
Total (7 wkts, declared)	250

Did Not Bat: PJ Martin, AA Barnett.
Fall of Wickets: 1-24, 2-34, 3-76, 4-144, 5-161, 6-185, 7-186.
Bowling: Holdsworth 12-0-58-1; Hughes 13-5-32-2; Warne 32.4-12-54-3; May 15-2-48-0; Zoehrer 8-2-26-0; Taylor 5-0-17-0.
Batting time: 310 minutes
Overs: 85.4

LANCASHIRE — Second Innings

GD Mendis c Taylor b Warne	24
JP Crawley c Slater b May	109
SP Titchard run out	11
NJ Speak not out	39
GD Lloyd run out	6
JER Gallian c Hayden b May	0
*M Watkinson not out	14
Extras (15 b, 4 lb, 6 nb)	25
Total (7 wkts)	228

Fall of Wickets: 1-81, 2-134, 3-196, 4-206, 5-211.
Bowling: Holdsworth 2-0-11-0; Hughes 6-1-20-0; Warne 24-7-61-1; May 25.2-3-99-2; ME Waugh 2-0-13-0; SR Waugh 1-0-5-0.
Batting time: 217 minutes
Overs: 60.2

Umpires: B Dudleston and MK Reed

LANCASHIRE WON BY FIVE WICKETS

Match 26 (July 31-August 2)

v Glamorgan, at Neath *(Australians won toss)*

AUSTRALIANS — First Innings

MJ Slater c and b Thomas	72
DC Boon c Cottey b Bastien	120
ME Waugh not out	152
DR Martyn b Phelps	38
#IA Healy c Morris b Dale	5
*AR Border not out	14
Extras (2 b, 7 lb, 4 nb)	13
Total (4 wkts, declared)	414

Did Not Bat: PR Reiffel, SK Warne, MG Hughes, TBA May, WJ Holdsworth.
Fall of Wickets: 1-158, 2-215, 3-328, 4-355.
Bowling: Thomas 20-2-93-1; Bastien 17-0-70-1; Croft 21-2-71-0; Dale 20-3-66-1; Phelps 23-3-105-1.
Batting time: 328 minutes
Overs: 101

AUSTRALIANS — Second Innings

MJ Slater c and b Croft	43
DR Martyn c Metson b Thomas	15
#IA Healy c Croft b Thomas	4
PR Reiffel c and b Thomas	52
SK Warne run out	18
MG Hughes b Dale	71
*AR Border b Dale	23
ME Waugh not out	2
DC Boon not out	2
Extras (5 lb)	5
Total (7 wkts, declared)	235

Fall of Wickets: 1-37, 2-45, 3-65, 4-100, 5-176, 6-213, 7-232.
Bowling: Thomas 18-2-95-3; Bastien 10-0-31-0; Dale 9-0-41-2; Croft 12-2-46-1; Phelps 3-0-17-0.
Batting time: 180 minutes
Overs: 52

GLAMORGAN — First Innings

JRA Williams c Healy b Hughes	0
*H Morris c Healy b Hughes	18
A Dale c Healy b Holdsworth	25
MP Maynard lbw ME Waugh	132
PA Cottey b Warne	68
DL Hemp b Warne	40
RBD Croft lbw Warne	17
#CP Metson not out	22
SD Thomas st Healy b Warne	9
Extras (2 b, 9 lb, 1 w, 20 nb)	32
Total (8 wkts, declared)	363

Did Not Bat: BS Phelps, S Bastien.
Fall of Wickets: 1-4, 2-37, 3-78, 4-254, 5-274, 6-318, 7-337, 8-363.
Bowling: Hughes 13-2-67-2; Holdsworth 22-5-91-1; Reiffel 8-0-58-0; ME Waugh 15-4-56-1; Warne 26.2-6-67-4, Border 5-1-13-0.
Batting time: 322 minutes
Overs: 89.2

GLAMORGAN — Second Innings

JRA Williams c Boon b Hughes	6
*H Morris c Boon b Holdsworth	2
A Dale c Healy b Warne	31
MP Maynard b Holdsworth	36
PA Cottey c Martyn b Border	38
DL Hemp b Warne	16
RBD Croft not out	11
#CP Metson not out	7
Extras (1 b, 12 lb, 1 w, 8 nb)	22
Total (6 wkts)	169

Fall of Wickets: 1-8, 2-8, 3-92, 4-96, 5-132, 6-158.
Bowling: Hughes 7-1-23-1; Holdsworth 12-2-43-2; Reiffel 10-1-34-0; Warne 17-3-44-2, Border 5-2-12-1.
Batting time: 193 minutes
Overs: 51

Umpires: AGT Whitehead and PB Wight

MATCH DRAWN

THE FIFTH TEST (August 5-9)

at **Edgbaston** *(England won toss)*

ENGLAND — First Innings

GA Gooch c Taylor b Reiffel	8
*MA Atherton b Reiffel	72
RA Smith b ME Waugh	21
MP Maynard c SR Waugh b May	0
#AJ Stewart c and b Warne	45
GP Thorpe c Healy b May	37
N Hussain b Reiffel	3
JE Emburey not out	55
MP Bicknell c ME Waugh b Reiffel	14
PM Such b Reiffel	1
MC Ilott c Healy b Reiffel	3
Extras (4b, 6 lb, 7 nb)	17
Total	**276**

Fall of Wickets: 1-17, 2-71, 3-76, 4-156, 5-156, 6-160, 7-215, 8-262, 9-264, 10-276.
Bowling: Hughes 19-4-53-0; Reiffel 22.5-3-71-6; ME Waugh 15-4-43-1; SR Waugh 5-2-4-0; May 19-9-32-2; Warne 21-7-63-1.
Batting time: 364 minutes
Overs: 101.5

ENGLAND — Second Innings

GA Gooch b Warne	48
*MA Atherton c Border b Warne	28
RA Smith lbw Warne	19
MP Maynard c Healy b May	10
#AJ Stewart lbw Warne	5
GP Thorpe st Healy b Warne	60
N Hussain c SR Waugh b May	0
JE Emburey c Healy b May	37
MP Bicknell c SR Waugh b May	0
PM Such not out	7
MC Ilott b May	15
Extras (11b, 9 lb, 2 nb)	22
Total	**251**

Fall of Wickets: 1-60, 2-104, 3-115, 4-115, 5-124, 6-125, 7-229, 8-229, 9-229, 10-251.
Bowling: Hughes 18-7-24-0; Reiffel 11-2-30-0; May 48.2-15-89-5; Warne 49-23-82-5; Border 2-1-1-0; ME Waugh 5-2-5-0.
Batting time: 461 minutes
Overs: 133.2

AUSTRALIA — First Innings

MA Taylor run out	19
MJ Slater c Smith b Such	22
DC Boon lbw Emburey	0
ME Waugh c Thorpe b Ilott	137
*AR Border c Hussain b Such	3
SR Waugh c Stewart b Bicknell	59
#IA Healy c Stewart b Bicknell	80
MG Hughes b Bicknell	38
PR Reiffel b Such	20
SK Warne c Stewart b Emburey	10
TBA May not out	3
Extras (7 b, 8 lb, 2 nb)	17
Total	**408**

Fall of Wickets: 1-34, 2-39, 3-69, 4-80, 5-233, 6-263, 7-370, 8-379, 9-398, 10-408.
Bowling: Bicknell 34-9-99-3; Ilott 24-4-85-1; Such 52.5-18-90-3; Emburey 39-9-119-2.
Batting time: 579 minutes
Overs: 149.5

AUSTRALIA — Second Innings

MJ Slater c Thorpe b Emburey	8
MA Taylor c Thorpe b Such	4
DC Boon not out	38
ME Waugh not out	62
Extras (3 b, 5 lb)	8
Total (2 wkts)	**120**

Fall of Wickets: 1-12, 2-12.
Bowling: Bicknell 3-0-9-0; Such 20.3-4-58-1; Emburey 18-4-31-1; Ilott 2-0-14-0.
Batting time: 149 minutes
Overs: 43.3

Umpires: JH Hampshire and DR Shepherd
Video-replay official: AGT Whitehead

Man of the Match: ME Waugh

AUSTRALIA WON BY EIGHT WICKETS

Match 28 (August 11-13)

v Kent, at Canterbury *(Australians won toss)*

AUSTRALIANS — First Innings

*MA Taylor c Cowdrey b Ellison	78
MJ Slater c Fulton b Ealham	7
ML Hayden c Igglesden b Ellison	31
SR Waugh b Igglesden	123
DR Martyn not out	105
#IA Healy not out	33
Extras (3 lb, 1 w, 10 nb)	14
Total (4 wkts, declared)	**391**

Did Not Bat: BP Julian, SK Warne, TJ Zoehrer, TBA May, WJ Holdsworth.
Fall of Wickets: 1-22, 2-90, 3-151, 4-315.
Bowling: Igglesden 22-4-59-1; Ealham 25-1-103-1; Ellison 30-6-97-2; Davis 35-12-96-0; Patel 10-1-33-0.
Batting time: 453 minutes
Overs: 122

AUSTRALIANS — Second Innings

BP Julian not out	15
SK Warne not out	17
Extras (2 lb)	2
Total (0 wkts, declared)	**34**

Bowling: Davis 5-0-22-0; Patel 4-1-10-0.
Batting time: 22 minutes
Overs: 9

KENT — First Innings

DP Fulton not out	40
GR Cowdrey lbw Warne	25
NJ Llong c Taylor b SR Waugh	15
#SA Marsh not out	16
Extras (3 lb, 1 w, 14 nb)	18
Total (2 wkts, declared)	**114**

Did Not Bat: *MR Benson, TR Ward, MA Ealham, RM Ellison, RP Davis, M Patel, AP Igglesden.
Fall of Wickets: 1-71, 2-90.
Bowling: Holdsworth 7-2-20-0; Julian 9-2-41-0; Warne 9-1-30-1; SR Waugh 6-3-13-1; Hayden 1-0-7-0.
Batting time: 121 minutes
Overs: 32

KENT — Second Innings

DP Fulton c Zoehrer b Holdsworth	4
*MR Benson c Warne b SR Waugh	14
TR Ward c Taylor b Warne	69
NJ Llong lbw SR Waugh	0
GR Cowdrey run out	51
#SA Marsh lbw May	14
MA Ealham lbw May	34
RM Ellison c and b Zoehrer	1
RP Davis b Taylor	6
M Patel st Healy b Zoehrer	2
AP Igglesden not out	0
Extras (12 lb, 1 w, 14 nb)	27
Total	**222**

Fall of Wickets: 1-21, 2-27, 3-29, 4-158, 5-168, 6-204, 7-211, 8-211, 9-220, 10-222.
Bowling: Holdsworth 16-4-35-1; Julian 8-1-49-0; Warne 20-6-50-1; SR Waugh 5-2-9-2; May 14-2-39-2; Zoehrer 9.2-1-24-2; Taylor 1-0-4-1.
Batting time: 260 minutes
Overs: 73.2

Umpires: P Adams and JW Holder

AUSTRALIANS WON BY 89 RUNS

Match 29 (August 14-16)

v Essex, at Chelmsford *(Australians won toss)*

AUSTRALIANS — First Innings

MJ Slater lbw Pringle	0
ML Hayden c Such b Pringle	111
DC Boon St Garnham b Childs	15
ME Waugh b Salim Malik	108
*AR Border c Pringle b Childs	57
#IA Healy c Hussain b Childs	32
TJ Zoehrer not out	17
BP Julian not out	1
Extras (6 lb, 10 nb)	16
Total (6 wkts, declared)	**357**

Did Not Bat: PR Reiffel, MG Hughes, TBA May.
Fall of Wickets: 1-3, 2-81, 3-198, 4-291, 5-325, 6-347.
Bowling: Ilott 19-2-52-0; Pringle 14-1-48-2; Gooch 6-2-14-0; Such 16-2-102-0; Childs 23-4-86-3; Salim Malik 12-0-49-1.
Batting time: 330 minutes
Overs: 90

AUSTRALIANS — Second Innings

BP Julian b Pringle	66
MJ Slater c Salim Malik b Ilott	0
DC Boon b Childs	26
PR Reiffel lbw Such	15
MG Hughes lbw Pringle	0
TJ Zoehrer c Knight b Such	38
#IA Healy c Ilott b Such	4
ME Waugh c Lewis b Pringle	9
*AR Border c Knight b Pringle	12
TBA May not out	0
Extras (2 lb, 10 nb)	12
Total	**218**

Fall of Wickets: 1-1, 2-98, 3-98, 4-99, 5-115, 6-127, 7-175, 8-196, 9-218, 10-218.
Bowling: Ilott 9-1-47-1; Pringle 19-4-65-4; Such 14.1-3-52-4; Childs 17-6-52-1.
Batting time: 235 minutes
Overs: 59.1

ESSEX — First Innings

*GA Gooch c and b Julian	61
NV Knight c Healy b Reiffel	1
PJ Prichard b Reiffel	21
Salim Malik c Border b May	17
N Hussain c Slater b May	57
JJB Lewis lbw Zoehrer	8
#MA Garnham run out	17
DR Pringle c Healy b Zoehrer	9
MC Ilott st Healy b Zoehrer	24
PM Such c Healy b May	15
JH Childs not out	11
Extras (4 b, 9 lb, 14 nb)	27
Total	**268**

Fall of Wickets: 1-10, 2-74, 3-96, 4-122, 5-153, 6-198, 7-205, 8-211, 9-240, 10-268.
Bowling: Hughes 10-1-55-0; Reiffel 14-5-32-2; May 29-10-71-3; Julian 8-2-40-1; Zoehrer 21.3-3-57-3.
Batting time: 255 minutes
Overs: 72.3

ESSEX — Second Innings

*GA Gooch c Hughes b May	73
NV Knight c Hayden b Zoehrer	87
PJ Prichard b May	1
Salim Malik lbw Zoehrer	39
N Hussain c Zoehrer b ME Waugh	32
DR Pringle b ME Waugh	1
MA Garnham run out	12
JJB Lewis not out	1
MC Ilott c sub (SK Warne) b Zoehrer	1
JH Childs st Healy b ME Waugh	0
PM Such not out	0
Extras (10 b, 14 lb, 6 nb)	30
Total (9 wkts)	**277**

Fall of Wickets: 1-121, 2-124, 3-198, 4-245, 5-249, 6-275, 7-275, 8-277, 9-277.
Bowling: Hughes 9-1-32-0; Reiffel 15-4-32-0; May 13-3-44-2; Julian 5-0-25-0; Zoehrer 16-1-71-3; Border 6-0-23-0; ME Waugh 8-1-26-3.
Batting time: 278 minutes *Overs:* 72

Umpires: JD Bond and MJ Harris

MATCH DRAWN

THE SIXTH TEST (August 5-9)

at The Oval *(England won toss)*

ENGLAND — First Innings

GA Gooch c Border b SR Waugh	56
*MA Atherton lbw SR Waugh	50
GA Hick c Warne b May	80
MP Maynard b Warne	20
N Hussain c Taylor b Warne	30
#AJ Stewart c Healy b Hughes	76
MR Ramprakash c Healy b Hughes	6
ARC Fraser b Reiffel	28
SL Watkin c SR Waugh b Reiffel	13
PM Such c ME Waugh b Hughes	4
DE Malcolm not out	0
Extras (7 lb, 1 w, 9 nb)	17
Total	**380**

Fall of Wickets: 1-88, 2-139, 3-177, 4-231, 5-253, 6-272, 7-339, 8-363, 9-374, 10-380.
Bowling: Hughes 30-7-121-3; Reiffel 28.5-4-88-2; SR Waugh 12-2-45-2; Warne 20-5-70-2; ME Waugh 1-0-17-0; May 10-3-32-1.
Batting time: 420 minutes *Overs:* 101.5

ENGLAND — Second Innings

GA Gooch c Healy b Warne	79
*MA Atherton c Warne b Reiffel	42
GA Hick c Boon b May	36
MP Maynard c Reiffel b Hughes	9
N Hussain c ME Waugh b Hughes	0
#AJ Stewart c ME Waugh b Reiffel	35
MR Ramprakash c Slater b Hughes	64
ARC Fraser c Healy b Reiffel	13
SL Watkin lbw Warne	4
PM Such lbw Warne	10
DE Malcolm not out	0
Extras (5 b, 12 lb, 1 w, 3 nb)	21
Total	**313**

Fall of Wickets: 1-77, 2-157, 3-180, 4-180, 5-186, 6-254, 7-276, 8-283, 9-313, 10-313.
Bowling: Hughes 31.2-9-110-3; Reiffel 24-8-55-3; Warne 40-15-78-3; May 24-6-53-1.
Batting time: 470 minutes *Overs:* 119.2

AUSTRALIA — First Innings

MA Taylor c Hussain b Malcolm	70
MJ Slater c Gooch b Malcolm	4
DC Boon c Gooch b Malcolm	13
ME Waugh c Stewart b Fraser	10
*AR Border c Stewart b Fraser	48
SR Waugh b Fraser	20
#IA Healy not out	83
MG Hughes c Ramprakash b Watkin	7
PR Reiffel c Maynard b Watkin	0
SK Warne c Stewart b Fraser	16
TBA May c Stewart b Fraser	15
Extras (5 b, 6 lb, 2 w, 4 nb)	17
Total	303

Fall of Wickets: 1-9, 2-30, 3-53, 4-132, 5-164, 6-181, 7-196, 8-196, 9-248, 10-303.
Bowling: Malcolm 26-5-86-3; Watkin 28-4-87-2; Fraser 26.4-4-87-5; Such 14-4-32-0.
Batting time: 408 minutes *Overs:* 94.4

AUSTRALIA — Second Innings

MA Taylor b Watkin	8
MJ Slater c Stewart b Watkin	12
DC Boon lbw Watkin	0
ME Waugh c Ramprakash b Malcolm	49
*AR Border c Stewart b Malcolm	17
SR Waugh lbw Malcolm	26
#IA Healy c Maynard b Watkin	5
MG Hughes c Watkin b Fraser	12
PR Reiffel c and b Fraser	42
SK Warne lbw Fraser	37
TBA May not out	4
Extras (2 b, 6 lb, 2 w, 7 nb)	17
Total	**229**

Fall of Wickets: 1-23, 2-23, 3-30, 4-92, 5-95, 6-106, 7-142, 8-143, 9-219, 10-229.
Bowling: Malcolm 20-3-84-3; Watkin 25-9-65-4; Fraser 19.1-5-44-3; Such 9-4-17-0; Hick 8-3-11-0.
Batting time: 334 minutes *Overs:* 81.1

Umpires: MJ Kitchen and BJ Meyer
Video-replay official: AA Jones
Man of the Match: ARC Fraser

ENGLAND WON BY 161 RUNS

TEST AVERAGES

AUSTRALIA — Batting and Fielding

Batsman	Mat	Inn	NO	Runs	HS	100	50	Avge	Ct	St
SR Waugh	6	9	4	416	157*	1	2	83.20	5	-
DC Boon	6	10	2	555	164*	3	1	69.37	5	-
ME Waugh	6	10	1	550	137	1	5	61.11	9	-
IA Healy	6	7	2	296	102*	1	2	59.20	21	5
AR Border	6	9	1	433	200*	1	1	54.12	8	-
MA Taylor	6	10	-	428	124	2	1	42.80	11	-
MJ Slater	6	10	-	416	152	1	2	41.60	2	-
SK Warne	6	5	2	113	35*	-	-	37.66	4	-
BP Julian	2	3	1	61	56*	-	1	30.50	2	-
PR Reiffel	3	3	-	62	42	-	-	20.66	1	-
MG Hughes	6	5	-	76	38	-	-	15.20	-	-
TBA May	5	4	2	23	15	-	-	11.50	2	-
CJ McDermott	2	1	-	8	8	-	-	8.00	-	-

AUSTRALIA — Bowling

Bowler	Overs	Mdns	Runs	Wkts	Best	5w	10w	Ave
PR Reiffel	140.4	31	396	19	6-71	2	-	20.84
SK Warne	439.5	178	877	34	5-82	1	-	25.79
MG Hughes	296.2	78	845	31	5-92	1	-	27.25
TBA May	278	90	592	21	5-89	1	-	28.19
AR Border	27	11	35	1	1-35	-	-	35.00
SR Waugh	32	9	82	2	2-45	-	-	41.00
BP Julian	82	16	291	5	2-30	-	-	58.20
ME Waugh	56	16	161	1	1-43	-	-	161.00
CJ McDermott	48	11	126	0	-	-	-	-

ENGLAND — Batting and Fielding

Batsman	Mat	Inn	NO	Runs	HS	100	50	Avge	Ct	St
JM Emburey	1	2	1	92	55*	-	1	92.00	-	-
GA Gooch	6	12	-	673	133	2	4	56.08	2	-
MA Atherton	6	12	-	553	99	-	6	46.08	1	-
GP Thorpe	3	6	1	230	114*	1	1	46.00	5	-
GA Hick	3	6	-	256	80	-	2	42.66	-	-
MR Ramprakash	1	2	-	70	64	-	1	35.00	2	-
AJ Stewart	6	12	-	378	78	-	3	31.50	14	2
N Hussain	4	8	2	184	71	-	1	30.66	2	-
RA Smith	5	10	-	283	86	-	2	28.30	2	-
MW Gatting	2	4	-	91	59	-	1	22.75	2	-
ARC Fraser	1	2	-	41	28	-	-	20.50	-	-
MN Lathwell	2	4	-	78	33	-	-	19.50	-	-
NA Foster	1	2	-	36	20	-	-	18.00	-	-
AR Caddick	4	8	1	101	25	-	-	14.42	2	-
CC Lewis	2	4	-	52	43	-	-	13.00	1	-
MP Maynard	2	4	-	39	20	-	-	9.75	2	-
PM Such	5	9	3	56	14*	-	-	9.33	2	-

Batsman	Mat	Inn	NO	Runs	HS	100	50	Avge	Ct	St
SL Watkin	1	2	-	17	13	-	-	8.50	1	-
MC Ilott	3	5	1	28	15	-	-	7.00	-	-
MJ McCague	2	3	-	20	11	-	-	6.66	1	-
MP Bicknell	2	4	-	26	14	-	-	6.50	-	-
PAJ De Freitas	1	2	-	12	7	-	-	6.00	1	-
PCR Tufnell	2	4	2	3	2*	-	-	1.50	1	-
DE Malcolm	1	2	2	0	0*	-	-	-	-	-

ENGLAND — Bowling

Bowler	Overs	Mdns	Runs	Wkts	Best	5w	10w	Ave
ARC Fraser	45.5	9	131	8	5-87	1	-	16.37
SL Watkin	53	13	152	6	4-65	-	-	25.33
DE Malcolm	46	8	170	6	3-84	-	-	28.33
PM Such	239.5	64	541	16	6-67	1	-	33.81
JE Emburey	57	13	150	3	2-119	-	-	50.00
MC Ilott	129	28	412	8	3-108	-	-	51.50
PAJ De Freitas	47	9	126	2	1-46	-	-	63.00
PCR Tufnell	104	12	319	5	2-78	-	-	63.80
MP Bicknell	87	17	263	4	3-99	-	-	65.75
MJ McCague	79.3	13	294	4	4-121	-	-	73.50
AR Caddick	153	28	488	5	3-32	-	-	97.60
CC Lewis	58	7	238	2	2-151	-	-	119.00
GP Thorpe	6	1	14	0	-	-	-	-
GA Hick	25	7	52	0	-	-	-	-
GA Gooch	25	6	66	0	-	-	-	-
NA Foster	30	4	94	0	-	-	-	-

indicates not out

Statistical Notes on the Test Series

FIRST TEST

Test Debuts:
Australia — MJ Slater, BP Julian
England — AR Caddick, PM Such

Centuries:
MA Taylor — 124 in 322 minutes, 234 balls, 12 fours, one six (ninth Test century, third v England).
IA Healy — 102* in 165 minutes, 133 balls, 12 fours (maiden Test and first-class century). This was the first Test century by an Australian wicketkeeper in England.
GA Gooch — 133 in 314 minutes, 247 balls, 21 fours, two sixes (18th Test century, third v Australia).
• PM Such returned the best innings bowling figures by an Englishman on debut since 1976-77 (JK Lever 7-46 v India at Delhi).
• SK Warne dismissed MW Gatting with his first ball in Ashes Tests. He was the third Australian to achieve this feat, after A Coningham, in Melbourne in 1894-95, and EL McCormick, in Brisbane in 1936-37.
• GA Gooch's handled the ball dismissal was the first by an Englishman in Test cricket, the first in Ashes Tests, and the fifth ever in Tests. The other instances were:
– WR Endean, South Africa v England, Cape Town, 1956-57.
– AMJ Hilditch, Australia v Pakistan, Perth, 1978-79.
– Mohsin Khan, Pakistan v Australia, Karachi, 1982-83.
– DL Haynes, West Indies v India, Bombay, 1983-84.

SECOND TEST

Centuries:
MA Taylor — 111 in 325 minutes, 245 balls, 10 fours, one six (10th Test century, fourth v England).
MJ Slater — 152 in 295 minutes, 263 balls, 18 fours (maiden Test century).
DC Boon — 164* in 474 minutes, 378 balls, 15 fours (15th Test century, fourth v England).
• The opening partnership of 260 between MA Taylor and MJ Slater was the highest for any wicket for Australia in a Test at Lord's.
• The instance of Australia's first three batsmen all scoring centuries in the one innings was the third time Australia's top three had done so in a Test, and the first time in England-Australia Test matches.
• ME Waugh was the third Australian to be dismissed for 99 in a Test match at Lord's, after CG Macartney (1912) and R Edwards (1975).
• ME Waugh's 99 was the highest score by an Australian opening bowler since 1955 (KR Miller, 109 v West Indies, at Kingston).
• CJ McDermott was taken to hospital after tea on the second day and played no further part in the match, or tour.
• RA Smith passed 3000 runs in Test cricket (42 Tests) when 2 in England's second innings.
• The instance of two individual scores of 99 occurring in the one Test was one short of the Test record three individual 99s that occurred in 1973 at Karachi (Majid Khan and Mushtaq Mohammad for Pakistan, DL Amiss for England).
• Australia maintained an unbeaten record at Lord's stretching back to 1934 (15 Tests,

seven wins, eight draws). England's loss was their seventh in succession (one v Pakistan, three v India, one v Sri Lanka, two v Australia).

THIRD TEST
June 4 was a rest day.
Test Debuts:
England — MC Ilott, MN Lathwell, MJ McCague, GP Thorpe.
Centuries:
DC Boon — 101 in 257 minutes, 177 balls, 17 fours (16th Test century, fifth v England).
GA Gooch — 120 in 324 minutes, 265 balls, 18 fours, one six (19th Test century, fourth v Australia).
• GP Thorpe — 114* in 334 minutes, 280 balls, 11 fours. Thorpe became the 14th Englishman to score a century on Test debut, and the first since FC Hayes scored 106* v West Indies, at The Oval, 1973.
• The number of English Test debutants (four) equalled the number at The Oval v Sri Lanka in 1988 (KJ Barnett, DV Lawrence, PJ Newport, RC Russell), which was the most since five Englishmen made their debuts in the first Test v India in 1951-52.
• At the commencement of the Test, GA Gooch had scored more Test runs (7859) than the entire rest of his team (6595) and taken more Test wickets (22) than the rest of his team (10).
• MG Hughes took five wickets in an innings for the seventh time in Tests, and first time v England.
• GA Gooch passed 2000 runs v Australia (in 34 Tests) when 9 in the second innings.

FOURTH TEST
Centuries:
DC Boon — 107 in 310 minutes, 225 balls, 17 fours (17th Test century, sixth v England). Boon became the first Australian to score centuries in three successive Tests in England since DG Bradman in 1938.
AR Border — 200* in 565 minutes, 399 balls, 26 fours (26th Test century, second Test double-century, eighth v England). Border's score was the highest by an Australian captain v England in England since RB Simpson's 311 at Old Trafford in 1964.
SR Waugh — 157* in 405 minutes, 305 balls, 19 fours (fifth Test century, third v England).
• Australia's first innings total (653) was the highest ever scored in an Ashes Test at Headingley. It was Australia's highest score in a Test since 1964 (8 (dec) 656 v England at Old Trafford), and the highest score by any country against England since 1987 (when Pakistan scored 708 at The Oval).
• AR Border's 200* was the third highest innings by an Australian at Headingley, after DG Bradman's 334 in 1930 and 304 in 1934.
• The partnership between AR Border and SR Waugh, 332* for the fifth wicket, was the highest for any Australian wicket since KD Walters and WM Lawry added 336 for the fourth wicket v West Indies in Sydney in 1968-69. It was the second-highest Australian Test fifth-wicket partnership on record, and the seventh highest for any Australian wicket in Tests.
• PR Reiffel's five wickets in the English first innings was the first time he had taken five wickets in a Test innings.
• MG Hughes' sixth wicket of the match (MJ McCague) was his 200th, in 49 Tests. He was the seventh Australian (after DK Lillee, R Benaud, GD McKenzie, RR Lindwall, CV Grimmett and JR Thomson) to achieve this feat.

- The Australian victory was the sixth biggest Australian win by an innings margin in Ashes Tests. The five more decisive were:

An innings and 332 runs — Brisbane, 1946-47
An innings and 200 runs — Melbourne, 1936-37
An innings and 180 runs — Nottingham, 1989
An innings and 154 runs — Brisbane, 1954-55
An innings and 149 runs — The Oval, 1948

FIFTH TEST

Centuries:
ME Waugh — 137 in 239 minutes, 219 balls, 18 fours (fourth Test century, second v England).

- GA Gooch having stepped down from the captaincy, this was MA Atherton's first Test as captain. Gooch was one of three ex-captains in the England side (AJ Stewart and JE Emburey were the others). Only India's M Azharuddin, in two Tests in Australia in 1991-92, has led a Test side containing more ex-captains (RJ Shastri, K Srikkanth, DB Vengsarkar and Kapil Dev).
- PR Reiffel's 6-71 was his second successive five-wicket innings haul, and the best innings figures by an Australian bowler in a Test at Edgbaston.
- The 153 partnership for the fifth wicket, between SR and ME Waugh, in the first Australian innings was the first instance of twins sharing a century partnership in Test cricket. It was the highest partnership by brothers since 1986-87 (156 for the third wicket by JJ and MD Crowe, for New Zealand v West Indies, at Christchurch). The highest Test partnership by brothers is 264 by IM and GS Chappell, v New Zealand at Wellington in 1974.
- SK Warne and TBA May each took their second five-wicket innings haul in Test cricket, and their first against England. The taking of five wickets each in the same Test innings by two Australian bowlers last occurred in the Tied Test in Madras in 1986 (GRJ Matthews and RJ Bright).
- ME Waugh's 199 runs (137 and 62*) were the most scored by an Australian in a Test match at Edgbaston.
- This Test was Australia's 38th Test victory in England, meaning Australia had won more Tests in England than they had lost (37).

SIXTH TEST

- AJ Stewart passed 2000 Test runs in his 32nd Test when 28 in the first innings.
- ARC Fraser took his fifth five-wicket innings haul in Tests, in his first Test for two-and-a-half years.
- GA Gooch, in his 107th Test, passed DI Gower's English Test aggregate runs record of 8231 runs when he reached 18 in the English second innings.

The last Ashes Test in England in which no individual century was scored was in the fourth Test of 1981, at Edgbaston, when JM Brearley top-scored for the match with 48.

- England's win was their first Test win against Australia since the 4th Test of the 1986-87 series — a run of 18 Tests without a win (5th Test in 1986-87, Bi centenary Test in 1988, six Tests in 1989, five in 1990-91, five in 1993). This represented the longest run without a win in England v Australia Test history. The previous longest run without a win was 14, by England, from the first Test in 1946-47 to the fifth Test in 1950-51.
- AR Border was the Australian captain in each of those 18 Tests. The next best undefeated run by a captain in Ashes Tests is 10, by the Australians, WW Armstrong (1920-

21) and DG Bradman (1946-48).

• MG Hughes, after 51 Tests, is one run away from becoming the seventh Australian to tally 1000 runs and 100 wickets in Test cricket. The six Australians to have achieved this feat are: G Giffen, MA Noble, KR Miller, RR Lindwall, R Benaud and AK Davidson.

THE SERIES

• At the conclusion of the sixth Test, SK Warne (Australia) and GA Gooch (England) were chosen as the Men of the Series.

• Australia's Test wins at Lord's and Headingley, for the loss of only four wickets, were the most decisive innings victories in Ashes Tests, in terms of fewest wickets lost.

• AR Border has now led Australia in 29 Tests against England. The next most appearances by an Australian captain is 19, by DG Bradman between 1936 and 1948. Border's record stands at 13 wins, 6 losses, 10 draws. Bradman's was 11 wins, 3 losses, 5 draws.

• The 10 individual centuries scored by Australians in the series were the most ever scored by an Australian team in an Ashes series in England, and equalled the record for the most by Australians in an Ashes series (10 individual Australian centuries were also scored in 1920-21 and 1946-47).

• For the second successive Ashes series in England, Australia's top seven batsmen were unchanged throughout the series (in 1989 the first seven were MA Taylor, GR Marsh, DC Boon, AR Border, DM Jones, SR Waugh and IA Healy). In 1989 Australia used 12 players in the six Tests, in 1993 they used 14.

• DC Boon became the fourth Australian batsman to score at least three centuries in an Ashes series in England. The others to do so were DG Bradman (four in 1930, three in 1938), CG Macartney (three in 1926), and AR Morris (three in 1948).

• In one innings of each of the first five Tests of 1993, DC Boon and ME Waugh put on a century partnership for the third Australian wicket.

• SK Warne's 2649 deliveries in the series (including eight no-balls and two wides) were the most ever bowled by one bowler in an Ashes series. Warne's 34 wickets were the most by an Australian slow bowler in a series in England, five more than the previous best by CV Grimmett in five Tests in 1930. The list of the most wickets taken by an Australian in an Ashes series in England is as follows:

Wkts	Tests	Bowler	Series	Wkts	Tests	Bowler	Series
42	6	TM Alderman	1981	31	6	MG Hughes	1993
41	6	TM Alderman	1989	30	6	CJ McDermott	1985
39	6	DK Lillee	1981	29	5	CV Grimmett	1930
34	6	SK Warne	1993	29	5	GD McKenzie	1964
31	5	DK Lillee	1972	29	6	GF Lawson	1989

• England used 24 players in the series. On only three occasions has England used more than 24 in an Ashes series — in 1921 (when they used 30), in 1989 (29) and 1909 (25).

• In the 1989 series, the only men to play for England in all six Tests were DI Gower (the captain) and RC Russell (the wicketkeeper). In 1993, the only England players to appear in all six Tests were GA Gooch and MA Atherton (the two captains) and AJ Stewart (the wicketkeeper).

• In each of the first four Tests in 1993, England's second innings was over 100 runs larger than its first innings.

• MA Atherton's 553 runs (including six half-centuries) in the series was the highest aggregate ever achieved in a Test series by a batsman not scoring a century. The previous best was 550 (including six half-centuries) by CC Hunte, for the West Indies v Australia in 1965 (five Tests).

AUSTRALIAN TOUR AVERAGES

FIRST-CLASS MATCHES

Batting and Fielding

Batsman	Mat	Inn	NO	Runs	HS	100	50	Avge	Ct	St
DC Boon	14	23	4	1437	164*	9	2	75.63	10	-
ME Waugh	16	25	6	1361	178	4	9	71.63	8	-
DR Martyn	12	15	3	838	138*	4	3	69.83	9	1
SR Waugh	16	21	8	875	157*	3	2	67.30	7	-
ML Hayden	13	21	1	1150	151*	3	7	57.50	9	-
MJ Slater	17	28	4	1275	152	4	8	53.12	6	-
AR Border	16	21	3	823	200*	1	4	45.72	15	-
MA Taylor	15	25	2	972	124	3	4	42.26	25	-
IA Healy	16	20	7	499	102*	1	3	38.38	42	11
MG Hughes	14	12	3	299	71	-	2	33.22	3	-
BP Julian	13	17	6	284	66	-	2	25.81	7	-
PR Reiffel	13	9	1	181	52	-	1	22.62	3	-
SK Warne	16	15	4	246	47	-	-	22.36	8	-
TJ Zoehrer	8	9	1	115	38	-	-	14.37	17	4
CJ McDermott	6	3	-	42	23	-	-	14.00	3	-
TBA May	17	9	5	31	15	-	-	7.75	5	-
WJ Holdsworth	9	3	-	17	12	-	-	5.66	2	-

* indicates not out

Bowling

Bowler	Overs	Mdns	Runs	Wkts	Best	5w	10w	Ave
TJ Zoehrer	87.2	21	250	12	3-16	-	-	20.83
SK Warne	765.5	281	1698	75	5-61	2	-	22.64
TBA May	562.2	156	1429	53	5-89	1	-	26.96
MG Hughes	470.2	113	1420	48	5-92	1	-	29.58
PR Reiffel	375.4	85	1113	37	6-71	2	-	30.08
ML Hayden	8.4	1	31	1	1-24	-	-	31.00
MA Taylor	9	0	31	1	1-4	-	-	31.00
SR Waugh	73.1	19	229	7	2-9	-	-	32.71
WJ Holdsworth	204.5	32	833	23	5-117	1	-	36.21
BP Julian	318.5	57	1158	29	5-63	1	-	39.93
AR Border	65	17	177	3	1-12	-	-	59.00
ME Waugh	121.1	28	403	6	3-26	-	-	67.16
CJ McDermott	143	26	449	6	2-36	-	-	74.83
DR Martyn	8	2	21	0	-	-	-	-

NOTABLE TOUR PERFORMANCES

Centuries (37):

DC Boon (9) —
108   v Worcestershire (first innings)
106   v Worcestershire (second innings)
123   v Leicestershire
164* v England (second Test)
146   v Hampshire
101   v England (third Test)
112   v Durham
107   v England (fourth Test)
120   v Glamorgan

ML Hayden (6) —
151#   v England Amateur XI
122#   v Middlesex
115   v Hampshire
133*# v Ireland
151*   v Durham
111   v Essex

ME Waugh (5) —
113#   v England (second limited-overs international)
178   v Surrey
152*   v Glamorgan
137   v England (fifth Test)
108   v Essex

DR Martyn (4) —
136   v Sussex
116   v Warwickshire
138*   v Combined Universities
105*   v Kent

MJ Slater (4) —
122   v Somerset
152   v England (second Test)
111   v Combined Universities
133*   v Derbyshire

MA Taylor (3) —
124   v England (first Test)
111   v England (second Test)
122   v Lancashire

SR Waugh (3) —
124   v Sussex
157*   v England (fourth Test)
123   v Kent

AR Border (2) —
111#   v Ireland
200*   v England (fourth Test)

IA Healy (1) —
102*   v England (first Test)

Five Wickets in an Innings (10):

PR Reiffel (3) —
5-28# v Minor Counties
5-65   v England (fourth Test)
6-71   v England (fifth Test)

SK Warne (2) —
5-61   v Gloucestershire
5-82   v England (fifth Test)

WJ Holdsworth (1) —
5-117 v Derbyshire (including hat-trick)

MG Hughes (1) —
5-92   v England (third Test)

BP Julian (1) —
5-63   v Sussex

TBA May (1) —
5-89   v England (fifth Test)

ME Waugh (1) —
5-32# v Duchess of Norfolk's XI

Five Dismissals in an Innings by a Wicketkeeper (3):

TJ Zoehrer (3)
8 (6 ct, 2 st)   v Surrey
6# (4 ct, 2 st) v Minor Counties
5# (5 ct)   v England Amateur Xi

* indicates not out
# indicates non-first-class

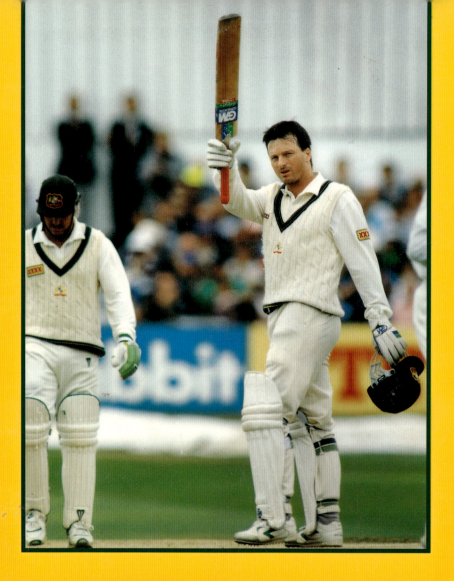

At the forefront of Australia's 1993 Ashes cricket triumph was Steve Waugh. This is his diary of that tour, a daily record of awesome performances by the Australian side. It is a rare and intimate "insider's" view of the international cricket scene.

After outstanding victories in the one-day internationals, Allan Border's side dominated the Test matches, to complete one of the most successful of all Australian cricket tours. In *Steve Waugh's Ashes Diary*, Steve shows himself to be an acute observer of his sport, not only in his descriptions of the many brilliant displays by the players, but also in capturing the side's characters, the funny moments, the glamour and not so glamorous aspects of the tour, and the sheer glory of being a successful Test cricketer in England.

With a foreword by the remarkable Shane Warne, a detailed statistical analysis, and more than 150 photographs -- many in colour and many taken behind the scenes by Steve himself -- *Steve Waugh's Ashes Diary* is the ultimate record of a famous tour.

'Steve Waugh joins another winning team'

ISBN 0-330-27465-1